Literature
of Tennessee

Literature of Tennessee

edited by

Ray Willbanks

MERCER
MUP

ISBN 0-86554-139-6

Literature of Tennessee
Copyright ©1984
Mercer University Press
All Rights Reserved
Printed in the United States of America

All books published by Mercer University Press are produced on acid-free paper that exceeds the minimum standards set by the National Historical Publications and Records Commission.

Library of Congress Cataloging in Publication Data

Main entry under title:

Literature of Tennessee.

    Includes bibliographies.
    1. American literature—Tennessee—History and criticism—Addresses, essays, lectures. 2. Tennessee in literature—Addresses, essays, lectures. 3. American literature—20th century—History and criticism—Addresses, essays, lectures. I. Willbanks, Ray.
PS266.T2L57   1984   810.9'9768   84-91155
ISBN 0-86554-139-6 (alk. paper)

CONTENTS

Introduction vii

Acknowledgments xiii

1 The Literature of Tennessee before 1920
  Elmo Howell 1

2 The Southern Renascence and the Writers
  of Tennessee, *Lloyd Davis* 21

3 John Crowe Ransom, *William Osborne* 37

4 Donald Davidson and Allen Tate
  Thomas Daniel Young 63

5 Cleanth Brooks and Robert Penn Warren
  Mark Royden Winchell 89

6 Andrew Lytle, *Charles C. Clark* 115

7 James Agee, *Victor A. Kramer* 133

8 Peter Taylor, *Clayton Robinson* 149

9 Shelby Foote, *Helen White* 163

10 Contemporary Writers, *Dennis Loyd* 183

INTRODUCTION

A sense of place has long been an identifiable aspect of Southern literature. One links Faulkner with Mississippi, Twain with Missouri, and O'Connor with Georgia, though certainly these writers have not limited the settings of their stories or the mobility of their personal lives to a particular state or region. Indeed, given the fact that few people have remained in one place for a lifetime during the nineteenth and twentieth centuries, it is to a certain extent an artificial construct to assign a group of men and women to a particular state using any exclusive or inclusive consistency. The closer one comes to the present the more difficult such an assignment becomes. Yet, allowing for entrances and exits, I believe it is quite plausible to identify a sizable group of men and women as Tennessee writers. It is possible because these writers, whether by childhood, educational experience, peer association, apprenticeship, or decades of residency, have brought to their work an infusion of sensibility and insight derived from their particular sojourn in Tennessee.

In the nineteenth century, and to some extent in the twentieth, the Tennessee writer has been influenced by where in the state he has lived, whether in the flatlands of the West, with its Indian lore, its river traffic, and its black culture; in the Cumberland Plateau of Central Tennessee, with its pasture and farm land; or in the hills and mountains of East Tennessee, an area rich in individuality and folklore. As was true elsewhere in the United States, one of the most popular forms of literature in Tennessee in the nineteenth century was frontier humor. Tennessee's best-known exponents were Davey Crockett and George Washington Harris—Crockett for the descriptions of his own backwoods adventures, particularly in the Reelfoot area of West Tennessee, and Harris for the comic sketches of Sut Lovingood, "a nat'ral born durn'd fool" living in the mining country of southeastern Tennessee. Lovingood's remarks on women, preachers, propriety, foreigners, and Yankees reveal the common prejudices of his day in a vernacular so realistic and with an imagery so vivid that he won the admiration of Mark Twain.

A second popular literary form practiced in Tennessee in the nineteenth century was Local Color. While there were several Memphis writers who published novels and poems set in West Tennessee, particularly romantic Old South plantation stories, the best Tennessee local colorist, in fact one of the best in the country, was Mary Noailles Murfree. Although her home was in Middle Tennessee, in Murfreesboro, she learned about mountain people at her family's summer residence at Beersheba Springs in the Cumberland Mountains and from later visits to the Great Smoky Mountains. Of the twenty-five volumes she had written by the time of her death in 1922, two brought her considerable fame. These novels, *In the Tennessee Mountains* and *The Prophet of the Great Smoky Mountains*, suggest in their titles the importance of East Tennessee as place in the work of their author.

In the first third of the twentieth century the greatest creative thrust in the state occurred in Middle Tennessee, in Nashville. In fact, three significant movements in American literature grew out of the association of a few Vanderbilt University teachers, students, and their friends. These movements were the Fugitives, the Agrarians, and New Criticism. The Nashville men began to gather to discuss literature and social issues as early as 1915, but it was not until after the war, in 1922, that they published the first issue of *The Fugitive*, a journal of poetry that was to become quite important. Of the sixteen Fugitives, the most important in terms of publications and later influence were John Crowe Ransom, Donald Davidson, Allen Tate, and Robert Penn Warren. Although Tate and Warren were not born in Tennessee, they had close Tennessee associations: Warren came from nearby Kentucky to Clarksville, Tennessee, for high school and later enrolled at Vanderbilt;

Tate was often in Tennessee during his youth and followed his two older brothers to Vanderbilt. Davidson and Ransom were the products of rural Middle Tennessee; both were educated at Vanderbilt; both became teachers at Vanderbilt.

What these men who called themselves Fugitives had in common was an awareness of their world in transition, the changing face of the South as it moved from agriculture toward industry, from traditional agrarian values to "progressive" business values. While wishing to preserve the best of the traditional South, these writers who gathered in Nashville also sought to reject the sentimental, worn-out poetic forms of the nineteenth century and to create new, carefully crafted poetry reflective of the ambiguity, incongruity, and irony readily apparent so early in the twentieth century. Though there were only nineteen issues of *The Fugitive* during its three years of publication, this Nashville journal, according to Frederick J. Hoffman, was the only magazine of its time that "rocketed its poets into the national spotlight." (Davis, p. 26)

"Then if you ask me why, of all places, at Nashville," Donald Davidson wrote in 1957, "and why not at Charleston, Charlottesville, Atlanta, Macon, Athens, New Orleans, I can say only that I can see no good reason why not if, granting ability and interest, the poets of such Southern centers had applied themselves to the art of poetry as exclusively as we did for a long while at Nashville." (Davis, pp. 23-24) And it was at Nashville that these particular talents came together again in 1930 to publish their Agrarian manifesto *I'll Take My Stand*. As Southerners, Ransom, Davidson, Tate, and Warren were concerned with the increasingly popular belief that science and technology were the answers to man's problems and that the South with its religious fundamentalism, its slower pace, its codes of conduct and manners was anachronistic and as such due for a pragmatic dose of Northern progress. What turned concern into action was the negative national publicity focused on Tennessee during the Scopes Trial of 1925. By association of place and self, these Tennessee writers felt under attack. The aforementioned Fugitives, two historians, a psychologist, and soon-to-be-novelist Andrew Lytle, joined others to write *I'll Take My Stand*. The work consists of twelve essays arguing from different points of view the dangers of industrialization in America and the necessity for the South to retain its agrarian character. Ransom's lead essay, "Reconstructed But Unregenerate," argues that "poetry, the arts, and religious myth function best in an agrarian culture consisting of small, self-supporting farms where man can enjoy a proper relationship to nature. Such a relationship, Ransom argued, was not easily found in an industrial society where Reason reigns over Sensibility." (Osborne, p. 53)

The third important movement, New Criticism, also grew out of the work of these Nashville writers. In particular, the ideas of New Criticism were expressed by John Crowe Ransom in early essays collected in *The World's Body* (1938) and again in *The New Criticism* (1941). Briefly stated, Ransom taught his students at Vanderbilt, and later wrote in his essays, that a poem should be given a close textual reading, with the reader avoiding biographical, historical, and psychological considerations. The poem was to be seen as an entity, not read in terms of something outside itself.

The importance of the Vanderbilt teachers and the dissemination of their ideas can be seen in the essay in this volume dealing with the Southern Renascence and in the essays that present John Crowe Ransom, Donald Davidson, Allen Tate, Cleanth Brooks, Robert Penn Warren, Andrew Lytle, and Peter Taylor. The ideals of New Criticism are echoed in Brooks and Warren's college textbooks *Understanding Fiction* and *Understanding Poetry*. The sense of place and the value of tradition defended in *I'll Take My Stand* are reflected in the Tennessee fiction of Andrew Lytle and Peter Taylor. Although when Ransom, the foremost Tennessee poet-scholar, left Vanderbilt in 1935 for Kenyon College many of his colleagues and students were already scattered beyond Nashville and the borders of Tennessee, what they had gained from their Vanderbilt experience continued to influence their work, whether it was teaching or writing criticism, poetry, or fiction.

Although there are a number of Tennessee writers in the twentieth century who had no connection with the Fugitives or the Agrarians—for example, T. S. Stribling, Evelyn Scott, Horace McCoy, James Agee, Shelby Foote, Nikki Giovanni, Ishmael Reed—it is interesting to see how frequently a Vanderbilt education figures in the lives of a number of significant contemporary writers, namely Randall Jarrell, Peter Taylor, Walter Sullivan, Madison Jones, and Jesse Hill Ford.

Apart from a similarity in education as a cohesive force in the lives of Tennessee writers, a sense of region has been important to Tennessee writers in the twentieth century, as it was in the nineteenth, and

Literature of Tennessee

by looking at the work of James Agee, Peter Taylor, and Shelby Foote one can observe this influence. James Agee's childhood in Knoxville and school years at St. Andrew's near Sewanee gave him material and setting for stories, for his novella, *The Morning Watch*, and for his posthumous novel, *A Death in the Family*. Peter Taylor, grandson of a three-term governor of Tennessee, has drawn heavily on his birthplace, Trenton, in West Tennessee, for the small-town settings of his stories, and on Memphis and Nashville, where he was educated, for his urban settings. Although as a writer Shelby Foote has shown a consistent interest in his native Washington County and Greenville, Mississippi, he has a prominent place in the literature of Tennessee because of his long residence in Memphis and his use of Tennessee places in several of his works, in particular in *Shiloh, The Civil War*, and *September September*. In East Tennessee the mountains have played a part in shaping character, and in West Tennessee, as Foote shows, the rich topsoil and the wide flatland of the Delta have been a power in the lives of both white and black.

In the final chapter of this volume, Dennis Loyd surveys literature in Tennessee since 1950. His list is a long one and from it he selects four writers: Jesse Hill Ford, Madison Jones, Ishmael Reed, and Nikki Giovanni. The first two writers, Ford and Jones, by virtue of their Vanderbilt educations, their long residences in Tennessee, and the settings of their fiction, are easily recognized as Tennessee writers. For the latter two, Reed and Giovanni, the Tennessee claim is not as strong and their inclusion in this volume indicates the problems inherent in geographical classification. Reed was born in Chattanooga, but moved out of the state in his childhood. It is not known how much his Tennessee experience influenced him, and his only acknowledgment of this tie comes in a 1973 volume of poems, *Chattanooga*. Although Nikki Giovanni has lived most of her life outside Tennessee, the poems reflective of her childhood in her birthplace, Knoxville, and her troublesome years at Fisk University in Nashville show the importance of Tennessee in her work.

Collectively, the essays in this volume illustrate several points about the literature of Tennessee: the importance of the geographical divisions within the state, the importance of the Vanderbilt associations formed in the 1920s, and the significance of Tennessee writers in the overall history of American literature.

ACKNOWLEDGMENTS

Special thanks to Helen White and Redding Sugg, Jr., for their assistance in the initial planning of this volume.

Considerable thanks also goes to Mary Ellen Pitts for her diligent and careful editorial assistance.

1

The Literature of Tennessee before 1920

Elmo Howell

Tennessee literature is part of Southern literature and follows its changing trends, with the Civil War as the watershed event. Before the war, the South was a confident, aggressive region with an ethos reflected in its literature—in the novels of William Gilmore Simms, for example, and in the sketches of the southwest humorists. After the war, writing became a genteel exercise practiced mostly by women until it found itself again in the twentieth century through a return to its beginnings. When William Faulkner paid tribute to Mark Twain and to Twain's mentors the prewar humorists—he singled out Tennessee's Sut Lovingood as a favorite character—the course of Southern letters had come full cycle.

In the first century of its statehood, Tennessee produced no well-known authors except David Crockett, whose reputation lies mainly outside literature. George Washington Harris, creator of Sut Lovingood, and local colorist Mary Noailles Murfree are mentioned in literary histories but are no longer read. Beyond these three there is nothing—except, of course, a vast body of forgotten work long out of print, some of it available only in archives and special collections. But the winnowing of time in the short space of a century is not always according to merit, and some of these volumes still surprise and delight. Moreover, they are the testimony of an age that anticipates and makes manifest the important literary flowering that began in Tennessee and the rest of the South sometime after 1920.

The most original achievement in the first half of the nineteenth century was the work of the humorists, most of them anonymous, who wrote thousands of sketches and stories for local papers and magazines and at least one well-known national publication, the New York *Spirit of the Times*, which gave special attention to the South in the generation before the war. Tennessee produced more than its share of this type of writing, including the sketches of Crockett, who set the tone for the whole school. Crockett, however, was in one respect unlike most of the writers who followed him; they were men of culture and professional standing, but he was a semiliterate backwoodsman reporting his own adventures, whether as a hunter in the devastated country of the New Madrid earthquake or as a stump politician or practical joker outwitting a Yankee peddler. He became a legend and was associated with works he never wrote, but *A Narrative of the Life of David Crockett of the State of Tennessee*, published in 1834, was his own production, written in part to repudiate another work attributed to him.

Though the usual way of publication was by magazine, several notable volumes of sketches appeared following Crockett's book: A. B. Longstreet's *Georgia Scenes* in 1834, Johnson Jones Hooper's *Captain Simon Suggs* in 1845, William T. Porter's *Big Bear of Arkansas* also in 1845, and—in Tennessee—John Tomlin's *Tales of the Caddo* in 1849. Like most of the frontier sketches, Tomlin's little volume has long disappeared from notice, even by historians of the movement. Tomlin was known in his own time as "literary postmaster of Jackson." He was author of *Shelley's Grave and Other Poems* (1843), inspired in part by a long correspondence with Edgar Allan Poe, for unlike Crockett, Tomlin was a man of culture in close touch with literary developments of his time. In 1848, he left Jackson for Texas—a lodestone for Southerners and particularly for Tennesseans—by way of the Red River to Lake Caddo and on to the thriving port of Jefferson ten miles away. Here he spent a few weeks with relatives and gathered material for his book, the earliest known fictional treatment of life in the Republic of Texas. The tales are related by one Jack Faraday, "the old man of the forest," who lives alone on an island in Lake Caddo. The purpose, says the author, is to reveal "Western manners and Western habits as they exist on the most extreme borders of civilization."[1] The events are crude enough, but Tomlin, who looked with the eye of a poet on the exotic natural world of the river and bayou of the Caddo region, has a pleasing literary style. He also has a sense of history and is sensitive to the Spanish heritage of the new nation of Texas.

If Tomlin's Jack Faraday deserves a better hearing, George Washington Harris's Sut Lovingood has been a byword since his first appearance in *Spirit of the Times* in 1854. Though ignored by literary solons, he was widely enjoyed in Harris's lifetime, and Mark Twain wrote a review of the volume of Sut yarns that appeared in 1867. It was not until the twentieth century, however, that Harris was taken seriously, and not always favorably. Edmund Wilson calls Sut "a dreadful half-bestial Cracker" and "the most repellent character in American literature." He regards the favorable commentary of fellow critics as "among the curiosities of American scholarship."[2] Nevertheless, Sut has had his day. He is in print again and the subject of academic study.

In sheer vigor and Rabelaisian good humor, the Lovingood sketches are the crowning achievement of frontier writing. Harris anticipates the comic incongruities of Mark Twain with a freedom of expression that Twain could not allow himself in the postwar era. His claim to art—again like Twain's—is primarily in the use of language: metaphors that rise inevitably from Southern life and a breathless volubility that carries all before it. At a Negro revival meeting, for example, Sut turns loose a nest of hornets among the worshipers. The description of what follows reveals much of a whole way of life.

> Sich nises—screechin like painters, cryin, hollerin, a few a-cussin, an' more a-jinin em, beggin, prayin, groanin, gruntin, nickerin, an' wun or two fool wuns singin. Ho'nets don't keer a durn fur music, when they's a-fitin, while abuv em a-flyin in the ar, jis' like they weighed nuthin, wer a desirabil 'sortmint ove hyme books, fans, hanketchers, hats, caps, umerellers, walkin-sticks, biskits, chicken-laigs, strings ove beads, Couber peas, year-rings, ginger-cakes, collars, garters, babies, terbacker-pipes, ridicules, littil baskits, popco'n, scent bottils, ribbons, hollyhawk bokays, pint ticklers, bits ove straw, an' wun shiff—how she got outen hit wifout takin off her frock, I be durn'd ef I ken tell;

---

[1] John Tomlin, *Tales of the Caddo* (Cincinnati: Office of the "Great West," 1849) 15.

[2] Edmund Wilson, *Patriotic Gore* (New York: Oxford University Press, 1962) 507-19.

but thar hit wer a-sailin roun wif a deck-load ove ho'nets ontu hit what wer the resarve I reckon. All this wer set off tu advantige by dus', an' millions ove insex, jis' a-hoverin over the sufferers an' then divin down fur a sting.[3]

He likes to bait pious churchgoers, white as well as black, and enjoys a joke at the expense of sheriffs, Yankees, women of a certain character, members of his own family, and especially himself. At heart an agreeable fellow, he admits that he is a coward whose long "laigs" have gotten him out of many a scrape. But he is more than a Cracker "squatting in his own filth," in Wilson's words; he is a disaffected moralist lampooning the hypocrisies of his time and as such becomes the mouthpiece of his creator. In this respect, Harris invites comparison not so much with contemporary humorists as with angry Elizabethan pamphleteers or eighteenth-century malcontents like Swift and Smollett. He has Smollett's salty prose and crude jokes and, more fundamentally, the dark trenchancy of Swift, who said his purpose was to vex the world rather than divert it. The moral dimension gives Harris a special place among the southwestern humorists.

The humorous frontier sketch is the South's most original contribution to literature. It began with William Byrd in the eighteenth century and reached full expression with Harris and his contemporaries, who stand as a seminal influence in Southern letters. But there are other modes woven around the dominant theme. The poetry of Poe and the fiction of Simms (insofar as Simms is a follower of Scott) are part of the Romantic expression of the age and look strangely out of place in settlements on the frontier. Yet every community of only a few hundred people had its own printing press and took pride in local authors, however imitative, since culture was something to be brought in from the outside. In the 1830s, for example, Knoxville boasted not of Crockett's homespun sketches but of John Robinson's *The Savage* (1833), a collection of Addisonian essays, and Charles W. Todd's *Woodville* (1832), a romance in the worn-out Gothic manner which has no connection with the state or region, but which the Knoxville *Register* declared would be a great book "if it had been composed in England

---

[3]George Washington Harris, *Sut Lovingood's Yarns Spun by a Nat'ral Born Durn'd Fool. Warped and Wove for Public Wear* (New York: Dick & Fitzgerald, 1867) 167.

and praised by the reviewers."[4] The local had little appeal to literary circles on the frontier. They preferred sentiment, romance, and the pious religiosity of a more sophisticated society on the Eastern seaboard.

The first important novelist in Tennessee was Mrs. Lucy Virginia French, whose work, in both poetry and prose, began to appear in the decade before the Civil War. Born in Virginia, she came to Memphis as a teacher in 1848. After her marriage in 1853, she moved to her husband's plantation near McMinnville, where she lived during the war. Being a woman of wide-ranging interests, she compiled an extensive journal of events, a still-unpublished manuscript of interest to historians as well as literary scholars. Her best-known novel, *My Roses: The Romance of a June Day* (1872), is set in New Orleans in 1852. Its appeal lay in the exotic Creole setting and in a subject taken directly from Victorian ethics: the reclamation of a "woman *mal-famée*" by a peerless heroine. Most of the novel can be anticipated, but not all. The heroine assumes the disguise of a man in order to visit the lovely creature in the Maison des Bijoux in the old Quarter, and in the course of time, as Monsieur Henri, falls in love with the girl herself.

> I had deliriously desired to *be* what I *seemed*, the boy-love of Coralie Lesueur. To me the wish appears neither unnatural nor unwomanly, because I really felt it.... The blood rushed in a tumultuous torrent to my brow, as I remembered that brief draught of an intoxicating madness which I had drained when a few hours before I had clasped her to my bosom, and forgotten, as in some weird exhilarating *hasheesh* dream—everything in earth or heaven, save that she was mine! And now—how was all this to end?[5]

Mrs. French does not explore these psychological difficulties but moves on to a conventional ending, although not without teasing the reader with hints of originality which never find full expression.

After the war, the sentimental novel took up the theme of the Lost Cause with a degree of respectability in writers like Thomas Nelson

---

[4]Knoxville *Register*, 18 July 1832. See Ulna Foster Park, "The Early Literature of East Tennessee: A Study of Literary Publications and Their Background from the Beginning to 1840" (M.A. thesis, University of Tennessee, 1954).

[5]L. Virginia French, *My Roses: The Romance of a June Day* (Philadelphia: Claxton, Remsen & Haffelfinger, 1872) 109-10.

Page of Virginia but dominated by, in the words of Jay B. Hubbell, "the subliterary novels of Southern women."[6] Tennessee produced no sensations in this vein, though most of the fiction of this period was touched by the war in some way, even that of Opie Read and John Trotwood Moore, whose main bent is not sentimental. In *Brokenburne* (1897), Mrs. Virginia Frazer Boyle of Memphis wrote "the most perfect idyl of the South ever written," according to Walter Hines Page. It is a sentimental romance in which a young Southerner and his Northern friend visit an old plantation after the war and listen to the black mammy who still holds the place together. The theme is one taken for granted in novels of the period—contemplation of lost grandeur and reconciliation with a former enemy. In *Serena* (1904), Mrs. Boyle goes back to the war itself as a young lady who rides through the story like Joan of Arc in defense of family honor.

But Mrs. Boyle was better known as a poet, having been dubbed the "poet laureate of the South" in a memorable interview with Jefferson Davis when she was a girl. Her volumes include *The Other Side* (1897), *Love Songs, Bugle Calls* (1906), and *Song Of Memphis* (1919), a canticle to celebrate the centennial year of the founding of the city. There were other poets, of course. Mrs. French, the novelist, first made a reputation as poet in *Wind Whispers* (1856), a volume obviously influenced by Poe and the English Romantics, particularly Byron. In Nashville, Mrs. Clara Coles, a shy, reclusive lady whose main appeal was in homeliness of subject matter, achieved local renown through contributions to the papers and in her one volume, *Clara's Poems* (1861). All three ladies appeal mainly to the domestic virtues and are representative of myriads of women in the South in the nineteenth century who wrote primarily, says Hubbell, "because they liked to write and wished to see their verses in print."[7]

One of the best-known poets of Tennessee before the appearance of the Fugitives in the twentieth century was Walter Malone of Memphis. Malone combined his literary activity with a career as an attorney and, during the last ten years of his life, was judge of the Second Circuit Court of Shelby County. He was a prolific writer, publishing his

---

[6] Jay B. Hubbell, *The South in American Literature, 1607-1900* (Durham NC: Duke University Press, 1954) 616.

[7] Ibid., 604.

Literature of Tennessee 7

first volume of more than three hundred pages when he was sixteen and a second volume before he was twenty. After his first volume, John Greenleaf Whittier wrote, "Why, at thy age, I could not make a respectable rhyme"; and the English poet laureate Alfred Austin approved of his deference to "the best traditions of English poetry."[8]

Malone's subjects are wide ranging. He traveled much about the world, but wrote best about everyday life at home ("An Unsent Letter," "The Churchyard," "The Bachelor," "Burial of an Old Slave") and the natural world of West Tennessee ("A Mississippi Swamp," "September in Tennessee," "A Storm in Summer," "The Dried-up Stream," "To a Mocking Bird Singing in October"). He liked historical subjects and in "Had Lincoln Lived" voiced the common sentiment that at Lincoln's death the South lost its best friend. He commended Johnny Reb and celebrated General Forrest's raid on the Gayoso Hotel in Memphis in 1864. A volume of Malone's short poetry still makes pleasant reading, though his faults are obvious: carelessness prompted by volume and devotion to the twin gods of the genteel tradition—propriety and sentiment. Long out of print, Malone is still remembered for at least one poem, "Opportunity," which says well what many people like to hear, and perhaps for the long narrative poem *Desoto*, though few have cared to read it through.

The Local Color Movement, dominant after the war, conformed to the romantic taste of the time, different only in its deliberate use of realism to help bring together a divided nation. In the South, the local colorists are literary descendants of the old southwest humorists, but their realism and humor, when humor exists at all, are directed toward a didactic purpose. The Negro was the most interesting cultural phenomenon, and Tennessee produced its share of plantation stories, notably those of John Trotwood Moore and Virginia Frazer Boyle, whose *Devil Tales* (1900), exploring the superstitious side of her characters with humor and stark realism, is perhaps her finest achievement.

But Tennessee stands out in the Local Color Movement because of another sort of character and in particular because of one writer. Mary Noailles Murfree of Murfreesboro was a major figure in the movement and enjoyed a national reputation. Her special interest was the moun-

---

[8]Frazer Hood, "Walter Malone—His Life and Works," in Walter Malone, *Selected Poems* (Louisville: John P. Morton & Co., 1919) xiii-xxvi.

tain country of East Tennessee. More than any other writer, she is responsible for calling attention to Appalachia, with its poverty and violence and, what some like to consider, its ties with Elizabethan England. Though no longer popularly read, Miss Murfree's work still turns up in anthologies and in the critical reviews. She is the best-known writer Tennessee produced before the Southern Renascence.

In one respect she was at a greater disadvantage than most of the local colorists in that she was not intimately acquainted with her subject. Born into a family of wealth and culture in Middle Tennessee, she learned about mountain people on summer holidays at her family's cottage at Beersheba Springs, the popular antebellum resort in the Cumberland Mountains. Later, she visited the Great Smokies, but the early experience in the Cumberlands set the pattern for her mountain fiction.

She began with short stories for magazines, using the name Charles Egbert Craddock, and in 1884 published eight of these stories in her first volume, *In the Tennessee Mountains*. The following year a novel appeared, *The Prophet of the Great Smoky Mountains*. Her fame principally rests on these two books, though she continued to write until her death in 1922, turning out a total of twenty-five volumes. In the central character in *The Prophet*, she deals with the popular subject of religious doubt, though equally attractive are the usual mountain types—a young man hiding out under suspicion of murder, a moonshiner and his three giant sons operating a still in a cave, a mountain girl pursuing her dream of love—along with bizarre minor characters that may owe something to Dickens, all of whom speak in idioms as alien as Cockney English.

At this point one must raise a question about Miss Murfree's dialect and its relation to her art. As in the Uncle Remus stories, the dialect gets in the way and becomes a problem; however, unlike Joel Chandler Harris's Georgia Negro speech, Murfree's does not ring true. No doubt she listened carefully when she invited the locals inside her cottage at Beersheba, but the result is only a parody of Southern country talk. Particularly offending is the consistent use of "you-uns," the country equivalent of "you all," as singular, as well as such locutions as "it do" and "I are." Her deafness to speech patterns qualifies her realism and supports the view that she was a romantic who saw her characters through a mountain mist, from the safe vantage point of a lady of quality.

Above all, she loved the mountains. A major delight of her fiction is the close observation of plant and animal life, canyons and pinnacles, the "bald" of Old Smoky rearing above the clouds, and far poetic vistas that remind one of Claude Lorrain and Mrs. Ann Radcliffe. She loved rustic people; however, in her books they were a means of getting into an exotic landscape that charmed her imagination.

> Always enwrapped in the illusory mists, always touching the evasive clouds, the peaks of the Great Smoky Mountains are like some barren ideal, that has bartered for the vague isolations of a higher atmosphere the material values of the warm world below. Upon those mighty and majestic domes no tree strikes root, no hearth is alight; humanity is an alien thing, and utility set at naught. Below, dense forests cover the massive, precipitous slopes of the range, and in the midst of the wilderness a clearing shows, here and there, and the roof of a humble log cabin; in the valley, far, far lower still, a red spark at dusk may suggest a home, nestling in the cove.[9]

Though inevitably associated with Local Color fiction, Miss Murfree tried her hand at other things—romance, history, children's stories—that must be taken into consideration in any final evaluation. *The Story of Old Fort Loudon* (1899), in the manner of Scott, deals with a chapter of colonial history in East Tennessee. *Where the Battle Was Fought* (1884) is in some ways a personal narrative of the Battle of Stone's River near Murfreesboro, which encircled and destroyed the Murfree home, although the author carefully avoids the personal element. She also wrote romances of the sort Mrs. French and later Mrs. Boyle wrote, still keeping clear of divisive issues. For example, in *The Fair Mississippian*, set only a few years after the war, the Delta planter families are apparently untouched by events of the time; the war might never have happened. What particularly engages Miss Murfree's interest in this novel is the plot, built around a fine point of law, in which she professed some competence under the direction of her lawyer father. The elaborate plotting, along with fear of emotional involvement, gives the work a sense of unreality, which to a large extent applies to

---

[9]Charles Egbert Craddock, *The Prophet of the Great Smoky Mountains* (Boston: Houghton, Mifflin and Co., 1885) 1.

the mountain stories as well. She was a novelist of the head rather than the heart.

Mary Noailles Murfree was only one of many Tennessee authors who wrote about the mountains. In "Lodusky," published in *Scribner's* in 1877 before the appearance of Miss Murfree's stories, English-born Frances Hodgson Burnett, living in New Market, wrote about a mountain girl from the point of view of a Northern tourist. Alice MacGowan, author of *Judith of the Cumberlands* (1908), was born in Ohio, but as a child she came to Chattanooga, where her father was part of the Federal occupying force. To learn about the region, she traveled on horseback through the mountains, "about a thousand miles of it," and the result was the popular *Judith*, in which Sinclair Lewis professed to see Elizabethan England "alive and thrilling." Miss MacGowan's sympathy is obvious but strained, and her dialect is as artificial as Miss Murfree's.

The stories of Will Allen Dromgoole of Murfreesboro are more authentic. His most famous story is "The Heart of Old Hickory" (*The Heart of Old Hickory and Other Stories of Tennessee*, 1895), based on the career of Governor Bob Taylor. In this story, Governor Taylor has been criticized in the papers for granting too many pardons. As another case is being considered, a street urchin reveals to the governor how much he is loved by the people. As Taylor muses on the statue of Old Hickory outside the capitol window and despite the Nashville *Banner*, he decides again for mercy. In "Fiddling His Way to Fame," Miss Dromgoole goes more directly to Taylor's mountain background. The governor tells his own story, relapsing easily into the speech of his boyhood, about one of the most famous gubernatorial contests in the state, in which his own brother, Alfred Taylor, was his opponent.

Most authentic of all is a small book, *The Spirit of the Mountains*, published in 1905, by Emma Bell Miles, an obscure but gifted artist in Chattanooga, whose understanding of the mountains is profound and whose sympathy is never patronizing. Her sketches of cabin, church, school, of men's work and women's work—the round of primitive existence—are vividly fresh. They are the impressions of a person who has lived life and loves it in spite of deprivations. She exults in the wholeness of a culture which in 1905 was beginning to be threatened from the outside. "My people, everywhere on the borders of the mountain country, are being laid hold of and swept away by the oncoming

Literature of Tennessee

tide of civilization, that drowns as many as it uplifts."[10] She calls for isolation and homogeneity, which alone can make her country "a peculiar and beneficent force" in the nation at large. Cities and the "summer people" and those who come in to "do good" are a threat. Like the later Agrarians, she saw an independent yeomanry as the basis of Jeffersonian democracy. "From the mountains will yet arise a quickening of American ideals and American life."[11]

For a couple of generations after the war, most Tennessee authors wrote about things as they might have been rather than as they were. They lived in a polite age, far removed from Crockett's frontier, with which they seemed to have nothing in common. New voices were beginning to be heard, but not loudly enough to break the pattern of the past. Beginning in 1911 with the popular *Queed*, Henry Sydnor Harrison of Sewanee wrote "modern" novels about smart young women who might have come out of Meredith. In these novels sentiment is concealed by cleverness. Maria Thompson Daviess of Nashville delighted her generation with light, tripping stories of maiden ladies; the most popular was *Miss Selina Lue* (1908), which evokes a whole community in the Harpeth Valley and recalls the village fiction of Mrs. Gaskell. But the resurgence of realism a few years later showed that the Genteel Age was only an interlude. The frontier spirit is the continuum that brings out the best in Southern letters.

The impulse toward realism continued to find expression after the war but received little critical notice because it was out of fashion. In 1881-1882, the Columbia *Herald* ran a series of war sketches by Sam R. Watkins of Columbia, published late in 1882 by the Cumberland Presbyterian Publishing Company in Nashville as *"Co. Aytch," First Tennessee Regiment: or, A Side Show of the Big Show*. "Us boys," says Watkins, "all took a small part in the fracas." At a time when the heroic was part of the approved formula, Watkins chose to give an earthy account of the daily life of the average soldier.

> The histories of the Lost Cause are all written out by the "big bugs," generals and renowned historians, and like the fellow who called a tur-

---

[10] Emma Bell Miles, *The Spirit of the Mountains* (New York: James Pott & Co., 1905) 190.

[11] Ibid., 200-201.

tle a "cooter," being told that no such word as cooter was in Mr. Webster's dictionary, remarked that he had as much right to make a dictionary as Mr. Webster or any other man; so have I to write a history.[12]

This neglected book—a second edition was issued in 1900 and quickly sold out—is the sort of thing David Crockett might have written. Watkins the private is not cynical about the war nor the ideals he fought for, nor proud that he was court-martialed for taking French leave to see his sweetheart, nor vain of the wounds he received in battles at Nashville, Murfreesboro, and Atlanta. Like Crockett, he makes no point of his experience; he writes because he has a story to tell and enjoys his quaint way of telling it. Watkins's book was no isolated instance of the continuing appeal of realism. Politicians throughout the South understood it. Governor Bob Taylor was famous for his campaign stories and in 1896 published a collection, *Gov. Bob Taylor's Tales*, in a decorative little volume reminiscent of the Crockett almanacs. The old happy informality was not dead but had gone underground in the wake of a new literary mode.

John Trotwood Moore (father of poet Merrill Moore) is remembered, if at all, as a sentimentalist on the fringe of the Local Color school, though his main impulse was toward realism. In *Songs and Stories from Tennessee* (1897), he is avowedly sentimental and patriotic—his best-known poem is about Sam Davis, the boy hero of Smyrna; but this book represents only one side of Moore's character. He was an active man of affairs very much involved with issues of his day. His novel *The Bishop of Cottontown* appeared in 1906, about the same time as Upton Sinclair's *The Jungle*. Like Sinclair's book it is an exposé of social injustice, in Moore's case the exploitation of child labor in the Southern cotton mills. Another of Moore's interests was conservation of natural resources, dealt with in *Jack Ballington: Forester* (1911).

In the meantime, Moore was establishing himself as a leading journalist of the South. In 1905, he founded *The Trotwood Monthly*, which later merged with *Bob Taylor's Magazine* to become *The Taylor-Trotwood Magazine* when Governor Taylor went to the U. S. Senate. Moore contributed stories and sketches as well as a column on literature and

---

[12]Sam R. Watkins, *"Co. Aytch," First Tennessee Regiment: or, A Side Show of the Big Show* (Nashville: Cumberland Presbyterian Publishing House, 1882) 11.

manners. Most important, he encouraged new writers, including the young T. S. Stribling, who became a member of the staff.

Like William Gilmore Simms before the war, Moore was an active agent in Southern letters whose significance goes beyond what he himself wrote, although his work, like Simms's, has been neglected, to a large extent because of partisan Southern attitudes. The constants in his fiction are the Negro, the horse, and the bluegrass, all of which add up to a portrayal of life in Middle Tennessee in the generation following the war. In stories of the turf, at a time when Tennessee was still known internationally for the breeding and racing of fine horses, Moore discovered his best character, Wash, who is his black alter ego, but who is also a distinctive creation and very much his own man. At first he was "Old Wash," but he became "Uncle Wash" through the influence of publishers who wanted to cash in on the popularity of Uncle Remus, though Moore wrote for those who liked their humor strong and racy, not for children and sentimentalists.

Old Wash has a shrewd, selfish side. He schemes to stand well with women, delights in liquor and good tobacco, and turns all to his own profit. Widows, mules, preachers, ghosts, goats, the Ku Klux Klan— Moore provides a potpourri more in keeping with Sut Lovingood yarns than the febrile fiction of the local colorists. In a review of *Uncle Wash* in 1910, the Louisville *Courier-Journal* said that Moore's stories were "full of surprise and originality; they disclose an unmistakably thoroughly conceivable personality, somewhat hard in outline but not untrue to a distinct phase of negro life and character. The author knows his Tennessee."[13]

In "Sis Ca'line's Enticement," for example, Wash sends his wife to visit her mother at Christmas and arranges a party with Sis Ca'line Hunter. The lovers are surprised by the Negro minister, who tries to blackmail Wash for money to support the church. Wash refuses to be blackmailed. He arranges for a young white friend to appear at the church trial dressed up as the devil and wins his case when the trial breaks up in a riot.

> Men fainted, wimmen hed fits, an' de chilluns jes' went inter er kommertose state an' stayed dar. Dem dat wan't so badly paralyzed dey

---

[13]Louisville *Courier-Journal*, 13 August 1910. See Claud B. Green, *John Trotwood Moore: Tennessee Man of Letters* (Athens: University of Georgia Press, 1957) 85.

cu'd use dey legs, made a rush fur de only winder in the house. But ole Aunt Fat Fereby, dat weighed fo' hundred an' sixty pounds, who happen to be settin' next to it, got dar fust an' started through without calculatin' on de rotundity uv her corporosity. Of course, she got stuck betwixt de jice an' de winder sill, an' shut off de air an' de exit at de same time. An' dar she stuck wid her legs flyin' lak windmills, an' tryin' ter kick de roof offen de house, go through or bust![14]

Moore (who chose his own middle name in admiration of Dickens) was old-fashioned at a time when the novel, under the influence of Henry James and his followers, was undergoing great change. The novelist, Moore said, must do two things: tell a story and create characters. James and Howells were emasculating fiction by insisting on principles "which exclude real genius and reduce all styles to mediocrity."[15] Moore's view reflects a cultural predilection that would reassert itself to greater effect a few years later. Like Faulkner, he held to the virile style, the quick metaphor and compulsive adjective, and the humor of character and incident.

In 1893, Opie Read, journalist of *Arkansas Traveler* fame, published a novel about his native country around Gallatin, the same country Moore wrote about. *A Tennessee Judge* is a good place to begin a study of one of the most interesting literary figures Tennessee has produced and certainly one of the most productive. His biographer, after providing a catalogue of fifty-seven books, adds that it is impossible to make a complete list of Read's works, so varied were his activities and so informal his methods of authorship.[16] Out of this mass of material—most of it the slapdash work of a newspaper man, like Mark Twain's and before him Daniel Defoe's—some of Read's work is still worth reading, not only as entertainment, but as the expression of a perceptive and thoughtful mind.

In *A Tennessee Judge*, a young Chicago man comes South on orders of his doctor, buys a plantation outside Gallatin, and enters the life of

---

[14]John Trotwood Moore, *Uncle Wash: His Stories* (Philadelphia: John C. Winston Co., 1910) 18.

[15]"The Blight of the Howells School," *Taylor-Trotwood Magazine* 7 (August 1908): 470.

[16]Robert L. Morris, *Opie Read: American Humorist* (New York: Helios Books, 1967) 238-40.

the region, expressed most vibrantly in one of his neighbors, the Tennessee Judge. He falls in love with the judge's granddaughter, but the love affair has second place to the old gentleman himself and the collection of personalities in the community, odds and ends of both races now taken for granted in the Southern novel. Read favors the rural South. His attitude is clearly romantic in that he looks on his country as a sort of oasis in an industrial wasteland. But he is not a sentimentalist. His instinct is down-to-earth and his experience is too broad to indulge in the pipe dreams of contemporary writers about the South's recent history. Like Faulkner, he was a realist as well as a romantic and also a moralist who believed that certain principles that informed the past could have meaning in modern life.

In a series of forgotten novels—*A Kentucky Colonel, On the Suwanee River, My Young Master, An Arkansas Planter, The Jucklins, The Waters of Caney Fork, A Romance of Tennessee*, all in the 1890s—Read pursues this theme, which, if not original, demands attention when presented by an original mind. He was, says Burton Rascoe,

> an articulator of the robust spirit of democratic individualism which permeated the people who settled and built the river towns of the Mississippi Valley: he expressed their mores, their idioms, their lusty appetites, their quick tempers, their code of behavior, their disposition toward homely philosophy, their delight in extravagance, expansiveness, and humorous exaggeration, and above all their essential recklessness, impatience with restraint, and open defiance of the Eastern seaboard's notion of culture and polish.[17]

The South once had the promise of a great literature, the Tennessee Judge tells his Chicago friend, but that time is past. "Where is the rollicking fun of Sut Lovingood? Where is the vivid fancy of Simms? What has become of the charming grotesqueness of *Major Jones' Courtship*? All gone, sir, and the drivil has taken their place."[18] What Read did not see was that the "drivil" of his time represented a passing phase and that he and Moore were not only inheritors of a distinctive tradition but precursors of a twentieth-century revival that found its roots in

---

[17]Burton Rascoe, "Opie Read and Zane Grey," *Saturday Review of Literature*, 11 November 1939, 8.

[18]Opie Read, *A Tennessee Judge* (Chicago: Laird & Lee, 1893) 193.

those writers of the past that they admired. William Gilmore Simms, George Washington Harris, Mark Twain, John Trotwood Moore, Opie Read, William Faulkner, and those who followed them mark an unbroken line of development. The war changed life in the South and affected the way men wrote, but the nostalgia and sentimental games of the postwar generations were effete expressions of an old manner that had no permanent bearing on the course of Southern literature.

Tennessee lies very much at the center of this development. Her contribution to frontier literature and to the Southern Renascence a century later is part of literary history. What is not so generally known is the long period that lies between. Moore and Read not only produced a respectable body of letters but kept alive the native bent of their region and attacked the incursive "realism" of the Jamesian school, as Faulkner did later when he called James a prig who gave no pleasure because he was "detached from life."[19] What Moore and Read share with their predecessors and those who followed is an inspiration solidly based on life at home and absolute indifference to the outside. Old Wash and the Tennessee Judge might have turned up in a novel by Simms or Faulkner, not only because they tap the life force of a whole culture but because they are part of its paradox and part of the larger paradox in the heart that Faulkner said was the only thing worth writing about.

---

[19]*Faulkner in the University*, ed. Frederick L. Gwynn and Joseph L. Blotner (Charlottesville: University of Virginia Press, 1959) 16, 169.

Selected Bibliography

Brock, Henry Irving. "Spirit of the Tennessee Mountains." *New York Times Book Review,* 17 March 1906, 165.

Cary, Richard. *Mary N. Murfree.* New York: Twayne Publishers, Inc., 1967.

Clark, Edwin. "Tastes of a Self-sufficient Woman." Review of *Seven Times Seven* by Maria Thompson Daviess, *New York Times Book Review*, 18 May 1924, 17.

Davenport, F. Garvin. *Cultural Life in Nashville on the Eve of the Civil War.* Chapel Hill: University of North Carolina Press, 1941.

Davidson, James W. *The Living Writers of the South.* New York: Carlton, 1869.

Daviess, Maria Thompson. "American Backgrounds for Fiction: Tennessee." *Bookman* 38 (December 1913): 394-99.

Forrest, Mary [Julia Deane Freeman]. *Women of the South Distinguished in Literature.* New York: Garrett Press, 1861.

Frank, Waldo. "Among the Southern Appalachians." *New England Magazine* 24 (May 1901): 231-47.

Green, Claud B. *John Trotwood Moore: Tennessee Man of Letters.* Athens: University of Georgia Press, 1954.

Harkness, David J. "Tennessee in Literature." *University of Tennessee News Letters* 27, no. 11 (November 1949).

Herrick, Robert. "Henry Sydnor Harrison." *New Republic*, 27 March 1915, 199-201.

Hubbell, Jay B. *The South in American Literature, 1607-1900.* Durham NC: Duke University Press, 1954.

Ingle, Edward. *Southern Sidelights: A Picture of Social and Economic Life in the South a Generation Before the War*. New York: T. Y. Crowell & Co., 1896.

James, W. P. "On the Theory and Practice of Local Color." *Living Age*, 12 June 1897, 743-48.

Landrum, Grace Warren. "Notes on the Reading of the Old South." *American Literature* 3 (March 1931): 60-71.

Lanier, Doris. "Mary Noailles Murfree: An Interview." *Tennessee Historical Quarterly* 31 (Fall 1972): 276-78.

MacGowan, Alice. "Preface," *Sword in the Mountains*. New York: G. P. Putnam's Sons, 1910.

Meeman, Edward J. "Introduction," Virginia Frazer Boyle, *Songs from the South*. Memphis: S. C. Toof & Co., 1939.

Morris, Robert L. *Opie Read: American Humorist*. New York: Helios Books, 1967.

Moses, Montrose J. *The Literature of the South*. New York: T. Y. Crowell & Co., 1910.

Park, Ulna Foster. "The Early Literature of East Tennessee: A Study of Literary Publications and Their Background from the Beginning to 1840." M.A. thesis, University of Tennessee, 1954.

Parks, Edd Winfield. *Charles Egbert Craddock*. Chapel Hill: University of North Carolina Press, 1941.

Phillips, Elizabeth C. "John Tomlin: The 'Literary Postmaster' of Jackson, Tennessee." *West Tennessee Historical Society Papers* 8 (1954): 39-54.

Rascoe, Burton. "Opie Read and Zane Grey." *Saturday Review of Literature*, 11 November 1939, 8.

Raymond, Ida [Mary T. Tardy]. *Living Female Writers of the South*. Philadelphia: Claxton, Remsen & Haffelfinger, 1872.

Rubin, Louis D., Jr. *A Bibliographical Guide to the Study of Southern Literature*. Baton Rouge: Louisiana State University Press, 1969.

Smith, Charles Forster. "Southern Dialect in Life and Literature." *Southern Bivouac*, n.s., 1 (November 1885): 343-51.

Starrett, Vincent. "Opie Read and the Great Novel." In *Buried Caesars: Essays in Literary Appreciation*. Chicago: Covici-McGee Co., 1923.

Warren, John W. and Adrian W. McClaren. *Tennessee Belles-Lettres: A Guide to Tennessee Literature*. Morristown TN: Morrison Printing Co., Inc., 1977.

Whisnant, David E. "Introduction," Emma Bell Miles, *The Spirit of the Mountains*. Knoxville: University of Tennessee Press, 1975.

Wiley, Bell Irvin. "Introduction," Sam R. Watkins, *"Co. Aytch," First Tennessee Regiment: or, A Side Show of the Big Show*. Jackson TN: McCowat-Mercer Press, 1952.

Wingfield, Marshall. *Literary Memphis: A Survey of Its Writers and Writings*. Memphis: West Tennessee Historical Society, 1942.

Wright, Nathalia. "Introduction," Mary Noailles Murfree, *In The Tennessee Mountains*. Knoxville: University of Tennessee Press, 1970.

The Southern Renascence and the Writers of Tennessee

Lloyd Davis

Beginning with the publication of Sherwood Anderson's *Winesburg, Ohio* in 1919, America entered its second golden age of literature. The first golden age had encompassed the decade of the 1850s, which produced *The Scarlet Letter, The House of the Seven Gables, Moby Dick, Walden*, and *Leaves of Grass*. The second golden age of the 1920s and 1930s gave us not only the works of Pound, Eliot, Hemingway, Fitzgerald, and other famous American expatriates, but also the works of a large number of American writers who, for the most part, chose to live and write in America. The vast majority of these writers were Southerners, such as William Faulkner, Thomas Wolfe, John Crowe Ransom, Allen Tate, and Robert Penn Warren. The tremendous outpouring of extremely high quality work by these and many other Southern writers in fiction, poetry, drama, and criticism in the period between the two world wars has come to be known as the Southern Renascence.[1]

This renascence was not, however, in the strict sense a "rebirth." The Southern literary tradition established during the first half of the nineteenth century had not died out completely with Lee's surrender at Appomattox in 1865, but it had declined to the extent that in 1917 H. L. Mencken had referred to the South as "the Sahara of the Bozart." In

---

[1] I have chosen to use the term *renascence* instead of *renaissance* or *resurgence* following the example of Louis D. Rubin, Jr., and Walter Sullivan, the two best-known commentators on this period.

a few short years, however, following the end of the First World War, this "Sahara" produced, in addition to Faulkner, Wolfe, Ransom, Tate, and Warren, such writers as Elizabeth Maddox Roberts, Katherine Anne Porter, Paul Green, Lillian Hellman, Jesse Stuart, and a host of other writers like Stark Young, William Alexander Percy, and Hamilton Basso, to name just three, who contributed significantly to the renascence without achieving reputations of the first rank.

The year 1918 is frequently cited as a turning point in the history of Western civilization, and it is convenient to date the inception of the Southern Renascence from this time. We must remember, however, that America's literary golden age of the 1920s, of which the Southern Renascence and the writers of Tennessee were such an important part, is in reality a later stage of an international cultural revolution, much of which took place on the Continent prior to the First World War. The music of Stravinsky, the sculpture of Brancusi, and the painting of Picasso antedate the war by several years. Although New York had been treated to the famous Armory Show of 1913, it was not until after 1918 that the rest of the country, perhaps especially the South, began to feel the revitalization of artistic creativity. For Southern writers, the Southern Renascence was, as Louis D. Rubin, Jr., has pointed out, "a part of a world literary movement, a worldwide artistic questioning of their time and place."[2]

But what was this "time and place" the Southern writers began to question and why were they questioning it? For one thing, the South, as well as most of the rest of the country, began to undergo technological and social changes. Its traditional institutions began to weaken under the impact of increasing industrialization. The Southern writers at the beginning of the renascence had all been born shortly before or shortly after the turn of the century. They had grown up in a traditional society characterized by an agrarian economy and a prescribed code of morals and manners. The social structure was rigid, and the Confederate states shared a painful memory of the Civil War and Reconstruction, of postwar poverty. The regional religion was largely Calvinistic, with its emphasis on original sin and the imperfectibility of man. There was a love of language, lore, and literature. There was a

---

[2]"Southern Literature: The Historical Image," in *South: Modern Literature in Its Cultural Setting*, ed. Rubin and Robert D. Jacobs (New York: Doubleday, 1961) 40.

sense of history, of tradition, in which the past was kept alive. Leisure was valued as an important aspect of everyday life. And finally, this society centered on the community life of the small town.

With the worldwide impact of the War of 1914-1918, however, this society could not avoid change. As Louis D. Rubin, Jr., has put it, "The Southern Literary Renascence occurred in a period of transition for the South. Certain young writers, reared in one kind of world, saw that world changing into another kind. They were themselves of that new, changed world, and yet apart from it, and conscious of the difference."[3]

It is impossible to say exactly when or where the Southern Renascence began, but the encouragement of creative writing by several Southern universities and the establishment of new "little" magazines were of significance. In the first two years of the 1920s four highly influential literary magazines were founded. In New Orleans *The Double Dealer* published its first issue in 1921 and later published poems by Faulkner and Hemingway. In the same year *The Review* appeared in Richmond and *The Lyric* in Norfolk. In April of 1922 *The Fugitive*, which was to become the most important magazine of the period, began publication in Nashville.

The Southern universities also contributed to the renascence. At Chapel Hill Professor Frederick Koch founded the Carolina Playmakers, where Thomas Wolfe and Paul Green came under his influence. The connection between the Faulkners and the University of Mississippi is well known. Without doubt, however, Vanderbilt, of all the universities, played the most significant role in the Southern Renascence; here the Fugitive group was formed and subsequently published *The Fugitive* from early 1922 until the end of 1925.[4]

"Then if you ask me why, of all places, at Nashville," Donald Davidson wrote in 1957, "and why not at Charleston, Charlottesville, Atlanta, Macon, Athens, New Orleans, I can say only that I can see no good reason why not if, granting ability and interest, the poets of such Southern

---

[3]Ibid., 36.

[4]See Louise Cowan's thoroughly researched and well-written *The Fugitive Group: A Literary History* (Baton Rouge: Louisiana State University Press, 1959).

centers had applied themselves to the art of poetry as exclusively as we did for a long while at Nashville."[5]

Before the Fugitive group even had a name, associations among several of the members had taken place. John Crowe Ransom, a native of Pulaski, Tennessee, entered Vanderbilt as a freshman in the fall of 1903. After two years he left the university to teach in Mississippi, returning to Vanderbilt in 1907 and graduating in 1909. That fall, another Tennessean, Donald Davidson of Campbellsville, entered Vanderbilt, but stayed only one year. After four years of teaching in private schools, Davidson came back to Vanderbilt in 1914. That year Ransom joined the Vanderbilt faculty, having received a B.A. as a Rhodes Scholar. In the meantime other soon-to-be Fugitives arrived. Stanley Johnson, from Nashville, entered Vanderbilt in 1911. Alec B. Stevenson, born in Canada, had come to Nashville shortly after his birth, and his father was a member of the Vanderbilt faculty. William Yandell Elliott, a native of Murfreesboro, Tennessee, entered the University in 1913, and Nathaniel Hirsch, of Nashville, entered the same year.

In the summer of 1915, Davidson, while a student, made the acquaintance of Sidney Mttron (pronounced Me-tat-tron) Hirsh and found his conversation so stimulating that Davidson invited Ransom to join in the soirees that began to be held at Hirsch's home. Walter Clyde Curry, a South Carolinian and a new instructor in Vanderbilt's English department, joined the group in the fall of 1915, along with Johnson, Stevenson, Elliott, and Hirsch's half-brother, Nathaniel. With the exception of Sidney Hirsch, these men, who formed the nucleus of the group later to be known as the Fugitives, were either students or faculty members at Vanderbilt.

The group was temporarily disbanded during the hostilities of 1917-1918 but was reformed after the Armistice. Ransom returned to his faculty post in 1919, and Davidson, who had taught at Kentucky Wesleyan during 1919-1920, accepted a graduate assistantship at Vanderbilt in 1920. In this year, too, Merrill Moore, a native of Columbia, Tennessee, entered Vanderbilt and later joined the Fugitives. (In later years, Moore, a psychiatrist, published *M*, a collection of a thousand sonnets, which gained recognition more for its quantity than for qual-

---

[5]*Southern Writers in the Modern World* (Athens: University of Georgia Press, 1958) 17.

ity.) In addition to the prewar members still in Nashville, there were two notable additions: Vanderbilt junior Allen Tate in 1921 and sophomore Robert Penn Warren in 1922.

From the initial get-together in the summer of 1915 to the publication of the first issue of *The Fugitive* in 1922, some members of the group had been discussing for as long as seven years the composition and criticism of poetry before any of it ever appeared in print, except for Ransom's *Poems About God* (New York: Henry Holt, 1919). Davidson remembered the typical Fugitive meeting like this:

> Generally we met once a week, on Saturday evenings. There was no formal organization. Each brought to the meeting whatever new poems he had composed during the days preceding, always providing typed copies for the circle. Each in turn read his poem or poems. Then all took part in a relentless critical discussion.[6]

Never before or since has any literary magazine emerged with so much planning and so much unity of purpose on the part of its contributors. With the launching of *The Fugitive* we see the combined influences of the university and the "little magazine" on the Southern Renascence.

In the early spring of 1922, at a meeting of the Fugitive group in the home of Hirsch's brother-in-law, James M. Frank, Alec Stevenson had suggested *The Fugitive* as a name for the new magazine. The title was agreed upon, and the word "fugitive" was explicated in Ransom's now-famous "Foreword" to the first issue:

> Official exception having been taken by the sovereign people to the mint julep, a literary phase known rather euphemistically as Southern literature has expired, like any other stream whose source is stopped up. The demise was not untimely: among other advantages THE FUGITIVE is enabled to come to birth in Nashville, Tennessee, under a star not entirely unsympathetic. THE FUGITIVE flees from nothing faster than from the high-caste Brahmins of the Old South. Without raising the question of whether the blood in the veins of its editors runs red, they at any rate are not advertising it as blue; indeed, as to

---

[6]Ibid., 18.

pedigree, they cheerfully invite the most unfavorable inference from the circumstances of their anonymity.[7]

Later, Donald Davidson gave his interpretation of the meaning of the title: "If there is a significance in the title of the magazine, it lies perhaps in the sentiment of the editors (on this point I am sure we all agree) to flee from the extremes of conventionalism, whether old or new. They hope to keep in touch with and to utilize in their work the best qualities of modern poetry, without at the same time casting aside as unworthy all that is established as good in the past."[8]

Here, then, are two Fugitive poet-critics writing in the early 1920s, Ransom emphasizing the break with the Old South and its sentimentality symbolized by the mint julep, and Davidson asserting the value of conserving "all that is established as good in the past." These positions may seem inconsistent, but they are not. In this period of taking stock, of looking back on the history of Southern literature from the point of view of the post-1918 "modern," we see the two men rejecting the worn-out forms, the techniques of the nineteenth century, in favor of those of the twentieth. But traditions of value were to be preserved.

The last of the nineteen issues of *The Fugitive* was published in December of 1925. In the end, Ransom, Davidson, Tate, and Warren were the only contributors to establish national reputations, but *The Fugitive* as a whole had attracted not only national but international attention as well. According to Frederick J. Hoffman, it was the only little magazine of its time that "rocketed its poets into the national spotlight."[9]

Two additional Tennessee writers who were not actually Fugitives but who were closely identified with the movement were Cleanth Brooks and Andrew Nelson Lytle. Brooks, who followed hard on the heels of the Fugitives, produced two milestones of poetry criticism—*Poetry and the Tradition* and *The Well Wrought Urn*—and joined with native-born Kentuckian Robert Penn Warren to produce college textbooks that dominated academia in the years following World War II. Ly-

---

[7]*The Fugitive*, 1, no. 1 (April 1922): 1.

[8]Unpublished letter to Corra A. Harris, 10 March 1923, as quoted in Cowan, 44.

[9]Charles Allen Hoffman and Carolyn F. Ulrich, *The Little Magazine: A History and a Bibliography* (Princeton NJ: Princeton University Press, 1946) 124.

tle, another Vanderbilt student who joined the Fugitives just as the group was disbanding, left the South for a brief career as playwright. He returned in 1930 to join the second Nashville-oriented group, the Agrarians, and contribute to *I'll Take My Stand*, the group's attack on industrialism. In the following years, Lytle established himself as one of the best of the Southern novelists.

Thus in the Southern Renascence, *The Fugitive* and the Fugitive group played extremely important roles. Following the success of *The Fugitive*, other literary periodicals, like *The Sewanee Review* and *The Southern Review*, began in the South. It is interesting to note that, after Poe and Lowell, the poet-critic had all but died out in America; now he had been reborn in Nashville, Tennessee.

The second major contribution to the Southern Renascence, as far as Tennessee was concerned at least, was the formation of a group of writers, historians, and social commentators who came to be known as the Nashville Agrarians, although not all were from Nashville nor were they all from Tennessee. In the five years between the cessation of *The Fugitive* and publication of the Agrarians' *I'll Take My Stand: The South and the Agrarian Tradition* in 1930, the four major Fugitives—Ransom, Davidson, Tate, and Warren—had become increasingly concerned with social developments in the South, chiefly the incursion of the idea of "progress" pushed by the encroachment of the industrial complex and the business community. Then, too, the Scopes Trial in Dayton, Tennessee, in the summer of 1925 had provoked much criticism of the South. According to Richard H. King, "It was in response to Mencken's attack on the South in Dayton that poets and intellectuals in Nashville readied the counterattack which was to appear in 1930 as *I'll Take My Stand*."[10]

In a partial reversal of the Fugitive position of fleeing from the traditions of the Old South, the Agrarians not only attacked growing industrialization and the philosophy of the perfectibility of man and advocated agrarianism as a way of life in the South, but also extended their criticism to include the New South Movement of the late nineteenth century. They resented the commercialization of the applied sciences and were critical of the pace of industrialism and its debili-

---

[10]*A Southern Renaissance: The Cultural Awakening of the American South, 1930-1955* (New York: Oxford University Press, 1980) 15.

tating effect on religion, art, and the everyday life-style of the South. They were especially concerned with the role of advertising, which they saw as an attempt to correct overproduction of consumer goods. Leisure was seen as one of the greatest of Southern values and labor was viewed as a joy and a mode of self-fullfillment. The Agrarian position was anticommunist and anticollective. They denigrated the "progressive" growth of cities and looked to the small towns as the proper cultural centers of an agrarian economy.

Although *I'll Take My Stand* was out of print for many years, it originally provoked a tremendous amount of controversy, comment, and criticism, because the issues raised by the twelve Southerners go far beyond their Southern focus. They were in effect dealing with the decline of a way of life in an industrial society. As Louis D. Rubin states in his introduction to the 1962 edition of *I'll Take My Stand*, the book "is a rebuke to materialism, a corrective to the workings of Progress, and a reaffirmation of man's aesthetic and spiritual needs."[11]

In the symposium the four major Fugitives mentioned above were joined by three other contributors who were non-Fugitives from Tennessee: soon-to-be-novelist Andrew Nelson Lytle; Lyle H. Lanier, a graduate in philosophy from Vanderbilt who later joined the faculty as a professor of psychology; and Henry Blue Kline, another Vanderbilt student who was greatly respected by Ransom and Davidson, who, after working for a number of federal agencies, became an editorial writer for the St. Louis *Post-Dispatch*.[12]

The collection begins with Ransom's "Reconstructed But Unregenerate," in which he describes the "gospel of Progress" and the "gospel of Service," which are changing the traditional life-style of the South. Ransom calls for the South to take a stronger political position as a region and sees the South as either a separate culture—by analogy with Scotland in the United Kingdom—or as part of an agrarian coalition with rural New England or the agrarian West.

---

[11]"Introduction," Harper Torchbook edition, 1962; reprinted in *I'll Take My Stand: The South and the Agrarian Tradition*, ed. Louis D. Rubin, Jr. (Baton Rouge: Louisiana State University Press, 1977) xxxi.

[12]Other contributors were historian Frank Lawrence Owsley, Imagist poet John Gould Fletcher, political scientist Herman Clarence Nixon, literary historian John Donald Wade, and novelist, translator, and drama critic Stark Young.

Ransom's essay is followed by Davidson's "A Mirror for Artists," in which Davidson raises this question: Is art possible in an industrial society? In the past, he says, art has been produced only by societies that are "stable, religious, and agrarian." He is critical of romantic art, although he sees it as the only kind possible in an industrial society. Davidson emphasizes the necessity for the alienation of the artist; however, he does not advocate an alienation of the wilderness but rather a withdrawal into the recesses of a tradition such as that of the South. Indeed, he sees conditions in the South as conducive to good art.

Lytle's essay, "The Hind Tit," emphasizes the role of the yeoman farmer as being central to an agrarian economy. He advocates a "Farming South" as opposed to a "Planting South" and deplores the creation of tenant farming and "the furnishing system" that came about with the breakup of large plantations following the Civil War. In describing the somewhat idealistic "typical" life of the freeholder, Lytle points to the joy in work and in play and notes the aesthetic values inherent in folk culture, such as singing, dancing, and play-parties. His argument is for the value of subsistence, all-round family farming, and he advocates returning to this system along with home manufacturing and turning away from the mass factory-facturing of industrialism.

Lyle H. Lanier, a native of Madison County, Tennessee, entered Vanderbilt in 1920 and was a faculty member in the Vanderbilt psychology department at the time of the Agrarian symposium. The title of Lanier's contribution is straightforward: "A Critique of the Philosophy of Progress." This essay reveals wide learning in the history of philosophy and would be instructive for that reason alone. In relation to the idea of Progress, however, Lanier indicates that progress usually means "business" that exploits the individual and advocates "progressive development toward some highly desired, but always undesignated, goal." Dating the idea of Progress from the Renaissance, and specifically from Francis Bacon, Lanier points out that "Man henceforth would be concerned not so much with saving his soul as with making himself comfortable." He then traces the history of Progress from Kant through Hegel and Comte to Marx and Darwin, at which point the theory of evolution can be seen as supporting human progress. Later the pragmatism of William James and the instrumentalism of John Dewey (that is, the concept of freeing the human being to fully realize his capacities) contributed to the popularity of the idea of Progress, especially in America.

Lanier is especially critical of Dewey's advocacy of industrialism and political socialism dedicated to remaking human nature, relying on collective behavior rather than individual leadership, and asserting the brotherhood of man through industrialism. Rather than Progress, Lanier says, Dewey's philosophy produces "personal isolation and fractionation of life functions into an ever-expanding and differentiating system of formalized institutions." Lanier's answer: Stabilize production in each industry and induce the unemployed to return to agriculture.

Another Tennessean, Henry Blue Kline, contributed "William Remington: A Study in Individualism." In this parable Remington (who bears a marked resemblance to Kline) is living an unhappy life in America closer to Detroit than to New Orleans, but somewhere in between. His friends are vivacious types with whom Remington does not quite fit in; although he is aware of his unhappy state, his friends are not aware of theirs.

In Remington's search for a meaningful occupation he considers teaching but rejects this idea when he perceives that "modern Socrateses are given the hemlock cup not at the end but at the beginning of their careers." He next considers art as a way of life until he encounters what a modern reader would call a "catch-22" situation: in a world of violent and rapid change the artist is forced to turn inward and express only personal concerns, *but* if the artist turns in upon himself he has nothing to express but "transitory states of feeling" which can never result in great art. Remington then considers entering the factory or the mill, occupations he has had on a part-time basis during the summers between his college years. He concludes, however, that the factory would be boring and he is too intellectual for the mill. When the Great Depression comes with its solution of *Buy!* Remington sees that, like his friends, the whole society vacillates between intoxication and depression. He has no desire for the needless gadgets offered by this industrial society, although he does like some of its products.

Becoming a "critical skeptic," he sees that if he enters society and works he will have no time for leisure. On the other hand, if he does not work he will not be able to benefit from any of the *things* he likes

Literature of Tennessee 31

and wants. His decision is to do a little of both, but to be selective; thus, he is a constant in a variable society.

At this point Remington decides to move farther South, this time closer to New Orleans than Detroit, but still somewhere in between. Here he finds congeniality. For the first time he feels he belongs: "And here was an audience, not a very large one, perhaps, but in sympathy with his own sense of human values." In this new environment he is willing to fight for his new-found home on these principles: (1) careful buying, (2) "civil and political activity to discourage promoters and exploiters from working their way in the section where Remington's group lives and prefers to live," and (3) ending the "aimless flux" of life and advocating the doctrine of self-acceptance and self-expression in favor of leading the sterotyped life.

Thus Lanier and Kline, as well as the better-known Tennesseans, made important contributions to the Agrarian Movement, itself an important aspect of the literary renascence of the South.

Although the Fugitives and Agrarians account for a large part of the success of the Southern Renascence, the work of individual Tennessee authors not directly connected with the two groups should not be overlooked. These nonaffiliated writers can be divided into two categories: those who achieved reputations between 1920 and World War II and those who appeared on the literary scene after 1945.

Of the first group, one of the earliest Tennessee writers to emerge was T. S. Stribling. Born Thomas Sigismund Stribling in Clifton, Tennessee, in 1881, he spent his formative years writing adventure stories. His first novel, *Birthright* (1922), dealt with race relations. This was followed by his most popular novel, *Teeftallow*, in 1924. In 1932 he was awarded the Pulitzer Prize for *The Store*, the second volume of a trilogy that included *The Forge* (1931) and *Unfinished Cathedral* (1934). Stribling, who has been compared to Erskine Caldwell, deals realistically with small town life in the South.

Evelyn Scott, born in 1893 in Clarksville, Tennessee, grew up in New Orleans and later traveled to South America and England, where she lived with her English husband. Her most famous works are her two volumes of autobiography, *Escapade* (1923) and *Background in Tennessee* (1937). Her novel *The Wave* (1929) was a notable contribution to the literature of the American Civil War.

Caroline Gordon, although born in Kentucky in 1895, spent most of her youth in Clarksville, Tennessee, where her father was headmaster of a school for the study of the classics. Miss Gordon claims to have received her early education from her father, who was the prototype for the main character of her second novel, *Aleck Maury, Sportsman* (1934). She received her bachelor's degree from Bethany College in West Virginia in 1916 and returned to the South. In 1924 she married Fugitive Allen Tate. Her first novel, *Penhally* (1931), was followed by numerous volumes, including *None Shall Look Back* (1937), a saga of the Civil War, and two excellent collections of short fiction, *The Forest of the South* (1945) and *Old Red and Other Stories* (1963).

Roark Bradford, born in Lauderdale County, Tennessee, in 1896, served as an artillery officer in World War I and was not released from active duty until 1920. In 1922 he settled in New Orleans, where he became the city editor of the *Times-Picayune*. His great interest in the American Negro, especially in the humor of the Southern Negro as it was expressed in dialect tales, resulted in his first collection of stories, *Ol' Man Adam an' His Chillun* (1928). Material from this volume was converted into the popular stage play and motion picture *Green Pastures* by Bradford's friend Marc Connelly. Although Bradford wrote several other books, including *This Side of Jordan* (1929), he never again achieved the success of his humorous initial work. He died in 1948 from a fever contracted while serving in Africa with the U.S. Navy during World War II.

Horace McCoy, born in Pegram, Tennessee, in 1897, wrote one of the most popular novels of the 1930s, *They Shoot Horses, Don't They?* The book was extremely popular in Europe before World War II. McCoy, who worked as a sports reporter in Dallas in the twenties before going to Hollywood to write screen scripts, had been a part-time expatriate and friend of F. Scott Fitzgerald. *They Shoot Horses, Don't They?* was followed by *No Pockets in a Shroud* (1937) and three other novels written before his death in 1955, but his first remained his best.

James Agee and Randall Jarrell were both published prior to World War II, but it was not until the country had settled into the peacetime era that these two Tennesseans emerged as important contributors to the second wave of writers who would continue the tradition of the Southern Renascence.

Agee, whose greatest fame was to be attained posthumously with the publication of his novel *A Death in the Family* (1957), began his career as a poet. Born in Knoxville in 1909, Agee attended Exeter Academy and Harvard, from which he graduated in 1932. Two years later his collection of poems, *Permit Me Voyage*, was published in the Yale Younger Poets Series. While working as a reporter for *Fortune* magazine, he became interested in the sharecroppers of Alabama. His book-length documentary was subsequently published in 1941 as *Let Us Now Praise Famous Men*, with photographs by Walker Evans. Agee later wrote reviews for *Nation* and *Time*, several screen scripts, notably *The African Queen*, and a four-part television series on the life of Abraham Lincoln.

Although Randall Jarrell had contributed to *Five Young American Poets* (1940) and had published *Blood for a Stranger* (1942) in the same year in which he entered the U.S. Army Air Forces, his early reputation was based primarily on the poems written out of his military experience: *Little Friend, Little Friend* (1945) and *Losses* (1948). Born in Nashville in 1914, Jarrell took two degrees from Vanderbilt, A.B. (1935) and M.A. (1938). In the period following World War II, Jarrell became well respected among American poets. In addition to poetry, he published a book of criticism, *Poetry and the Age* (1953); a novel, *Pictures from an Institution* (1954); and two children's books, *The Gingerbread Rabbit* (1963) and *The Bat Poet* (1964). Like his mentor, John Crowe Ransom, with whom he taught at Kenyon College (1937-1939), Jarrell was proficient in teaching, poetry, and criticism, although his reputation rests primarily on his poetry, which includes two later volumes, *The Woman at the Washington Zoo* (1960) and *The Lost World* (1965), published in the year of his death.

Poet George Scarbrough, born in Benton, Tennessee, in 1915, was a newspaperman and farmer for several years before becoming a teacher in the secondary schools of Tennessee. He published *Tellico Blue* (1949), *The Course Is Upward* (1951), and *Summer So-Called* (1956) before beginning a second teaching career at the college level at Hiwassee College and later at Chattanooga City College. His *New and Selected Poems* was published in 1977.

Peter Taylor, although primarily a practitioner of the short story, also writes plays and is the author of one novel. Born in Trenton, Tennessee, in 1919, he attended Vanderbilt and Southwestern at Memphis before earning his A.B. at Kenyon in 1940. Taylor's first collection of stories, *A Long Fourth and Other Stories* (1948), was followed by a novel, *A Woman of Means* (1950), and a book containing short stories and one play, *The Widows of Thornton* (1954). *Happy Families Are All Alike* appeared in 1960, *The Collected Stories* in 1969, and *In the Miro District* in 1977.

Walter Sullivan, born in Nashville in 1924, has spent the greater part of his life as a teacher at Vanderbilt, where he received his B.A. in 1947. Before beginning his teaching career there in 1949, however, he served with the U.S. Marine Corps and earned the M.F.A. degree at the University of Iowa. Sullivan's novels include *Sojourn of a Stranger* (1957) and *The Long, Long Love* (1959). His books of literary criticism are *Death by Melancholy* (1972) and *Requiem for the Renascence* (1976).

Another Nashville native, Madison Jones, born in 1925, received his bachelor's degree from Vanderbilt in 1949. Jones's best-known novels are *The Exile* (1967) and *Passage Through Gehenna* (1978). Others include *The Innocent* (1957), *Forest of the Night* (1960), *A Buried Land* (1963), and *A Cry of Absence* (1971).

One of the youngest of the Tennessee writers is Jesse Hill Ford. Born in Troy, Alabama, in 1928, he graduated from Vanderbilt in 1951. Ford is perhaps best known for his 1965 novel *The Liberation of Lord Byron Jones*. In addition to novels like *Mountains of Gilead* (1961), *The Feast of Saint Barnabas* (1969), and *The Raider* (1975), Ford is the author of a television drama, *The Conversion of Buster Drumwright*, produced on network television and published in 1964.

Looking back at the Fugitives, the Agrarians, and the individual, nonaffiliated writers of the last sixty years, we can see that from the very beginning of the Southern Renascence the writers of Tennessee have made a monumental contribution. When we consider the accomplishments of the Fugitives in poetry, fiction, and literary criticism; the catalytic effect of the Agrarians' eloquently stating a thesis against which Southern industrial and agrarian development could be measured, the idea of Progress could be evaluated, and America at large could assess its life-style; and, finally, the quantity and quality of the achievements of the writers between wars as well as those of more recent times, would it not be difficult to argue that no other state has contributed more to the Southern Renascence than Tennessee?

Selected Bibliography*

Bradbury, John M. *Renaissance in the South: A Critical History of the Literature, 1920-1960.* Chapel Hill: University of North Carolina Press, 1963.

Core, George, ed. *Southern Fiction Today: Renascence and Beyond.* Athens: University of Georgia Press, 1969.

Cowan, Louise. *The Fugitive Group: A Literary History.* Baton Rouge: Louisiana State University Press, 1959.

King, Richard H. *A Southern Renaissance: The Cultural Awakening of the American South, 1930-1955.* New York: Oxford University Press, 1980.

Pratt, William, ed. *The Fugitive Poets: Modern Southern Literature in Perspective.* New York: Dutton, 1965.

Rubin, Louis D., Jr. "Introduction," *I'll Take My Stand* by Twelve Southerners. Baton Rouge: Louisiana State University Press, 1977.

——————. *The Southern Renascence.* Taped lecture. De Land FL: Everett/Edwards, Inc., 1976. Cassette curriculum No. 905. Summarizes much of Rubin's earlier writing on the subject.

——————. *The Wary Fugitives.* Baton Rouge: Louisiana State University Press, 1978.

——————. *The Writer in the South: Studies in a Literary Community.* Athens: University of Georgia Press, 1965.

---

*See also Louis D. Rubin, Jr., ed., *A Bibliographical Guide to the Study of Southern Literature* (Baton Rouge: Louisiana State University Press, 1969) and Jerry T. Williams, ed.,*Southern Literature 1968-1975: A Checklist of Scholarship* (Boston: G. K. Hall, 1978).

Stewart, John L. *The Burden of Time: The Fugitives and Agrarians*. Princeton NJ: Princeton University Press, 1965.

Sullivan, Walter. *Death By Melancholy: Essays on Modern Southern Fiction*. Baton Rouge: Louisiana State University Press, 1972.

_____. *A Requiem for the Renascence: The State of Fiction in the Modern South*. Athens: University of Georgia Press, 1976.

3

John Crowe Ransom

William Osborne

The Southern Renascence, with all its brilliance and diversity, would have been a less powerful, less cogent literary movement had John Crowe Ransom, Tennessee's foremost poet and critic, not been at its center. Ransom's scholastic integrity, intellectual toughness, and humanistic camaraderie were qualities that brought focus and direction to some of the central concerns of that important movement.

To be more specific, John Crowe Ransom's principal contributions were these: he constructed an original and intriguing poetic idiom and wrote a number of first-rate poems that in all likelihood will find a permanent place in American literature; he founded and edited the *Kenyon Review*, making it one of America's most prestigious journals of literature, aesthetics, and philosophy; he defined some of the main tenets of the New Criticism, using his own poetry, essays, and reviews (almost four hundred published pieces) to elaborate his theories; and, finally, as teacher, organizer, and friend, he exerted an enormous influence on the productivity of such notable writers as Cleanth Brooks, Randall Jarrell, Robert Lowell, Andrew Lytle, Allen Tate, Peter Taylor, and Robert Penn Warren.

Genial, quiet-spoken, self-deprecating, studious, Ransom constantly played down his personal impact on the world of letters, preferring instead to let his works be judged on their own merits, independent of himself as a person existing in a given place and time.

Implicit in this stance was one of his most important and influential critical ideas—the necessity of reading a literary text closely, without undue attention to biographical, historical, or social considerations. Generations of students were to be influenced markedly by this strong emphasis on close textual reading, an emphasis that insisted on a careful study of every word and mark of punctuation in the poem; on a minute examination of word order, denotation, and connotation; on rhythm, rhyme, and sound; and on a painstaking search for what Ransom later called the "structure" and "texture" of the poem. The purpose of such a study and search was to learn what poetry, as opposed to science, could teach of the richness around us and to enjoy what we had come to understand of the "world's body."

John Crowe Ransom was born on 30 April 1888, in Pulaski, Tennessee. His father, John James Ransom, was a Methodist minister with an intellectual and scholarly disposition. Though the family moved frequently from one agricultural community to another in Middle Tennessee, the children's education was never neglected. In the home, great attention was paid to books and learning. To prepare himself for Vanderbilt University, Ransom was sent to the Bowen School in Nashville, a private college preparatory school noted for its rigorous training in mathematics, Latin, Greek, and science.

After graduating with honors from Vanderbilt, Ransom became a Rhodes Scholar at Oxford, where from 1910 to 1913 he studied philosophy, history, and languages to prepare himself for a scholarly career. In 1914 when he was invited to become a member of the English department at Vanderbilt, he gladly accepted, although his studies at Oxford were not directly related to the teaching of English literature and composition. During his early years as an English professor his career as a poet and his connection with the Fugitive Movement began.

The Fugitive Affiliation

If Ransom found himself teaching in a field that was alien to much of his classical training at Oxford, he nevertheless overcame whatever problems he encountered by diligent study and through the stimulation of classroom discussions. Ransom brought to his teaching a philosophical habit of mind that soon attracted a group of students who already had been meeting informally with some of their teachers in the evenings to discuss a wide range of ideas that were prompted by courses they were taking or books they were reading. The group (which was shortly to become known as the Fugitives) consisted of not only students and their professors, but of townspeople as well. Their discussions covered a wide variety of subjects, at first more philosophical than literary.

The meetings of this group (among whom were Donald Davidson, Sidney Hirsch, William Yandell Elliott, Stanley Johnson, Alec Stevenson, and Ransom) were interrupted by the First World War, but after the war, meetings resumed. By 1921, Allen Tate had been added to the number, which finally totaled sixteen Fugitives. After 1920, their meetings became more literary, more frequent, and more carefully structured, with their own poetry providing the center of their discussions. Donald Davidson has described the pattern most of their sessions assumed:

> First we gave strict attention, from the beginning, to the *form* of poetry ... Every poem was read aloud by the poet himself, while the members of the group had before them typed copies of the poem. The reading aloud might be followed by a murmur of compliments, but often enough there was a period of ruminative silence.... Then discussion began, and it was likely to be ruthless in its exposure of any technical weakness.... [1]

Allen Tate later recalled that Ransom regularly brought a poem to read at Fugitive meetings, "and when his turn came he read it in a dry tone of understatement. I can only describe his manner in those days as irony which was both brisk and bland."[2]

Although outsiders were inclined to give Ransom more credit for the work of the Fugitives than was actually the case, he nevertheless was the acknowledged leader of the group. Donald Davidson has described Ransom's position as follows:

> His performance was authoritative, and so was his criticism. It was natural that some of the prominent public notices we received should single out Ransom, the already mature and published writer, as the

---

[1] Thomas Daniel Young, *Gentleman in a Dustcoat* (Baton Rouge: Louisiana State University Press, 1976) 122.

[2] Ibid., 123.

leader of a coterie in which the rest seemed in greater or less degree satellites.[3]

It was not Ransom, however, but Sidney Hirsch who proposed that the group publish their work, and in April 1922, *The Fugitive*, a journal of poetry, was launched. There would be nineteen issues. To the first issue Ransom contributed three poems and an unsigned editorial in which he announced that

> ... THE FUGITIVE flees from nothing faster than from the high-caste Brahmins of the Old South. Without raising the question of whether the blood in the veins of its editors runs red, they at any rate are not advertising it as blue.[4]

Such flourishes prompted Tate to state later that the launching of *The Fugitive* was "a project of utmost temerity, if not of folly."[5] It is interesting that all of the poets used pseudonyms in the first two issues of the magazine, names such as "Robin Gallivant," "Henry Feathertop," and "L. Oafer." Ransom called himself "Roger Prim." The disguises were dropped, however, when a critic suggested that all the poems were probably written by the same person.

The Fugitive received mixed reviews. The *New York Times* noted that it was an "extremely mediocre" journal, while the *Nashville Tennessean* praised the poetry for its "considerable breadth and scope of imaginative imagery." H. L. Mencken, writing in the *Baltimore Sun*, remarked characteristically that *The Fugitive* was "at the moment, the entire literature of Tennessee."[6] Whatever final assessment is made of *The Fugitive*, the journal obviously served as an important vehicle for Ransom's poetic development, and there can be no doubt that it gave nourishment to the emerging Southern Renascence. By December 1925, the journal had run its course, and by that time Ransom had written some of the finest poems he would write.

---

[3]Ibid.

[4]Ibid.

[5]Ibid.

[6]John L. Stewart, *The Burden of Time* (Princeton NJ: Princeton University Press, 1967) 26.

The Poetry

Ransom's earliest verse was less impressive than the poems he began publishing in *The Fugitive* in 1922. Donald Davidson, Ransom's student at Vanderbilt, records the incident in which he was shown Ransom's first poem. The time was May 1916, and Ransom, a young assistant professor of English, had already been meeting for philosophical discussions with his Nashville friends.

> One day of the days I remember well. My teacher, John Ransom, beckoned me aside and led me to a shady spot on the campus.... Ransom drew a sheet of paper from his pocket. Almost blushingly, he announced that he had written a poem. It was his very first, he said. He wanted to read it to me. He read it, and I listened—admiringly, you may be sure. The title of the poem was "Sunset."[7]

The poem was about a young man's irritation because his sweetheart seemed unreasonably preoccupied with God. A few lines will show something of its blandness and melodramatic posturing.

> I thought you would someday begin to love me,
> But now I doubt it badly;
> It is no man-rival I am afraid of,
> It is God.

Davidson did not care for the poem but would not tell Ransom so, and the poet felt encouraged to continue writing. Other poems quickly followed, and Ransom was able to publish them in various little magazines and newspapers. Prior to his sailing for Europe after the outbreak of the First World War, Ransom sent copies of many of his early poems to Christopher Morley, his American friend from Oxford years, and Morley succeeded in finding a publisher for Ransom's juvenilia. Ransom's first volume of poetry was called *Poems About God*; Henry Holt published the book in 1919, while Ransom was serving in France as a first lieutenant in the field artillery.

The volume was not one that Ransom was particularly proud of, and even before it was published, the poet found himself doubting its merit. The preface to the volume contained some of his disclaimers, and afterward he did not bother to collect any of the poems for re-

---

[7]Young, 112.

printing as part of his collected volumes until many years later when his attitude toward his juvenilia had mellowed. His critical judgment of the volume was accurate. The poems are derivative, obvious, folksy, sentimental, and didactic—qualities absent from his mature verse. Indeed, these poems seem to have provided Ransom with models of what he did not later wish to write. For example, at his worst, Ransom could write "Noon Day Grace," a poem celebrating Nature, Country Cooking, Mother, and God.

> Mother, you're keeping a secret back!
> I see the pie-pan through the crack,
> Incrusted thick in gold and black.
> ....
> There's no telling what the pie can be,
> But tell me that it's blackberry!
> As long as I keep topside the sod,
> I'll love you always, mother and God.

Even "Sunset," which was included in *Poems About God*, was superior to this. The vocabulary, diction, and rhyme bear almost no resemblance to the mature manner Ransom very soon developed, though hints of that manner can be found from time to time in this early volume. In "Under the Locusts," for example, Ransom's celebrated irony can be seen in an early form.

> Dick's a sturdy little lad
> Yonder throwing stones:
> Agues and rheumatic pains
> Will fiddle on his bones.
> ....
> Jenny and Will go arm in arm,
> He's a lucky fellow:
> Jenny's cheeks are pink as rose,
> Her mother's cheeks are yellow.

This is more like what Ransom was becoming—a reflective poet making ironic comments about the inevitable diminution of youth and beauty and the grim onset of old age and death. Unfortunately, the strength of *Poems About God* is outweighed by its many excesses. Ransom was probably glad to leave this volume behind as he moved toward using a less obvious and facile idiom, fewer rural landscapes, and a more effective method of handling sentiment. The poems that followed this volume are almost as subtle and "inconclusive" (to use Ransom's term) as his earlier poems are obvious and didactic.

From about 1920 to 1927 the changes that took place in Ransom's poetry were dramatic. What brought about those changes cannot be known precisely, but Ransom dedicated much time and effort to developing an idiom that would be appropriate for his philosophical speculations. Further, following his return from France, he had been reading widely in nineteenth-century and contemporary literature—British, American, and French. To prepare himself for the course he would teach in Milton as a new professor in the English department at Vanderbilt, he steeped himself in the works of Renaissance scholars such as William Caxton and Sir Thomas Malory.

Whatever the effect of this reading on his poetic manner, a particular poem he read at a Fugitive session in November of 1921 revealed that important changes had taken place. Allen Tate describes the "conversion" as follows:

> Before we began to think of a magazine John had written a poem which foreshadowed the style for which he has become famous; it was "Necrological," still one of his best poems; I marvelled at it because it seemed to me that overnight he had left behind him the style of his first book and, without confusion, had mastered a new style.[8]

The difference between "Necrological" and the manner of *Poems About God* is worth examining.

"Necrological" is about a medieval friar who views first-hand the scene of a battle that has taken place outside the shelter of his monastery. The warriors who triumphed have departed; but dead men, dead horses, and birds of prey remain for the friar to confront. The poem presents the clash between the friar's ideological, religious view of the world and the stern reality he sees as he walks among the dead. The clash of disparate ideologies is reinforced by Ransom's language, rhythm, and rhyme. For example, biblical language is played off modern phrasing, and polysyllabic Greek or Latin words are posed against terse Anglo-Saxon ones; loose iambic pentameter rhythms strain against regular metrical patterns; and the *abab* rhyme scheme estab-

---

[8] Stewart, *Burden*, 216.

lished in the first stanza is promptly altered in stanza two with slant rhymes, but not again.

Note, for example, this instance of ironic biblical allusion in stanza three.

> The dead men wore no raiment against the air,
> Bartholomew's men had spoiled them where they fell;
> In defeat the heroes' bodies were whitely bare,
> The field was white like meads of asphodel.

The biblical "raiment" heightens the irony of the dead men lying naked against the morning coolness, while "meads of asphodel" with its honorific connotations assumes a grimness it was never intended to assume when it is linked with a mead filled not with lilies but with dead warriors.

And note in stanza six this curious blending of formal and Latinate language:

> Beneath the blue ogive of the firmament
> Was a dead warrior, clutching whose mighty knees
> Was a leman, who with her flame had warmed his tent,
> For him enduring all men's pleasantries.

The word "ogive" sends the reader to the dictionary (not an unusual activity when one reads Ransom's mature verse, particularly the longer poems), where he learns that the word refers to a diagonal arch or rib across a Gothic vault. This architectural term seems to relocate the battlefield within a cathedral-like setting, thus providing another of Ransom's many ironic contrasts. The medieval "leman" carries archaic connotations beyond the dictionary definition of "sweetheart" or "mistress," but, in addition, serves to elaborate the title of the poem. "Necrological," pertaining to a roll or list of the dead, can now be seen to include not only men and animals but a leman as well.

The young friar's conflict is made more complicated and subtle in the next-to-last stanza when he uncharacteristically retrieves a sword or knife from the stomach of a dead warrior.

> The youth possessed him then of a crooked blade
> Deep in the belly of a lugubrious wight;
> He fingered it well, and it was cunningly made;
> But strange apparatus was it for a Carmelite.

Ransom's reading of Willam Caxton and Sir Thomas Malory seems evident in this passage with its formal, Latinate diction that effectively summons up the heroic past. For example, instead of noting that the friar "took" the knife from the dead man, Ransom writes that he "possessed him" of the blade. Rather than calling the dead warrior just that, Ransom draws on the Latinate word for "sorrowful" and the Middle English word for "creature" and gives us the quaint "lugubrious wight," a phrase that could be taken ironically, sympathetically, or both. "Apparatus" is a stronger, more suggestive word than one we might be inclined to use—"weapon." And the heroic tradition is evoked in the idea that the weapon was "cunningly made." Epic poetry abounds in the careful description of any weapon that had served the warrior particularly well, with the poet often digressing to give the history of the making of the weapon and to describe in detail the intricacy of its construction. The friar's dilemma in wanting to own ("possess") the weapon in opposition to the Church's teaching contributes one more level of meaning to a poem whose subject matter and technique are filled with significant implication. The poem concludes with this:

> He sat upon a hill and bowed his head
> As under a riddle, and in a deep surmise
> So still that he likened himself unto those dead
> Whom the kites of Heaven solicited with sweet cries.

The poet sympathizes with the friar but will not permit the poem to conclude didactically or with the kind of direct statement that characterized *Poems About God*. Instead, Ransom steps back, suggests what goes on in the friar's mind, and permits the vultures to clean up the battlefield. The purging is accomplished by Nature, while Man sits pondering the meaning of it all. Calling the vultures "kites of Heaven" pulls together in a brief phrase one of the central conflicts of the poem: the friar's idealistic conception of the world versus the brutality of the actual.

The friar thus takes his place beside the host of other characters in Ransom's poems who are defeated or who in some way lose. They are people, as he described in "Man Without Sense of Direction," who cannot "fathom" or "perform" their natures. Ransom's attitude toward them hovers between sympathy and objectivity, his language and diction controlling the tone, as in "Necrological."

In this poem and others written during the early twenties, it is clear that Ransom's thinking centered on the various dualities, contradictions, and discrepancies he saw in the world around him. Indeed, the foundation of his thinking, following his return to Vanderbilt after the First World War, was that modern man is beset with a "dissociation of sensibility" that creates an imbalance with Reason, the imperious one, attempting to dominate Sensibility, the innocent one. By dramatizing in his poetry man's attempts to unify these warring elements (or man's inability to perceive this dissociation), Ransom found both a substantial thesis and a flexible medium for the exploration of man's dilemma. The best poems he wrote between 1920 and 1927 touched on man's struggle for a kind of unity of being and commented ironically on the claims and counterclaims of those forces within his nature that seemed most dominant: Reason and Sensibility, What Is and What Ought to Be, and Desire and Honor.

A pivotal year in Ransom's development as a poet was 1924, when he published *Chills and Fever* (New York: Knopf) in August and three months later *Grace After Meat* (London: Hogarth). This unusual feat was accomplished with the aid of his American friend Christopher Morley and his British friend and fellow poet Robert Graves. Ransom was jubilant. He wrote Graves, "You and Morley . . . are birds of a feather and a credit to ornithology."[9] Reviews of both books here and abroad were spirited and for the most part complimentary, and with this double publication Ransom's poetic career was well launched.

Of the forty-nine poems in *Chills and Fever*, thirty-six (including "Necrological") had already appeared in *The Fugitive*. *Grace After Meat* contained ten poems from *Chills and Fever* but suffered from the inclusion of nine poems from *Poems About God*, these nine comprising almost half the volume. The poems that attracted most interest were those that had already appeared in *Chills and Fever*—"Winter Remembered," "Necrological," and "Judith of Bethulia," to mention three.

Chills and Fever contains more poems that were later anthologized than any other volume he published during his most productive years—1916 to 1927. The title was taken from his poem "Here Lies a Lady." "Bells for John Whiteside's Daughter," "Spectral Lovers," "Miriam Tazewell," "Good Ships," "Necrological," "Captain Carpenter," and

---

[9]Young, 129.

"First Travels of Max" are other well-known poems from this volume. Most of these are little narratives about people—children, lovers, the aged and aging—who, like the friar in "Necrological," cannot reconcile the warring factions within their personalities. Particular moments in their lives serve as Ransom's focal points: the friar's confrontation with the brutally slain, the prim manner in which a lady dies in "Here Lies a Lady," the effect of a young girl's death on the startled adults in "Bells for John Whiteside's Daughter." Whatever moment Ransom seizes, his tone varies interestingly from poem to poem as he exploits various ironic stances in his attempt to control and restrain emotion.

As a matter of fact, it is the controlled irony of *Chills and Fever* that distinguishes it from the seemingly uncontrolled didacticism of *Poems About God*. This new tone of detachment was announced in the opening poem of *Chills and Fever* in which, in "Agitato ma non troppo" (agitated or shaken, but not too much), he concluded,

> I will be brief,
> Assuredly I have a grief
> And I am shaken; but not as a leaf.

Ransom did not attempt to deny emotion but to control it so that he could move easily back and forth between involvement and detachment, modulating his tone at will. The result of such a stance is an intellectual poetry that constantly proves the quality of life. Rather than taking a final, firm position against or for a proposition, his poetry explores the compelling claims of both views, now seeming to favor one, now the other.

A letter Ransom wrote Allen Tate in 1927, when his poetic power was at its height, is helpful in defining some of Ransom's poetic objectives.

> My object as a poet might be something like the following, though I won't promise to stick by my analysis: (1) I want to find the experience that is in the common actuals; (2) I want this experience to carry (by association of course) the dearest possible values to which we have attached ourselves; (3) I want to face the disintegration or multiplication of those values as calmly and religiously as possible. Art is our refusal to yield to the blandishments of "constructive" philosophy and permit the poignant and actual Dichotomy to be dissipated in a Tri-

chotomy. . . . And here's a slogan: Give us Dualism or we'll give you no Art.[10]

In light of this letter and of Ransom's interest in contraries and oppositions, it is not surprising that he developed a theory of poetic composition that pitted one primary aspect of his being with another, so that during the making of poetry he would sense a dualism at work. In a conversation in later years with Cleanth Brooks and Robert Penn Warren, he spoke of how he composed poetry and what happened within him during the process. He said that first he got himself involved in theoretical, philosophical questions until he had engaged his whole mind. Next, he would make rough drafts of the composition in its earliest form. And then, after about a week

> . . . maybe I'd worked up . . . a tension in me which made my reason, my thinking for the argument, and my imagination for the sensibility, more compatible with each other. They began to try to please each other. And then I found I could knock off a pretty fair poem and while I was still at that height I might do three or four poems.[11]

Poems that illustrate Ransom's poetic theories abound in the volumes published during his mature period. The tone of modulating objectivity and subjectivity is particularly prominent, and one example should show how well this device contributed to the complexity of the poem.

"Captain Carpenter," from *Chills and Fever*, is a balladlike poem about a chivalric captain of courtly, gentlemanly disposition who sallies forth into the world to do battle with the adversary, but who is defeated ignominiously at every turn. With each defeat he loses a part of his anatomy, but nevertheless carries on bravely with what is left of his ravaged body until finally only his heart remains. At last, the enemy divests him of his heart, leaving the corpse for the birds of prey. Grim as this surrealistic poem sounds, Ransom controls the tone by employing a courtly language that keeps insisting that all will be well in the end. Moreover, the speaker in the poem appears to side with the captain through all the battles, and near the end even assumes a protective role.

---

[10]Stewart, *Burden*, 223.

[11]Ibid., 213.

> God's mercy rest on Captain Carpenter now
> I thought him Sirs an honest gentleman
> Citizen husband soldier and scholar enow
> Let jangling kites eat of him if they can.

But the kites have their way, and the final stanza shows them clacking their beaks in anticipation. The tone of the poem moves skillfully from an objective, brutal account of the captain's losses to a subjective, shocked response to the captain's fate, leaving the reader to ponder this Don Quixote-like character whose heroic stance has fared no better than cowardice would have fared. Language and tone have given fresh perspective to the conflict between Innocence and Experience.

Following publication of *Chills and Fever* and *Grace After Meat*, Ransom continued to seek an audience for his verse. At the same time, however, he was actively engaged in developing some of the critical ideas that would soon be published in his books of social and literary criticism—an activity that would remove him almost completely from writing new poems. In 1926-1927 he had failed in his attempt to obtain a Guggenheim Fellowship that would have enabled him to complete a thesis he had tentatively called "The Gothic Principle in the English Literary Tradition," a thesis which contained some of the basic ideas of his best-known critical works—*God Without Thunder* and *The World's Body*. While he was reading proofs for his next volume of poetry—*Two Gentlemen in Bonds*—he strove to pull together the critical, aesthetic, and philosophical ideas about literature that had dominated his thinking for the past several years.

Two Gentlemen in Bonds (Knopf), published in January 1927, was arranged in three sections: "The Innocent Doves," fourteen poems concerned with the clash of innocence and experience; "The Manliness of Men," sixteen poems in which males struggle, with varying degrees of success, with the vicissitudes of life; and "Two Gentlemen in Bonds," a polished but unmoving sequence of twenty sonnets dealing with two brothers, Paul and Abbott, who though kin, are opposites—Paul representing the Flesh and Abbott representing the Spirit. The first two sections of the volume are the best; they contain, moreover, some of Ransom's finest lyrics. The sonnet sequence, though carefully wrought, has not elicited the same interest and enthusiasm as poems such as "Blue Girls," "Janet Waking," "Vision by Sweetwater," "Dead

Boy," and the powerful metaphysical poem called "The Equilibrists." Despite the problems of the sonnet sequence, this volume received even higher praise than *Chills and Fever*.

"Dead Boy" and "Blue Girls" are good examples of Ransom's mature control of sentiment and his mastery of the lyric form. The opening stanza of "Dead Boy" will illustrate:

> The little cousin is dead by foul subtraction,
> A green bough from Virginia's aged tree,
> And none of the county kin like the transaction,
> Nor some of the world of outer dark, like me.

The opening words introduce a sentimental note that is counterbalanced with "foul subtraction," an ambiguous phrase that seems to mock the boy's death while lamenting it. Line two intones the stock utterance that might have been made by the preacher, but this sentimental note is neutralized by the Latinate "transaction," a word associated with commerce and used in line three to heighten the understated verb "like." Indeed, understatement such as this is frequently used by Ransom to underplay the strong emotion that is actually present. The colloquial "county kin" beside the heavier "transaction" again reveals Ransom's fondness for odd juxtapositions. The poem succinctly defines the position of a Southern family whose homely, fesity, pestiferous son has died, but whose hearts nevertheless "are hurt with a deep dynastic wound."

"Blue Girls" is perhaps Ransom's finest lyric, one in which there are no ironic tensions created by odd linguistic juxtapositions or esoteric words chosen for their historical allusiveness. It is Ransom's simplest, most straightforward handling of the *carpe diem* formula, and the poem suffers from almost any paraphrase. The speaker in the poem watches young girls strolling across their campus, twirling their skirts and chattering like bluebirds. As an older, more knowledgeable person, the speaker becomes poignantly aware of the distance separating their two generations. She wishes she could tell them that although they are lovely now, in time they will lose their beauty. What she would like to say, they would not believe, but she nevertheless says it to herself.

> Practice your beauty, blue girls, before it fail;
> And I will cry with my loud lips and publish

> Beauty which all our power shall never establish,
> It is so frail.

Interestingly, this unabashed display of emotion, this conclusive statement about the transient character of beauty, is held within the speaker's consciousness where there is no need for ironic qualification. Or is there? The final stanza provides the speaker with a rueful recollection that permits the entrance of a harsh reality.

> For I could tell you a story which is true;
> I know a woman with a terrible tongue,
> Blear eyes fallen from blue,
> All her perfections tarnished—yet it is not long
> Since she was lovelier than any of you.

The Criticism

Ransom's career as a social and political critic might be said to have begun when he was caught up in the controversy surrounding the Scopes Trial in 1925, a trial dealing with a public school teacher's right to teach the Darwinian theory of evolution in Tennessee. During the trial and afterward, the South came under attack by the Northern press, and during these years Ransom developed the views that would link him intellectually and emotionally to his native region.

Specifically, Ransom came to believe that science and industrial technology were not the answer to man's problems, despite the North's insistence that they were. The South, with its more leisurely pace, its religious rituals, codes of conduct, myths, manners, and traditions, possessed a vastly more satisfying life than the progressive North could offer. Indeed, these typically Southern characteristics brought order and meaning to the lives of Southerners, as did their religious Fundamentalism. When this Fundamentalism came under attack for its backwardness and superstition, Ransom defended it on the grounds that it was superior to the North's new Rationalism because it used the supernatural "to represent the fullness of the natural" in ways that Rationalism could not.[12]

---

[12] John L. Stewart, *John Crowe Ransom* (Minneapolis: University of Minnesota Press, 1962) 36.

In other words, Ransom was affirming not only the existence of man's world, but also an inscrutable, mysterious, metaphysical world that science and its sects did not take into account. Science's view of the universe, therefore, was not a complete and accurate one, Ransom argued: it could neither account for evil nor prepare man for the vicissitudes of life and the uncertainties of fate. Religion and myth, on the other hand, addressed themselves to both worlds, contended with the problem of evil, and prepared man for his often imponderable fate. In short, religious myth established a bridge between the physical and metaphysical, a bridge that science was unable or unwilling to cross.

Ransom put these ideas into his first book of criticism, *God Without Thunder: An Unorthodox Defense of Orthodoxy* (1930). Adopting the persona of a Southern fundamentalist, he argued the superiority of a conservative religious stance over scientific Rationalism. More than that, he boldly offered a concrete program to anyone of his time wishing to find a satisfying religious position.

> With whatever religious motivation a modern man may be connected, let him try to turn it back towards orthodoxy.
> Let him insist on a virile and concrete God, and accept no Principle as a substitute.
> Let him restore to God the Thunder.
> Let him resist the usurpation of the Godhead by the soft modern version of the Christ, and try to keep the Christ for what he professed to be: the demigod who came to do honor to the God.[13]

It is interesting that the case Ransom made here for religion would be used later for poetry—that it was superior to abstract science as a means of understanding man's relationship to nature.

Between 1926 and 1930 Ransom did not confine himself solely to a defense of religious Fundamentalism. Other aspects of the Northern attack on the South provoked his interest. The letters he wrote to Allen Tate during this period point to the beginning of what has been called the Southern Agrarian Movement, a movement that attracted several of the Fugitives but was distinct from that particular effort. The Agrarians, in fact, included not only literary people, but two historians and a psychologist as well. One of the tangible outcomes of the conversa-

---

[13]Young, 196-97.

tions and correspondence of the Agrarians was the 1930 publication of their collection of essays entitled *I'll Take My Stand: The South and the Agrarian Tradition, by Twelve Southerners*. The twelve separate essays of the book argued from different points of view about the dangers of industrialization in America and the necessity for the South to retain its agrarian character.

Ransom contributed the introductory "Statement of Principles" and the leading essay, "Reconstructed But Unregenerate," to *I'll Take My Stand*. His philosophical defense of Agrarianism had already been stated in *God Without Thunder*: poetry, the arts, and religious myth function best in an agrarian culture consisting of small, self-supporting farms where man can enjoy a proper relationship to nature. Such a relationship, Ransom argued, was not easily found in an industrial society where Reason reigns over Sensibility.

Such ideas may have been blunted when Ransom linked Reason with the Industrial North and Sensibility with the Agrarian South, a generalization that could not be defended very easily. The Agrarian point of view suffered in other ways, too, for how could it find acceptance in the South where so many farmers and others close to the soil were suffering from the Depression? The mystical link between Man and Nature was a bit difficult to achieve when one was hungry. And finally, the book offered no program capable of translation into legislative or community action, though it had the positive effect of stimulating a great deal of regional self-analysis, North and South. And, too, in the present age when Americans are considering more seriously than ever the claims of an agrarian atmosphere over the regimentation of city living, one is inclined to judge the volume less harshly.

Following *I'll Take My Stand* and *God Without Thunder*, Ransom continued to publish essays and reviews and to devote himself to his teaching. In 1935 he brought forward a departure from his usual publications, *Topics for Freshman Writing*, a college textbook with materials for writing exercises. Though his last publications had tended to link him with his native region, he was nevertheless attaining a national reputation as a poet and critic. To the disappointment of many of his friends, he chose to leave Vanderbilt in 1937. After a great deal of consideration, he accepted a position as Carnegie Professor of Poetry at Kenyon College in Gambier, Ohio, where he would continue his work in criticism and teaching and where he was to spend the rest of his life.

Even during his Agrarian period, Ransom's writing and thinking had been directed toward the broader world of literature, philosophy, and aesthetics, a world which his training at Oxford had well prepared him to confront. His next important book, which appeared in 1938, was a collection of fifteen essays written during the previous five-year period. He called his book *The World's Body* (Charles Scribner's Sons), and though the essays do not make for a particularly easy unity (they were not originally intended to make a single book), they do present some of his most important critical ideas.

Of central concern in the book is what Ransom called the "ontology" of poetry, by which he appears to have meant the nature of a poem's "being" or "thingness." It was important for Ransom to establish the poem's ontology, because he wished to make a strong case for the superiority of the poem's account of the world to the account of the world rendered by science. John L. Stewart succinctly describes the issue at stake.

> All art, he had come to believe, originates in a sentimental attachment for beloved objects which the artist wishes to honor through his labor. It is essentially imitative; selection and arrangement of material are governed first by the need for verisimilitude, and the test of success is the accuracy with which it suggests the whole substance of the precious object. As a source of knowledge about the qualities of that object, a work of art is superior to any scientific account. Indeed, it is even better than the object itself because it cannot be used, it can only be contemplated.[14]

Plainly, science was Ransom's villain, for it tended to distort the world by reducing it to abstract formulas and concepts; such operations omitted a wealth of ever-changing details and particularities. Poetry tried to represent the wholeness of the object and to restore the world's body by its concrete presentation of the exciting, contingent particulars of nature.

The poem, then, is superior even to the object it describes, because the poem cannot be used: it is a good in itself, has its own being,

---

[14]Stewart, *Ransom*, 37-38.

or thingness, and is an object for our contemplation. But Ransom did not mean just any poem; he meant poems that had no moral, political, or psychological biases, that did not attempt to instruct or persuade, but existed for their own sakes and for the knowledge they contributed to our understanding and enjoyment of the world, and especially to our understanding. Of utmost importance in the reader's experience of a poem was understanding, or cognition. This understanding could be impeded by those critics whose scholarship was based on historical, social, or psychological considerations to the detriment of the formal, textual examination of the poem itself—the ontological poem.

Two years after Ransom moved his family to Kenyon College he was asked to edit the *Kenyon Review*, which was to become one of the most prestigious journals of literature and criticism in America, with an impressive number of prominent British and American writers publishing their work in the magazine. It is not surprising that the dialogue that began between these publishing critics would be encouraged by Ransom for the benefit of the students at Kenyon. The concrete result of that dialogue was Ransom's founding the Kenyon School of English. Begun in 1948, this summer school in literary criticism gave qualified graduate students the opportunity to study under well-known writers and critics.

For three years a Rockefeller Grant funded this summer program, after which it became the School of Letters at Indiana University, continuing with some of the features that Ransom had instituted. Ransom's program brought to Kenyon College such figures as F. O. Matthiessen, Lionel Trilling, Jacques Barzun, R. P. Blackmur, Kenneth Burke, William Empson, Austin Warren, René Wellek, Basil Willey, and Yvor Winters, not to mention such "locals" as Cleanth Brooks, Robert Penn Warren, and, of course, Ransom himself.

The New Criticism (1941), Ransom's last book of criticism, contained four essays dealing with I. A. Richards, William Empson, T. S. Eliot, and Yvor Winters. Many of the ideas articulated in the book were not particularly new ones, the book serving to focus on such earlier ideas as the importance of close textual reading; avoidance of biographical, historical, and psychological considerations; and poetry as a source of unique and individual knowledge, worthy of comparison with scientific pronouncements (his quarrel with science had become less agitated, his attitude more compromising). The term "New Criticism" became widely known in the years following the publication of Ransom's book, and though there was no official party headquarters or even an official roster of names (the Fugitives were far better defined), almost anyone who believed in the close, formal reading of literary texts without much attention given to "outside" concerns was a "New Critic." Possibly it was Ransom's break with older methods of criticism and his relentless, almost scientific approach to analysis that gave the movement sanction, respect, and authority for nearly two decades, until it too gave way to other approaches.

As noted earlier, some of the critical ideas of *The New Criticism* were touched on in *God Without Thunder* and *The World's Body*. In his final essay of *The New Criticism*, Ransom provided critical terminology that has become widely influential today—notably his "structure-texture formulation," which helped him describe the difference between poetic and scientific discourse as he proceeded toward the ontological analysis of poetry.

By "structure" he meant the logical discourse or argument of the poem, the prose of the poem, including rhyme and meter. "Texture" referred to such local details or "excitements" as imagery, diction, and sound, those specific features that were "obstructive" to and were carried along by the structure as a kind of baggage. The structure was needed "in order to support a local texture." He summed up by saying that the poem "is a loose logical structure with an irrelevant local texture."[15]

Between structure and texture there was a necessary tension and a need for compromise of some kind, though not necessarily an equal distribution of authority. "The more difficult the final structure," he noted, "the less rich should be the distraction of the texture; and the richer the texture as we proceed towards the structure, the more generalized and simple may be the structure in the end."[16] Though this formulation is difficult to quantify, John L. Stewart believes that "the poetic interest and aesthetic value of a poem were proportionate to the amount of local texture the structure managed to support." This is a reasonable judgment of the principal feature of Ransom's struc-

---

[15]Young, 355.

[16]Stewart, *Ransom*, 42-43.

ture-texture formulation.[17] Distinguishing carefully between these elements, Ransom believed, was the critic's chief duty.

The structure-texture formula has been widely practiced by students and critics in recent years, although Ransom later modified his views concerning its relevance. In 1947, for example, when he was discussing Cleanth Brooks's *The Well Wrought Urn*, he wrote,

> About fifteen years ago I was thinking of the poem as having a logical structure or framework, and a texture whose character was partly irrelevant to the logical form and purpose. My "texture" in particular has given offense, and the fact is that I no sooner uttered it than it struck me as a flat and inadequate figure for that vivid and easily felt part of a poem which we associate peculiarly with poetic language.[18]

From this reconsideration he formulated his organic theory of poetry, in which he saw at work a physiology consisting of a head, heart, and feet. The parts worked together separately but produced a whole, ". . . the head in an intellectual language, the heart in an affective language, the feet in a rhythmical language."[19]

In this modification of an earlier stance, Ransom was attempting to reverse a trend on the part of the New Critics to give short shrift to the structure or "theoretical constitution" of poetry in favor of the texture or specific connotations of words and phrases, a practice he believed was making the poem fragmentary and disjointed. To correct this tendency Ransom encouraged the use of logical paraphrase in analysis, a practice he had not always approved of, but which in 1954 he brought forward in support of structure, along with Hegel's phrase "Concrete Universal," to describe how heterogenous parts worked together to produce wholeness. In making these adjustments and compromises to an earlier position, we see evidence once more of

---

[17]Stewart, *Burden*, 282. Stewart further notes that Ransom added four other components: D M, Determinate Meaning (intellectual meaning before meter and other requirements have affected it); I M, Indeterminate Meaning (final meaning stemming from interplay of structure and texture); D S S, Determinate Sound Structure (especially meter); and I S S, Indeterminate Sound Structure (phonetic intensives without regard to metrics).

[18]Young, 422.

[19]Ibid., 423.

Ransom's need to check and recheck evidence before settling on a position. It was a habit of mind that made final belief nearly impossible.

The Last Years

By 1954, Ransom had made his critical and poetic statements to the world and would concentrate his remaining energies on developing the *Kenyon Review* and the School of English, on lecturing at various campuses around the country, and on writing essays and reviews that appeared in America's most prestigious journals and newspapers. Though he would write no more new poems after 1945, he would revise and republish many of the old ones. For example, in 1954, Knopf published Ransom's *Selected Poems*, a volume consisting of thirty-seven poems chosen from *Chills and Fever* and *Two Gentlemen in Bonds*, plus five new poems. In 1955, he published *Poems and Essays*, which contained eight critical essays but no new poems or revisions. In 1963, he published an enlarged edition of *Selected Poems* containing fifty-three poems previously published, adding five stanzas to "Prelude to an Evening" and substantially revising "Conrad in Twilight," which he renamed "Master's in the Garden Again." And finally, in 1969, he published his last *Selected Poems*, eighty poems in all from the 1963 *Selected Poems*, thirty of them revised.

In light of Ransom's frequent "tinkering" (his word) with poems written earlier, it would be useful to look at a few of the revisions, some of which were relatively minor, such as altering punctuation slightly or changing a word or two, but others of which were major. For example, "Necrological" was altered extensively after it appeared in *Chills and Fever*. For good measure, he altered it once more before it appeared in the 1954 *Selected Poems*. In line eleven he changed "bosoms" to "bodies" to make the line read, "In defeat the heroes' bodies were whitely bare." He also changed a verb in line seventeen from "were" to "lay," the line finally reading, "The lords of chivalry lay prone and shattered." Both changes were improvements.

Other changes were extensive; some of them involved eliminating whole stanzas and retitling the poem. An example is "The Equilibrists," earlier a much longer poem entitled "A History of Two Simple Lovers." These changes made the poem tighter and less direct. Finally, in his last *Selected Poems* (1969), he devoted forty pages to a section called "Sixteen Poems in Eight Pairings, with original and final versions studied comparatively." This section of the book serves as a reminder of Ransom's perennial interest in poetic analysis and interpretation. Whether or not the reader accepts Ransom's "final" version of a poem as the definitive one will depend upon the reader's judgment. Certainly some of these changes were improvements, but other changes have been questioned, each anthologist selecting the version he wished to print.

Arguing the strengths of one version over another is an activity that Ransom would certainly have applauded, and he would also have applauded the debate which must naturally accompany discussions of this sort—whether or not the artist has the right to make basic changes in a text after the text is in the public domain and whether or not the artist's testimony about the meaning and intention of a work is relevant. Such matters are discussed from various angles in Ransom's critical essays, and it is safe to say that whatever position he arrived at in his earlier literary and critical efforts, he was always willing to look at them again in the light of his new knowledge and experience.

Though Ransom retired from teaching and editing in 1958, he continued to be professionally active for the next ten years. His last two volumes of *Selected Poems* appeared in 1963 and 1969, and in 1972 *New Directions* published *Beating the Bushes*, a selection of his unpublished essays from the *Kenyon Review*, plus the essay "Wanted: An Ontological Critic." Also, during this period he was much in demand as a visiting professor and as a guest lecturer at various campuses around the country. Projects of particular interest to him at this time were assessments of the poetry of Hardy, Blake, and Wallace Stevens.

Between 1950 and his death in 1974, Ransom was the recipient of numerous honors and awards. Among the awards he received were Yale's Bollingen Award in Poetry (1951), an Academy of American Poets Fellowship (1962), election to the American Academy of Arts and Letters in 1966, and a $10,000 grant from the National Endowment for the Arts (1967). On the occasion of his eightieth birthday, he was honored by Kenyon College with a party that received national press coverage, with *Life* magazine devoting several pages to the celebration. Finally, during his lifetime Ransom saw several collections of essays contributed in his honor by some of his best-known critics. A good example of such a collection is one that appeared in 1968, edited by Thomas

Daniel Young and entitled *John Crowe Ransom: Critical Essays and a Bibliography* (Louisiana State University Press).

Because of an ear problem that produced vertigo, Ransom's activities from 1967 onward became more and more limited. Almost to the last, however, he continued to work on a new volume of his selected poems. He died quietly in his sleep on 3 July 1974.

Of the many tributes, one of the finest was written by Robert Penn Warren and delivered to the American Academy of Arts and Letters on 6 December 1974.

> Of his own poetry, John more than once said that he wanted to be a "domestic poet," that was his phrase, and most of his subjects are, on the surface at least, small, common, domestic. . . . But beyond his domestic poetry, there was, willy-nilly, another range of thought and feeling. There was the philosopher with a profound awareness of the tensions of his age, and an ironist to whom irony was the only antidote for the tragedy of life. And this fact is what gives the peculiar resonance and indefinable sweetness and pang and the individuality even to poems most obviously domestic. John Crowe Ransom is a writer about the small whose poems loom larger and larger—more inimitable, more indispensable, more powerful—as the years pass. A poet, in fact, in whom classic clarity of outline and modern intensities and tensions find their unique fusion. . . . [20]

Ransom's blending of reason and emotion, a trait most evident in his writings, can also be seen in these characteristic remarks he made to a *Time* reporter on the occasion of his seventy-fifth birthday.

> We survive the seasons of a year and we survive even the passing years, but not the span of life allotted to us. The poet knows that he will die, but he is prepared for it, he accepts it in advance. If he lives out his three score and ten he will come into the peace which accompanies the sense of having achieved all the wisdom that was available for him, and he will be happy to subside, happy but used up, into the annihilation of death.[21]

---

[20] Ibid., 478.

[21] Ibid., 475.

Selected Bibliography

There is no standard edition of Ransom's works. Individual titles, dates of publication, and publishers are cited in the foregoing essay. The titles below should provide the reader with a substantial introduction to John Crowe Ransom.

Stewart, John L. *The Burden of Time: The Fugitives and Agrarians*. Princeton NJ: Princeton University Press, 1965.

Williams, Miller. *The Poetry of John Crowe Ransom*. New Brunswick NJ: Rutgers University Press, 1972.

Young, Thomas Daniel. *Gentleman in a Dustcoat: A Biography of John Crowe Ransom*. Baton Rouge: Louisiana State University Press, 1976.

Young, Thomas Daniel, ed. *John Crowe Ransom: Critical Essays and a Bibliography*. Baton Rouge: Louisiana State University Press, 1968.

Donald Davidson and Allen Tate

Thomas Daniel Young

Donald Davidson

Born in Campellsville, Tennessee, 18 April 1893, Donald Davidson grew up in the communities of Middle Tennessee in which his father taught school. He entered Lynnville Academy in 1901 and transferred to the Branham and Hughes Academy in Spring Hill, Tennessee, in 1905. He graduated from the latter institution in June 1909, after having studied four years of Latin, three of Greek, and four of English and mathematics. In 1909 the family moved to Bell Buckle, Tennessee, when Davidson's father accepted a position as principal of the local public secondary school. On a scholarship arranged by Sawney Webb, headmaster of the Webb School in Bell Buckle, "$100 and a little odd cash," Davidson entered Vanderbilt in September 1909.

At Vanderbilt, a fascinating world opened for him. Ben and Varnell Tate, the two older brothers of Allen Tate, introduced Davidson to the dramas of Shaw and to the important European novelists of the late nineteenth and early twentieth centuries. After one year at Vanderbilt, however, a lack of funds forced his withdrawal. For the next four years he taught school, first at the Cedar Hill Institute and then at the Mooresville Training School, carefully saving his money so that he could complete his degree. While he was at Cedar Hill, he first tried his hand at writing, composing words and music for an operetta based on the Pandora myth.

When he returned to Vanderbilt in the fall of 1914, he found his savings were insufficient to pay university fees and living expenses, so he took a part-time position teaching French and English at the Wallace University School. These were exciting times for Davidson. He had classes with Walter Clyde Curry, John Crowe Ransom, and Edwin Mims. Although Ransom, with whom he would form a lasting friendship, had little effect on him at the time—he thought Ransom's classroom manner was too halting and indecisive—Curry taught him not only Chaucer and Shakespeare but introduced him to Ibsen, Strindberg, Rostand, Hauptmann, and Sudermann. In Edwin Mims's classes he learned that America and the South had a "literature that could be taught as a subject in school." From Alec B. Stevenson, a fellow student and the son of a Vanderbilt faculty member, he borrowed the novels of Joseph Conrad, whose works, along with those of Dostoyevsky (which he borrowed from another student), first taught him something of the art of modern fiction. Perhaps the enduring influence of Davidson's Vanderbilt years was the time he spent with his friends Alec Stevenson and William Yandell Elliott and his professor John Crowe Ransom engaged in literary and intellectual conversation in the apartment of Sidney Mttron Hirsch. Those attending these informal meetings would later form the nucleus of the Fugitive Movement.

At Vanderbilt Davidson was not much interested in poetry. At the meetings at the Hirsch apartment, he later wrote, "I felt myself destined to be but a shy guest at the feast of the world's great culture if the banquet were to consist of the categories of Kant and the heresies of Hegel." His first love was music—his mother, Emma Wells Davidson, an accomplished musician, early taught him to play the piano—and he had applied to Harvard for a fellowship in musicology when World War I began. Like Ransom, he went to Officer's Training School at Fort Oglethorpe, Georgia. After completing his training, he took a brief furlough to marry Theresa Sherrer, a girl from Ohio, and was sent overseas with the 81st Infantry Division. He carried with him a manuscript copy of some of the poems Ransom later published as *Poems about God* (1919). As Davidson pored over these poems, he later wrote, their meaning "came to me dim and distorted like the shapes glimpsed at the bottom of a Tennessee creek."

After the armistice, Davidson taught one year at Kentucky Wesleyan College before moving his family to Nashville, where he would be an instructor in English and work on his master's degree. The meetings of the Fugitive group—now the sessions were devoted to technical discussions of poetry—were held at the home of Hirsch's brother-in-law, James M. Frank, at 3802 Whitland Avenue. The first issue of *The Fugitive* appeared in April 1922, and publication of the journal continued until December 1925. Before the last issue was printed, the group contained fourteen poets, including Ransom, Davidson, Allen Tate, and Robert Penn Warren.

Most of Davidson's first poetry was published in *The Fugitive*. Influenced by the early works of Yeats, its tone was lyrical and romantic, concerning fairies, tigers, dragons, and demons. For a while, following the style and insistence of Allen Tate, Davidson experimented with modernistic techniques, wrote poems about flappers, dryads, and naiads, and even toyed with Baudelaire's "Theory of Correspondences." Only a few poems in *The Fugitive* or in *An Outland Piper* (1924), Davidson's first book of verse, are written in his later characteristic style; neither are they concerned with the almost obsessive subject matter of his mature verse. One of these poems is "A Demon Brother," later revised and renamed "An Outland Piper"; it details Davidson's lifelong concern for art. The first stanza of the poem sets the tone.

> *Old Man, what are you looking for?*
> *Why do you tremble so, at the*
>   *window peering in?*
> *—A Brother of Mine! That's what*
>   *I'm looking for!*
> *Some one I sought and lost of noble kin.*[1]

The piper answers the narrator's question: "I heard strange songs when I was young / Piping songs of an outland tongue." This haunting song, despite his efforts, drew the young man after the piper and held him. Now all he can tell the narrator is that for a long lifetime he has searched for "A Brother of Mine!" This poem, as Louis D. Rubin, Jr., points out, is an adequate announcement of "Davidson's career as a

---

[1] *The Fugitive* 1 (April 1922): 6.

poet." Another of the early poems, "Old Harp," treats Davidson's fundamental interest in the oral and musical qualities of traditional poetry.

After the Fugitives discontinued their regular meetings, Davidson and other members of the group searched for projects that would engage the interests of everyone, as the publication of the magazine had. In 1925 Davidson attempted to find a publisher for a collection of the best verse that had appeared in *The Fugitive*. Then he investigated the possibilities of establishing a Fugitive Press. After he was convinced that such an undertaking was much too ambitious, he threw his support to a venture first suggested by Allen Tate—an anthology of Fugitive verse, including "the best of the past and a sample of the present."

A manuscript was prepared from the poems submitted by various members and offered to several publishers before it was accepted by Harcourt. The volume, which includes nine poems by Davidson, appeared on 8 January 1928. Even a cursory glance through this collection reveals that Davidson's poetic career had taken a new direction. Although it contains only one piece written by Davidson after the discontinuance of *The Fugitive*, that one poem is a section from a book-length narrative that had consumed almost all of the poet's creative energies for two years or longer. This new poem, "Fire on Belmont Street," Davidson wrote Tate, made him very much dissatisfied with the verse he had contributed to *The Fugitive*.

About 1926, under the apparent influence of the Scopes Trial and the correspondence, meditation, and discussion leading to the Agrarian symposium *I'll Take My Stand* (1930), to which he contributed "A Mirror for Artists," Davidson began to write a different kind of poetry, which became *The Tall Men* (1927). Despite Tate's insistence that Davidson was trying to infuse into the poems a theme that they cannot communicate, except through bald statement, Davidson composed an interconnected series of narratives very much in the style of all his later poetry—a carefully controlled blank verse that suggests the heightened and intensified idiom of common speech. Its subject matter would dominate Davidson's creative powers for the rest of his career: the spiritual disorder and lack of purpose of the aimless present contrasted with the heroic purposefulness of the traditional past. This volume, like all of Davidson's later poetry, is intended to convince his reader of the accessibililty of this past.

Although Tate did not approve of the sections of the long poem Davidson sent him—Tate insisted that his old friend was "attempting to envisage an experience of the first order with a symbolism of lower order"—"The Long Street," the title by which Davidson was then referring to the poem, reveals clearly and convincingly the poet's compelling desire to integrate his personal past with that of the region to which he belonged. Davidson suggests this intention in a letter to his publisher: "It [*The Tall Men*] is a blend of what I learned from my folks . . . what I learned from history, and what I myself experienced." The poem was not intentionally autobiographical; instead, Davidson proposed "to draw a portrait in what the relativists now call 'time-space' of a 'western' American of Southern antecedents and affiliations who had been obliged by the crisis of modern times to examine both his traditional heritage and his future prospects." The ten sections of the poem (reduced to nine in later editions) reiterate one theme: the aimlessness and purposelessness of modern life are the result of the efforts of an enemy more definite and deadly than chance or circumstance. The concrete, specific nature of this enemy is most explicitly presented in "Epilogue: Fire on Belmont Street."

The poem opens with a devout Rotarian or Kiwanian rushing down the street, fearing his house is burning, and yelling, "Where is the Fire? . . . *Out Belmont Street*? My God, that's where I live!" But the persona interrupts the burgher's excited babbling to explain that the fire that is destroying his home, his family, his church, all elements of his civilization, is a different kind of conflagration.

> "The Fire," I cried. "What fire? No gables burn,
> Nor is that redness some unusual dawn
> Sprawled against moonrise, nor a dragon's breath
> Spurted from some old sewer you forgot,
> Nor ghosts of Red Men that your fathers knew,
> Come back with devil-medicine to bombard
> Your bungalows. Choctaw and Cherokee
> Lie where the spitting Decherd rifles planted
> Under the Tennessee grass, their tired bones. . . ."[2]

---

[2]Donald Davidson, *Poems, 1922-1961* (Minneapolis: University of Minnesota Press, 1966) 179.

The tragedy is that the modern enemy cannot be confronted as the dragon or the Indian was. The creeping, insidious, soul-destroying enemy of contemporary society is solipsism, man's inability to live except in the present moment, his loss of faith in a traditional society, and his disbelief in myth as a means of acquiring the truth that lies beyond the facts circumscribed by the senses and the reason. Man has surrendered the weapons he needs to fight the enemies that threaten to destroy his civilization.

> Who can conquer wheels
> Gigantically rolled with mass of iron
> Against frail human fingers? Who can quench
> The white-hot fury of the tameless atoms
> Bursting the secret jungle of their cells?
> Oh, who can stay or ever chain the dull
> Gnaw of the firey smoke, eternally settling
> Into the beating heart? There is no fire?
> Only, perhaps, the breath of a Southern wind
> That I have known too well in many a summer,
> Drying the pulse, stopping the weary pulse,
> Blowing the faint blood back in the curdled veins
> Till there is no way to think of what might be
> Better or worse. Yet maybe it were better
> Climbing the tallest hill to cry at night:
> "Citizens, awake! Fire is upon you, fire
> That will not rest, invisible fire that feeds
> On your quick brains, your beds, your homes,
>   your steeples,
> Fire in your sons' veins and in your daughters',
> Fire like a dream of Hell in all your world...."[3]

In 1936 Davidson contributed "That This Nation May Endure: The Need for Political Regionalism" to *Who Owns America?* and in 1938 he published *The Attack on Leviathan: Regionalism and Naturalism*, a reasoned defense of sectionalism and a passionate rebuke of big government, big business, and industrial capitalism. In the latter year he brought out his third book of poems, *Lee in the Mountains and Other Poems*. This volume contains Davidson's best-known poem, "Lee in

---

[3]Davidson, *Poems*, 180.

the Mountains," which covers a few minutes of a typical day in Robert E. Lee's life between 1865 and 1870, the period when he was president of Washington College. Beginning with Lee's arrival at his office to devote a few minutes to revising his father's memoirs, the poem explores Lee's consciousness as his psyche is torn apart by the deeply disturbing question that plagues him throughout this period: Rather than revising his father's memoirs, why does he not write his own? Knowing that if he does compose an honest account of his reactions to his experiences as leader of the Confederate forces, he will have to indicate his disagreement with President Davis in the closing days of the war, and realizing that he will have to express his conviction that the "gentlemen's agreement" that ended the war was being violated, he keeps his peace. To explore either of these subjects, he knows, might cause the "sunken flag . . . / to kindle on wild hills." His heart filled with the devastating belief that he might have violated the trust placed in him by not continuing to fight until the enemy *wanted* peace, he goes to morning chapel to insure his boys that they must face the future with the Christian conviction that a loving God will not disregard "the fierce faith undying / And the love quenchless" of those who fought for a just and sacred cause.

In 1946 and 1948 Davidson published his two-volume history *The Tennessee* in the Rinehart Rivers of America Series. Although some of the conclusions reached in these books have been challenged by some modern historians, the richly evocative prose in which they are written furnishes irrefutable proof that Davidson's prose is among the best written in the twentieth century. It is "not merely correct," as Gerald Johnson once noted, "it . . . [is] lucid, smooth, supple." His style is "carefully chiseled," "agreeable to the eye and ear without falling into puerility." A collection of his essays, *Still Rebels, Still Yankees*, which appeared in 1956, demonstrates that Davidson was a perceptive reader of literature and that he was an entertaining and convincing literary critic. This book, along with *The Attack on Leviathan: Regionalism and Naturalism*, established Davidson as one of the ablest exponents of intelligent conservatism. Like *I'll Take My Stand*, both books are thought today to be more instructive, wise, and provocative than when they were first published. In "Poetry as Tradition," from *Still Rebels, Still Yankees*, Davidson argues that poetry is not a means of intelligible communication in modern society because the poets have adopted a "guarded style" filled with so many obscure and esoteric references and literary allusions that it can be understood only by other poets and interpreted adequately only by professional critics. It does not reach a wide public, but "only the literary elite of poets, critics, professors of English," and college English majors.

> The general public does not know that science is hostile to poetry, and furthermore harbors a suspicion, inherited from some old rumors about the behavior of Byron or Poe, that poets are queer. The guarded style does nothing to dispel the suspicion. . . . Unless specially schooled, . . . [the modern citizen] may feel himself becoming a stranger to poetry when his son returns from studying under Ransom at Kenyon or Brooks at Yale and tells him that "The Dry Salvages" and "Sailing to Byzantium" are great poems . . . [4]

"The Traditional Basis of Thomas Hardy's Fiction" is now regarded as a classic of its kind, and certainly Davidson's essay "Theme and Method in *So Red the Rose*" is the point at which most students interested in criticism of Stark Young's classic novel begin. The sections of this collection of essays entitled "The South" and "Regionalism and Nationalism" reveal how closely Davidson maintained the position he adopted in *I'll Take My Stand* throughout the remainder of his literary career.

In 1957 Davidson delivered the Eugenia Dorothy Blount Lamar Memorial lectures at Mercer University (published as *Southern Writers in the Modern World* in 1958). His fourth volume of verse, *The Long Street* (1961), reflects his interest in New England landscape and manners fostered by nearly forty summers of living there. His *Poems: 1922-61,* containing all the verse he wished to keep in print, appeared in 1966. He died in Nashville on 25 April 1968. His faith in the virtues of a traditional society was as strong as ever, but he was saddened by the realization that his countrymen were unwilling to make the sacrifices and unable to produce the courage and conviction necessary to restore such a social order.

---

[4]Donald Davidson, *Still Rebels, Still Yankees and Other Essays* (Baton Rouge: Louisiana State University Press, 1957) 8.

Allen Tate

Few writers in American literature have shared Allen Tate's concern for the relationship between the artist and the tradition from which he comes and to which he should maintain a firm attachment. Not only did Tate feel a deep need for a sense of belonging to a specific place, but his art is always profoundly concerned with the past.

Perhaps his need to be a part of an individualized, concrete community was fostered in part by the rootlessness of his early life. Born in Winchester, Kentucky, on 19 November 1899—although his mother had always left with him the impression, until he was past thirty years of age, that he had been born in Fairfax County, Virginia—Tate's childhood was filled with so many brief stops at temporary abodes that he never really settled in one place. His father, John Orley Tate, was a man of no real professional interest, although he moved from town to town mismanaging the family timber business. Each year it deteriorated more and more until by Tate's early youth it had disappeared altogether. The elder Mr. Tate finally withdrew almost entirely from any active participation in human affairs (much like Jarman Posey in Tate's novel *The Fathers*). The family was supported by Ben, an older son, and young Allen's life was almost completely dominated by his mother, Eleanor Varnell Tate.

Because of his unusual and rather chaotic home life, Tate's early education was irregular and sporadic. Taught to read by his mother, he devoured family copies of the works of Dickens, Poe, and Scott, as well as Wordsworth's *Prelude*, before he had received much standardized schooling. When Ben and Varnell, the older Tate children, entered Vanderbilt, their mother moved with them to Nashville and enrolled Allen in the Tarbox School. After a semester there, he entered a private school in Louisville for a brief period where the primary emphasis was on the classics. After leaving this institution, he spent his winters in three other high schools in Kentucky and Indiana and his summers with his mother in various resorts in Tennessee and Virginia, before he graduated from Georgetown University Preparatory School. Even this highly irregular educational program was interrupted briefly while he studied violin with Jean Ten Have and Eugen Ysaye with an idea of becoming a professional violinist. Only when he was told that although his fingering was good he had no real musical talent did he give up his desire for a career in music and begin serious preparation for college.

In October 1918, Tate entered Vanderbilt University. After employing a tutor to prepare him for the admissions examination, he barely passed mathematics but excelled in Latin. For the first time, Tate began to write poetry seriously. One of his early efforts, "Red Stains," published in the *American Poetry Magazine* of Autumn 1921, bears the unmistakable stamp of his mature work.

> In a pyloned desert where the scorpion reigns
> My love and I plucked poppies breathing tales
> Of crimes now long asleep, whose once-red stains
> Dyed stabbing men, at sea with bloody sails.
> The golden sand drowsed. There a dog yelped loud;
> And in his cry rattled a hollow note
> Of deep uncanny knowledge of that crowd
> That loved and bled in winy times remote.
> The poppies fainted when the moon came wide;
> The cur lay still. Our passionate review
> Of red wise folly dreamed on. . . . She by my side
> Stared at the Moon; and then I knew he knew.
>   And then he smiled at *her*; to him 'twas funny—
>   Her calm steel eyes, her earth-old throat of honey![5]

In *Jade*, a humor magazine of the Calumet Club, a literary society at Vanderbilt, he published "A Ballade of the Lugubrious Wench," a satire in the style of Villon. This poem first brought Tate's poetic ability to the attention of Donald Davidson. Davidson invited Tate to a meeting of the Fugitives and, as Louise Cowan has pointed out, that group was never the same again. Tate brought to the meetings a deep interest in modernism based on a close reading of Arthur Symon's *The Symbolist Movement in Literature* and an intense study of the poems of Mallarmé, Laforgue, Rimbaud, and Ezra Pound, and, later, T. S. Eliot.

At Vanderbilt, Tate was influenced by three of his teachers. First there was Herbert Cushing Tolman, with whom he had four years of Greek. Professor Tolman provided Tate with such a solid foundation in classical Greek that he could read and write this difficult language for

---

[5]Allen Tate, *Collected Poems, 1919-1976* (New York: Farrar, Straus and Giroux, 1977) 171.

the remainder of his life with enviable ease. Then there was Herbert Charles Sandborn, who instilled in Tate a respect for and an insatiable interest in formal philosophy. Of more importance, however, was John Crowe Ransom, whom in later years Tate listed with T. S. Eliot as his "two masters." Unlike Davidson, Tate found Ransom a superb teacher.

> The civility of his demeanor was a gentle but severe reminder that we must try to behave as gentlemen, even when we were not. His role was that of *par inter pares*, a character to emulate not to imitate; for nothing would have disturbed John Ransom so much as to turn out diminutive copies of himself. His courtesy relieved us of the necessity to commit regicide in order to be ourselves.[6]

When Tate left Vanderbilt in 1925 to go to New York for a career in free-lance literary journalism, he took with him a deep knowledge of and an abiding interest in classical languages and literature, philosophical studies, and modernism. He had also had the profoundly influential experience of associating with and having his poems criticized by some of the most talented poets and critics of his day. In addition, he was a published poet. His early poems, contrasting a vital past with the purposeless present, had appeared not only in the *American Poetry Magazine* but also in *The Fugitive, The Double-Dealer,* and elsewhere. Most of all, he arrived in the literary center of the country with the sincere conviction that he must devote the remainder of his life to the profession of letters. For the first few years he eked out the barest existence by working for a pulp magazine, by reviewing books for such journals as *The Nation, The New Republic*, and the New York *Herald-Tribune*, and by writing brief articles on subjects of current literary interest for various journals. He also formed lasting literary friendships with Edmund Wilson, Malcolm Cowley, Mark Van Doren, Hart Crane, and others. To indulge his interest in contrasting a strong and vigorous past with an impotent and vitiated present, he wrote two biographies: *Stonewall Jackson: The Good Soldier* (1928) and *Jefferson Davis: His Rise and Fall* (1929). In 1926 he began working on "Ode to the Confederate Dead," one of his best-known poems, and in 1927 he published "Poetry and the Absolute," the first of his important critical essays.

---

[6]"Gentleman in a Dustcoat," *Sewanee Review* 76:381.

These early reviews and essays, as well as the poetry, reiterate one theme: as Oswald Spengler has insisted, a dying culture cannot produce vital art. Tate's work of this period also calls for an end to romantic, subjective, confessional poetry and a concentration on the concrete, particularized image. The latter concept reflects Tate's interest in the thought of T. E. Hulme and John Crowe Ransom. His contribution to *Fugitives: An Anthology of Verse* and the later poems in *Mr. Pope and Other Poems* (1928), particularly the title poem, demonstrate Tate's concern for the relationship of the artist to his society, a subject that would command his attention for the remainder of his career.

One of the most distinguished of Tate's early poems, "Mr. Pope," delineates with care and precision the timelessness of art. During Alexander Pope's lifetime, his warped and deformed body inspired fear in those who saw him. This feeling lives on in the hearts of those who read his crisp, highly mannered, satiric couplets. None of Tate's early poems has evoked as much critical commentary as this one. Radcliffe Squires argues that the essence of Pope's poetry, despite the contentions of many readers, is not to be found in the physical disfigurement of its creator. For Furman Bishop the image of the crooked tree is the poet's attempt to identify "organic nature with the moral essence of Pope," thereby expressing the belief that art can overcome the transcendence of nature. " 'Mr. Pope,' " according to Louis D. Rubin, Jr., "is probably Allen Tate's most finished poem; there are others that have more to say and in both content and range are more important than it, but in this, the first poem of his maturity, there is a formal expertness that he would never surpass." Pope's use of traditional rhyme and meter gave form and order to his art that the modern poet is denied. The carefully controlled work of art is important, not the imperfect, helplessly deformed creature who created it.

> And he who dribbled couplets like a snake
> Coiled to a lithe precision in the sun
> Is missing. The jar is empty; you may break
> It only to find that Mr. Pope is gone.
>
> What requisitions of a verity
> Prompted the wit and rage between his teeth
> One cannot say. Around a crooked tree
> A moral climbs whose name shall be a wreath.[7]

Literature of Tennessee 75

Tate's "Ode to the Confederate Dead" describes a world without a sense of purpose, one in which religious principles have become confused with social values. The poet is unable to celebrate the bravery of the Confederate dead because he belongs to a social order that has lost its sense of tradition, and in such a society the artist cannot produce a poem incorporating an integrated, steady vision.

In his essay "What Is a Traditional Society?" Tate unmistakably indicates the magnitude of his loss because he is a modern dissociated man.

> It means that in ages which suffer the decay of manners, religion, morals, codes, our indestructible vitality demands expression in violence and chaos; it means that men who have lost both the higher myth of religion and the lower myth of historical dramatization have lost the forms of human action; it means that they are no longer capable of defining a human objective, of forming a dramatic conception of human nature; it means that they capitulate from their human role to a series of pragmatic conquests which, taken alone, are true only in some other world than that inhabited by man.[8]

Like the blind crab in Tate's "Ode," modern man has movement without direction, energy but no purposeful world in which to use it. In a late essay, "Several Thousand Books," Tate gives a portrait of a man who was an integrated, functional member of a traditional society.

> As a small boy I knew a man who lived on a farm a few miles from a Kentucky county-seat, the population of which was about five hundred. . . . He was a lawyer whose office was up a dingy flight of stairs above the feed store on the courthouse square. He had "read" law after the war in the office of an older lawyer; but before the war he had been graduated from a small sectarian college, a day's buggy-ride from the family farm; and while he was reading law for the state bar examinations he taught mathematics at his *Alma Mater*. (I once had his books on Conic Sections and the Integral Calculus.) I think I must have seen him last when I was about twelve or thirteen. It was summertime. He wore a shapeless, sweat-stained panama, black alpaca

---

[7]Tate, *Collected Poems*, 6.

[8]Allen Tate, *Essays of Four Decades* (Chicago: Swallow Press, 1968) 554.

> coat, unpressed broadcloth trousers, and string tie; he was very tall and very fat, with a smooth round face and unkept white hair. I could not then have understood that he saw no difference between his vocation and his avocation, or that he did not know which was which....
> He might have answered questions with obvious appeal to authority—"As Plato *says* in the *Phaidros*"—putting the verb in the present tense because Plato had lived only recently; or he might quote the *Georgics* and look hurt if the company kept an uncomprehending silence.[9]

Although the lawyer was not a scholar, Tate continues, he was informed on many subjects—mathematics, science, the ancient classics, agronomy, and the law. All he knew formed an integral part of his daily life and was constantly brought to bear on the human condition. In the real meaning of the term he was an educated man. His life and his livelihood were the same. The way he made his living strongly affected the way he lived.

In New York and in France, where Tate had gone on a Guggenheim Fellowship in 1928 to complete the biography of Jefferson Davis and to begin a biography of Robert E. Lee, Tate became increasingly aware that as an artist he was working *against* not *with* society. Alarmed, too, by his increasing awareness of a rapidly disintegrating society, he became more and more conscious of his rootlessness, his dislocation. Tate's meditations on the life of Davis convinced him that the Mississippian was temperamentally unsuited to lead the Confederacy. A dissociated man in the contemporary use of that term, Jefferson Davis did not have the will to make appropriate judgments based on the knowledge and information he had at his disposal. This Hamlet-like incapacity for action rendered him impotent and resulted in his providing poor leadership for the Southerners' attempt to achieve independence. Tate's search for his own identity, first given effective expression in the "Ode" and even more overtly a shaping force in the Davis biography, made him more introspective. Three thousand miles from home he decided, as M. E. Bradford has observed, that he could not solve his problem of self-definition, as Joyce and James had theirs, by surrendering everything to art.

In November 1929 he wrote "Message from Abroad," addressed to Andrew Lytle, in which he considers the reasons some traditions are

---

[9] Allen Tate, "Several Thousand Books," *Sewanee Review* 75: 376.

Literature of Tennessee

handed down intact from one generation to another while others disappear without a trace. Because of his long absence from home, Tate writes, he has lost some of his sense of belonging to that line of "bony, red-faced" men who were his ancestors. He is acutely aware of his separation from his tradition. Why, he asks, do some cultures such as "Provence, The Renascence, the Age of Pericles" move clearly and completely from one generation to the next, their art preserved, whereas others are lost completely?

> I cannot see you
> The incorruptibles,
> Yours was a secret fate,
> The stiff-backed liars, the dupes:
> The universal blue
> Of heaven rots,
> Your anger is out of date—
> What did you say mornings?
> Evenings, what?
> The bent eaves
> On the cracked house,
> The ghost of a hound. . . .
> The man red-faced and tall
> Will cast no shadow
> From the province of the drowned.[10]

Shortly after the completion of this poem, Tate sailed for America, settled at Benfolly—an antebellum farmhouse near Clarksville, Tennessee, the first real home Tate had ever known—and threw himself wholeheartedly into the Agrarian venture, along with Ransom, Davidson, Warren, and others. His contribution to the Agrarian symposium *I'll Take My Stand* is an essay entitled "Remarks on the Southern Religion," in which he argues that the antebellum Southern society was destroyed because it lacked an appropriate religion.

> They had a religious life, but it was not enough organized with a right mythology. In fact, their rational life was not powerfully united to the religious experience, as it was in medieval society, and they are a fine specimen of the tragic pitfall upon which the Western mind has always hovered. Lacking a rational system for the defense of their religious

---

[10]Tate, *Collected Poems*, 40-42.

attitude and its base in a feudal society, they elaborated no rational system whatever, no full-grown philosophy; so that, when the postbellum temptations of the devil, who is the exploiter of nature, confronted them, they had no defense.[11]

In fact, the Jamestown project may be seen as "the symbol of what later happened to this country," for it was a capitalistic enterprise undertaken for material gain, and the religion the colony developed was one to support its economic aims.

After the publication of this symposium, Tate actively supported the endeavors of the Agrarians, publishing essays and reviews in *The American Review*, *The Southern Review*, and elsewhere. With Herbert Agar he edited a second symposium entitled *Who Owns America?* (1936). Like the other Agrarians, Tate was protesting against the obsessive material acquisitiveness that seemed to dominate the American economic system, but, as he said repeatedly, he was not advocating the restoration of an antebellum Southern society. Basically, he was arguing for the return of religious humanism. This conviction of the incompleteness of the modern world and the desire for a social order founded on the traditional virtues caused him to abandon the biography of Lee, which he had begun working on in 1929. On 19 October 1932, he wrote John Peale Bishop that "Lee did not love power... because he was profoundly cynical of all action for the public good. He could not see beyond his own salvation." After working on the book for three or four years, Tate put it aside because, as Radcliffe Squires has written, it began "to turn into a species of autobiography or even of fiction." Then Tate undertook a novel with the working title *Ancestors of Exile*, in which he planned to trace his own ancestry by contrasting two American types—the Tidewater aristocrat and the pioneer—stability opposed to unorganized and undirected energy. This project was also abandoned, because, as Tate wrote Bishop on 30 October 1933, he had found that he could not complete it "without faking either the significance or the material." However, he did preserve enough of the material for two short stories: "The Immortal Woman" (1932) and "The Migration" (1934), which presage in important ways Tate's only novel, *The Fathers* (1938).

---

[11] Allen Tate, "Remarks on Southern Religion," *I'll Take My Stand* by Twelve Southerners (Baton Rouge: Louisiana State University Press, 1977) 173.

The narrative of *The Fathers* is written from the point of view of an eyewitness narrator who recalls the events of the plot fifty years later. It details the conflict between a classical hero, who is so deeply immersed in the forms of his traditional society that he has no outlet for his private feeling except through these forms, and a romantic hero, who will permit no kind of restraint on his own private, instinctive urges. The inevitable result of the clash between the forces represented by these two men is the destruction of the society to which they belong, the antebellum South. George Posey, the romantic hero, the traditionless man, can be contrasted at every point with Major Lewis Buchan, the classical hero.

George believes the world's actions are intended for his private consumption. He is a man, Tate's narrator says, "who received the shock of the world at the end of his nerves." All actions are intensely personal to him. At his mother-in-law's funeral, he cannot participate in the ceremonious acts of the religious community because he is obsessed with the putrifying corpse. It seems he is forever flirting with personal destruction because he is unaware of the protection offered by a civilized society: its rituals, rites, manners, customs, and ceremonies. Because he is caught up in "time's monotone"—he has no tradition and must live only in the present—the slightest problems become matters of major significance. He must approach even the most mundane decision as if he were the only man in history to have been confronted with such a problem. His life, then, moves from crisis to crisis and inevitably leads to useless violence. He reacts against the discipline of the formal society, with its fundamentally civilizing influences—its codes, rituals, and ceremonies—and is left naked and alone. In this respect he is very much the modern man who feels he can neither deny nor restrain his natural impulses.

Major Lewis Buchan's life is strictly controlled by the demands of the traditional society to which he belongs. In fact, this society has become so rigid and unyielding in its demands that Major Buchan cannot see the Civil War as the devastating human tragedy that it is; it has become merely an abstract struggle between "the 'government' and the sons of his neighbors and kin in the Northern neck of Virginia." Although, as Tate says, Major Buchan is the "classical hero, whose *hubris* destroys him," he has committed himself so completely to the traditional society of which he is an essential part that he can express no human feelings, not even the love he feels for his son Lacy, except through the rituals of that society. Somewhere between the extremes represented by these two men is the position of the vital, living society.

Since the late 1920s Tate's search for his rightful heritage had strongly drawn him toward Catholicism, but in "The Cross," a poem of this period, he suggested that a deeply religious experience might be "soul destroying," and for a time he had turned toward Agrarianism. This attempt to broaden and universalize personal feeling through religious experience suggested, perhaps, other areas of investigation. In 1933 he published "The Mediterranean," based on an actual picnic he had had with some friends at Cassis and some imaginative meditations motivated by reading a passage from the *Aeneid*. In this poem he suggests that his ancestors came not only from the South but from Western Europe; thus, his heritage is that of Western European civilization. Modern man must travel Eastward and backward in an attempt to find his spiritual roots. The poem demonstrates unmistakably that Tate believes if contemporary man is to find his bearings he must break out of "time's monotone" and reestablish his relationship to his traditional heritage. The final stanza clearly shows that Tate is not in sympathy with the degree of emphasis modern man places on material acquisitiveness.

> Westward, westward till the barbarous brine
> Whelms us to the tired land where tasseling corn,
> Fat beans, grapes sweeter than muscadine
> Rot on the vine: in that land were we born.[12]

As in "The Mediterranean" Tate broadened his vision through rereading Vergil, in "The Seasons of the Soul," his most ambitious poem and the best explanation he gives for joining the Roman Catholic Church, he goes back to Dante. Written in the canzone stanza and rhyming *ab ac bd ed de*, the poem contains four sections of six stanzas each. Each section is roughly equivalent to one of the four natural elements of ancient philosophy: "Summer" (air), "Autumn" (earth), "Winter" (water), and "Spring" (fire). The basic myth around which each section is organized comes from *The Divine Comedy*: the omnipresence of sin and the only means by which man may be relieved

---

[12]Tate, *Collected Poems*, 66-67.

from it. The "Summer" section deals with Tate's long-standing interest in the dissociation of thought and feeling. "Autumn" delineates man's inevitable separateness, his imprisonment within his solipsistic self. "Winter" depicts the harrowing spectacle of a world from which God has withdrawn, from which He has disappeared because man no longer believes. "Spring" is concerned with an impotent, intellectualized, abstract, depersonalized religion, but there is also "the mother of silences," Saint Monica, the mother of Saint Augustine. In the *Confessions*, St. Augustine communicates with his dead mother though no words pass between them. Tate seems to be ending his poem by fusing thought and feeling and providing for the possibility of a redeeming faith.

> Speak, that we may hear;
> Listen, while we confess
> That we conceal our fear;
> Regard us, while the eye
> Discerns by sight or guess
> Whether, as sheep foregather
> Upon their crooked knees,
> We have begun to die;
> Whether your kindness, mother,
> Is mother of silences.[13]

The poem is deeply moving and, as Squires says, "one of the most magnificently sustained" of the twentieth century.

At his death, on 9 February 1979, Tate left only three parts of a proposed long autobiographical poem in terza rima: "The Maimed Man," "The Swimmers," and "The Buried Lake." What we have of this poem demonstrates that Tate's poetic talent was as powerful and original as ever, and many critics have suggested that it is potentially the poet's masterpiece. The completed portions of the work offer convincing evidence that Tate's poetic and critical contributions to American letters are of enduring value.

---

[13]Tate, *Collected Poems*, 122.

Selected Bibliography

Donald Davidson

For an exhaustive bibliography of Davidson's books, pamphlets, poems, essays, and book reviews, and an annotated list of biographical and critical material, through 1964, see *Donald Davidson: An Essay and a Bibliography*, Thomas Daniel Young and M. Thomas Inge (Nashville: Vanderbilt University Press, 1965).

Primary Sources

An Outland Piper. (Poems) Boston and New York: Houghton Mifflin Company, 1924.

The Tall Men. (Poems) Boston and New York: Houghton Mifflin Company, 1927.

The Attack on Leviathan: Regionalism and Nationalism in the United States. (Essays) Chapel Hill: University of North Carolina Press, 1938.

Lee in the Mountains and Other Poems, Including The Tall Men. (Poems) Boston and New York: Houghton Mifflin Company, 1938. Reissued by Charles Scribner's Sons, 1949.

The Tennessee. 2 volumes. The Rivers of America Series. New York and Toronto: Rinehart & Company, 1946 and 1948. Reissued by University of Tennessee Press, 1978.

Still Rebels, Still Yankees. (Essays) Baton Rouge: Louisiana State University Press, 1957.

Southern Writers in the Modern World. Lamar Memorial Lectures. Athens: University of Georgia Press, 1958.

The Long Street. (Poems) Nashville: Vanderbilt University Press, 1961.

Literature of Tennessee

The Spyglass: Views and Reviews, 1924-1930. (Book reviews and essays) Selected and edited by John Tyree Fain. Nashville: Vanderbilt University Press, 1963.

Poems: 1922-1961. Minneapolis: University of Minnesota Press, 1966.

Secondary Sources

Beatty, Richmond Croom. "Donald Davidson as Fugitive-Agrarian." *Hopkins Review* 5 (Winter 1952): 12-27. Reprinted in Louis D. Rubin, Jr., and Robert D. Jacobs, eds. *Southern Renascence.* Baltimore: Johns Hopkins Press, 1953.

Bowling, Lawrence E. "Analysis of Davidson's 'Lee in the Mountains.' " *Georgia Review* 6 (Spring 1952): 69-88.

Bradford, M. E. "A Comment on the Poetry of Davidson." *Mississippi Quarterly* 19 (Winter 1965-1966): 41-43.

_____. "Donald Davidson: 1893-1968." *Southern Review* 4 (Autumn 1968): 1110-11.

_____. "A Durable Fire: Donald Davidson and the Profession of Letters." *Southern Review* 3 (Summer 1967): 721-41.

_____. "Meaning and Metaphor in Donald Davidson's 'A Touch of Snow.' " *Southern Review* 2 (Summer 1966): 516-23.

Cowan, Louise. "Donald Davidson: The 'Long Street.' " In *Reality and Myth: Essays in American Literature in Memory of Richmond Croom Beatty,* edited by William E. Walker and Robert L. Walker. Nashville: University Press, 1964.

_____. "The Communal World of Southern Literature." *Georgia Review* 14 (Fall 1960): 248-57.

_____. *The Fugitive Group: A Literary History.* Baton Rouge: Louisiana State University Press, 1959.

_____. "The *Pietas* of Southern Poetry." In *South: Modern Southern Literature in Its Cultural Setting,* edited by Louis D. Rubin, Jr., and Robert D. Jacobs. Garden City NY: Dolphin Books, Doubleday and Company, 1961.

_____. *The Southern Critics.* Irving TX: University of Dallas Press, 1972.

Doyle, John Robert, Jr. "Pacing the Long Street with Donald Davidson." *Sewanee Review* 74 (Autumn 1966): 946-50.

Drake, Robert. "Donald Davidson and the Ancient Mariner." *Vanderbilt Alumnus* 49 (January-February 1964): 18-22.

Eaton, Charles Edward. "Donald Davidson and the Dynamics of Nostalgia." *Georgia Review* 20 (Fall 1966): 261-69.

Fain, John Tyree and Thomas Daniel Young, eds. *The Literary Correspondence of Donald Davidson and Allen Tate.* Athens: University of Georgia Press, 1974.

Inge, M. Thomas. "Donald Davidson on Faulkner: An Early Recognition." *Georgia Review* 20 (Winter 1966): 454-62.

_____. "The Unheeding South: Donald Davidson on James Branch Cabell." *The Cabellian* 2 (Autumn 1969): 17-20.

Karanikas, Alexander. *Tillers of a Myth: Southern Agrarians as Social and Literary Critics*. Madison: University of Wisconsin Press, 1966.

Lasseter, Rollin A., III. "The Southern Myth in Donald Davidson's Poetry." *Kentucky Review* 1 (Fall 1967): 31-43.

Montgomery, Marion. "Bells for John Stewart's Burden." *Georgia Review* 20 (Summer 1966): 145-81.

Pratt, William, ed. *The Fugitive Poets: Modern Southern Poets in Perspective*. New York: E. P. Dutton & Co., 1965.

Purdy, Rob Roy, ed. *Fugitives' Reunion: Conversations at Vanderbilt, May 3-5, 1956*. Nashville: Vanderbilt University Press, 1959.

Ransom, John Crowe. "The Most Southern Poet." *Sewanee Review* 70 (Spring 1962): 202-207.

Rock, Virginia. "The Making and Meaning of *I'll Take My Stand*: A Study in Utopian-Conservatism, 1925-1939." Ph.D. dissertation, University of Minnesota, 1961.

Rubin, Louis D., Jr. "Four Southerners." In *American Poetry*, edited by John Russell Brown, Irving Ehrenpreis, and Bernard Harris. New York: St. Martin's Press, 1965.

_____. "The Concept of Nature in Modern Southern Poetry." *American Quarterly* 9 (Spring 1957): 63-71.

_____. *The Faraway Country: Writers of the Modern South*. Seattle: University of Washington Press, 1963.

_____. *The Wary Fugitives*. Baton Rouge: Louisiana State University Press, 1978.

Stewart, John Lincoln. *The Burden of Time: The Fugitives and Agrarians*. Princeton NJ: Princeton University Press, 1965.

Stewart, Randall. "Donald Davidson." In *South: Modern Southern Literature in Its Cultural Setting*, edited by Louis D. Rubin, Jr., and Robert D. Jacobs. Garden City NY: Dolphin Books, Doubleday and Company, 1961.

Tate, Allen. "The Gaze Past, The Glance Present." *Sewanee Review* 70 (Autumn 1962): 671-73.

Wade, John Donald. "Oasis." *Sewanee Review* 70 (Spring 1962): 208-12.

Warren, Robert Penn. "A Note on Three Southern Poets." *Poetry* 40 (May 1932): 103-13.

Young, Thomas Daniel, and M. Thomas Inge. " 'Lee in the Mountains': The Making of a Poem." In *Donald Davidson: An Essay and a Bibliography*. Nashville: Vanderbilt University Press, 1965.

_____. *Donald Davidson.* New York: Twayne Publishers, Inc., 1971.

Allen Tate

For a complete listing of Tate's editing and writing and an annotated checklist of secondary sources, consult *Allen Tate: A Bibliography*, edited by Marshall Fallwell. Fugitive Bibliographies, Thomas Daniel Young, general editor. New York: David Lewis, 1969.

Primary Sources

The Golden Mean and Other Poems. Allen Tate and Ridley Wills. Nashville: Privately printed, 1923.

Stonewall Jackson: The Good Soldier. New York: Minton, Balch and Co., 1928.

Mr. Pope and Other Poems. New York: Minton, Balch and Co., 1928.

Jefferson Davis: His Rise and Fall. New York: Minton, Balch and Co., 1929.

Poems: 1928-1931. New York and London: Charles Scribner's Sons, 1932.

Reactionary Essays on Poetry and Ideas. New York: Charles Scribner's Sons, 1936.

The Mediterranean and Other Poems. New York: Alcestis Press, 1936.

Selected Poems. New York and London: Charles Scribner's Sons, 1937.

The Fathers. New York: G. P. Putnam's Sons, 1938. Reissued as *The Fathers and Other Fiction*, with a new introduction by Thomas Daniel Young. Baton Rouge: Louisiana State University Press, 1977.

Reason in Madness, Critical Essays. New York: G. P. Putnam's Sons, 1941.

Poems: 1922-1947. New York: Charles Scribner's Sons, 1948.

On the Limits of Poetry, Selected Essays 1928-1948. New York: The Swallow Press and William Morrow and Co., 1948.

The Hovering Fly and Other Essays. Cummington MA: Cummington Press, 1949.

Two Conceits for the Eye to Sing, If Possible. Cummington MA: Cummington Press, 1950.

The Forlorn Demon: Didactic and Critical Essays. Chicago: Henry Regnery Co., 1953.

The Man of Letters in the Modern World, Selected Essays: 1928-1955. New York: Meridian Books, 1955.

Collected Essays. Denver: Alan Swallow, 1959.

Poems. New York: Charles Scribner's Sons, 1960.

Essays of Four Decades. Chicago: Swallow, 1968.

Memoirs and Opinions. Chicago: Swallow, 1976.

Collected Poems, 1919-1976. New York: Farrar, Straus and Giroux, 1977.

Secondary Sources

Amyx, Clifford. "The Aesthetics of Allen Tate." *Western Review* 13 (Spring 1949): 135-44.

Beatty, Richmond C. "Allen Tate as a Man of Letters." *South Atlantic Quarterly* 47 (April 1948): 226-41.

Berland, Alwyn. "Violence in the Poetry of Allen Tate." *Accent* 11 (Summer 1951): 161-71.

Blackmur, R. P. *"San Giovanni in Venere*: Allen Tate as Man of Letters." *Sewanee Review* 47 (Autumn 1959): 614-31.

Brooks, Cleanth. "Allen Tate." *Poetry* 66 (September 1945): 324-29.

Cowan, Louise. *The Fugitive Group: A Literary History*. Baton Rouge: Louisiana State University Press, 1959.

———. *The Southern Critics*. Irving TX: University of Dallas Press, 1972.

Cowley, Malcolm. "Two Winters with Hart Crane." *Sewanee Review* 67 (Autumn 1959): 547-56.

Davis, Robert Gorham. "The New Criticism and the Democratic Tradition." *American Scholar* 19 (Winter 1950): 9-19.

Feder, Lillian. "Allen Tate's Use of Classical Literature." *The Centennial Review* 4 (Winter 1960): 89-114.

Foster, Richard. *The New Romantics: A Reappraisal of the New Criticism*. Bloomington: Indiana University Press, 1962.

Greenhut, Morris. "Sources of Obscurity in Modern Poetry: The Examples of Eliot, Stevens, and Tate." *Centennial Review of Arts and Sciences* 7 (1963): 171-90.

Hemphill, George. *Allen Tate* (UMPAW, 39). Minneapolis: University of Minnesota Press, 1964.

Kermode, Frank. "The Dissociation of Sensibility." *Kenyon Review* 19 (Spring 1957): 169-94.

———. "Old Orders Changing." *Encounter* 15 (August 1960): 72-76.

———. "Contemplation and Method." *Sewanee Review* 72 (1963).

Koch, Vivienne. "The Poetry of Allen Tate." *Kenyon Review* 11 (Summer 1949): 355-78.

Meiners, R. K. *The Last Alternatives: A Study of the Works of Allen Tate*. Denver: Alan Swallow, 1962.

Mizener, Arthur. *"The Fathers* and Realistic Fiction." *Accent* 7 (Winter 1947): 101-109.

Nemerov, Howard. "The Current of the Frozen Stream: An Essay on the Poetry of Allen Tate." *Furioso* 3 (February 1948): 50-61.

Ransom, John Crowe. *"In Amicitia."* *Sewanee Review* 67 (Autumn 1959): 528-39.

Rubin, Louis D., Jr. *The Wary Fugitives*. Baton Rouge: Louisiana State University Press, 1978.

Schwartz, Delmore. "The Poetry of Allen Tate." *Southern Review* 5 (Winter 1940): 419-38.

Spears, Monroe K. "The Criticism of Allen Tate." *Sewanee Review* 67 (Spring 1949): 317-34.

Vivas, Eliseo. "Allen Tate as Man of Letters." *Sewanee Review* 62 (Winter 1954): 131-43.

Young, Thomas Daniel. *The Past in the Present: Thematic Studies in the Modern Novel*. Baton Rouge: Louisiana State University Press, 1981.

——————. *Waking Their Neighbors Up: The Function of the Agrarians Today*. The Lamar Lectures, 1980. Athens: University of Georgia Press, 1982.

Cleanth Brooks and Robert Penn Warren[1]

Mark Royden Winchell

Cleanth Brooks and Robert Penn Warren first met during their undergraduate days at Vanderbilt University in the mid-1920s, and for the ensuing six decades their paths have continually crossed. Warren was born in Gutherie, Kentucky, in 1905 and attended high school in nearby Clarksville, Tennessee. In 1921 he enrolled at Vanderbilt, a precocious if somewhat awkward young man of sixteen. At that time, Allen Tate would later recall, "Red" Warren "was tall and thin, and when he walked across the room he made a sliding shuffle, as if his bones didn't belong to one another. He had a long quivering nose, large brown eyes, and a long chin—all topped by curly red hair."[2] Already attending meetings of the Fugitives as a sophomore, Warren—in his junior year—became the youngest member of one of the most influential literary groups of the twentieth century.

Born in 1906, a year later than Warren, Brooks entered Vanderbilt in 1924 and as a sophomore enrolled in John Crowe Ransom's modern literature class. Unfortunately, Brooks was "too much in awe" of Ransom and dropped the course because he did not feel that he was prepared for the work the class was doing. Although he did complete

---

[1] A few sentences in this essay have appeared in slightly different form in my article "O Happy Sin!: *Felix Culpa* in *All the King's Men*," *Mississippi Quarterly* 31 (Fall 1978): 570-85.

[2] See Charles H. Bohner, *Robert Penn Warren* (New York: Twayne, 1964) 26.

Ransom's advanced composition course during his junior year, Brooks's undergraduate contact with the Fugitive Movement was more vicarious than direct.[3] Apparently, he relished the literary ambience created by Ransom and company without being sufficiently assertive to make himself part of it. Young Cleanth Brooks was quiet and introspective and, according to Allen Tate, when "he was wearing his thick spectacles . . . one had the fleeting thought that like Eliot's Donne he was looking into one's skull beneath the skin."[4]

After his graduation from Vanderbilt in 1928, Brooks earned his M.A. from Tulane (1929) and proceeded to Oxford on a Rhodes Scholarship, arriving there a year after another Rhodes Scholar from Tennessee—Robert Penn Warren. (Since his own graduation from Vanderbilt in 1925 Warren had earned an M.A. at Berkeley and had done a year's graduate work at Yale.) Upon completing his B.A. (1931) and B.Litt. (1932) at Exeter College, Oxford, Brooks returned to the United States to teach at Louisiana State University. In 1934 he was joined there by Warren, who had previously taught for brief periods at Vanderbilt and at Southwestern at Memphis. At LSU in 1935—under the unlikely patronage of Huey P. Long—Brooks and Warren founded one of the most prestigious literary journals in America, *The Southern Review*.

During the late 1930s and early 1940s a relatively homogeneous group of Southern scholars—Ransom, Tate, and Brooks and Warren—edited, respectively, the *Kenyon, Sewanee,* and *Southern Reviews*,[5] thus exerting a profound influence upon the criticism of literature in this country. In addition, these journals published some of the best creative writing being done at the time. One could find in the pages of *The Southern Review* the work of such established poets as T. S. Eliot, W. H. Auden, and Wallace Stevens and such major fictionists as Ford Madox Ford, Aldous Huxley, and Katherine Anne Porter, as well as the work of

---

[3]See Thomas Daniel Young, "A Little Divergence: The Critical Theories of John Crowe Ransom and Cleanth Brooks," in *The Possibilities of Order: Cleanth Brooks and His Work*, ed. Lewis P. Simpson (Baton Rouge: Louisiana State University Press, 1976) 168-69.

[4]Allen Tate, "What I Owe to Cleanth Brooks," in Simpson, 125.

[5]Ransom edited *The Kenyon Review* from 1937 to 1959; Tate, *The Sewanee Review* from 1944 to 1946; and Brooks and Warren, *The Southern Review* from 1935 to 1942.

Literature of Tennessee 91

new talents like Nelson Algren, Randall Jarrell, Mary McCarthy, Delmore Schwartz, and Eudora Welty. Indeed, it may be that the South's claim to literary preeminence during the period between the two world wars rests as much on the critical and editorial labors of Ransom, Tate, Brooks, and Warren as it does on the creative efforts of even so great a writer as Faulkner. The Midwest and the Northeast gave us a larger number of major novelists and poets than did the South; yet, it is doubtful that any group from any region did more to shape the nation's literary tastes during the second quarter of this century than the New Critics from Nashville.

The collaboration of Brooks and Warren was not confined to editing *The Southern Review*, however; nor did that collaboration end with the *Review*'s demise in 1942.[6] Over the years these teacher-critics have edited several textbooks, the best known of which are *Understanding Poetry* (1938, revised 1950, 1960), *Understanding Fiction* (1943, revised 1959), *Modern Rhetoric* (1949, revised 1958, 1972), and—with R. W. B. Lewis—*American Literature: The Makers and the Making* (2 volumes, 1973).

It is difficult to overestimate the influence that *Understanding Poetry*, in particular, has had on the teaching of literature in the four decades since its publication. Essentially, this book is applied New Criticism. In a lengthy introduction it defines the uniqueness of poetic discourse and the formal characteristics that go into the making of poetry; then it provides the student with a large selection of individual poems, complete with commentary and a glossary of useful literary terms.[7] In its insistence on close reading, *Understanding Poetry* reflects the critical bias of its editors, a bias articulated and defended by Brooks and Warren at the very outset of their work. Quoting Louis Cazamian, they contend that if the "student of literature is to be capable of an intelligent appreciation, he must go beyond the passive enjoy-

---

[6]*The Southern Review* as it existed under Brooks and Warren ceased publication in 1942; however, it has since been revived.

[7]Walter Sutton points out that the selection and definition of terms in this glossary reflects a "new critical" bias. See Sutton's *Modern American Criticism* (Westport CT: Greenwood Press, 1977) 117.

ment of what he reads; he must be instructed, partly at least, in the mysteries of the art."[8]

What Brooks Hath Wrought

In his first major critical work, *Modern Poetry and the Tradition* (1939), Brooks proposes nothing less than a revisionist history of English poetry. Like Eliot, Brooks believes that our poetry took a wrong turn at the end of the seventeenth century and is only now beginning to find its way again. He contends that the eighteenth and nineteenth centuries developed certain aesthetic assumptions that the metaphysical poets did not share and the modern poets have rejected. Among these assumptions is a belief in an inherently poetic subject matter and the repudiation of intellect as being antagonistic to the poetic faculty.

Ultimately, Brooks argues, the conception of poetry that flourished in the eighteenth and nineteenth centuries derives from Hobbes's view that the poet is a mere *copyist*, not a *maker*. If it is the poet's function simply to hold the mirror up to nature, then he can please his audience most by holding that mirror up to pleasant objects. With the Romantic Movement and its emphasis on inspiration and emotion, reason itself fell into disrepute and became a hopelessly mundane form of apprehension. (As a corollary of this second development, wit was expunged from poetry to make room for "high seriousness.")

In contrast to the position of Hobbes and his followers, Brooks does not find any subject matter to be inherently poetic or unpoetic. Like I. A. Richards, he believes in a poetry that can accommodate a wide range of human experience—a poetry of inclusion, not of exclusion. The essence of poetry is not to be found in the subject matter of a poem, nor even in the paraphrasable statement a poem makes about its subject matter. Rather, it is the play of language and concept, the exploitation of irony and paradox, that makes a poem a poem. Not surprisingly, Brooks values the metaphysical poets for their insistence on the centrality of the metaphor in poetry. He tells us that "we cannot remove the comparisons from their poems, as we might remove ornaments or illustrations attached to a statement, without demolishing

---

[8]*Understanding Poetry*, ed. Cleanth Brooks and Robert Penn Warren (New York: Holt, Rinehart and Winston, 1938, 1950) xx.

the poems." "The comparison," he concludes, "*is* the poem in a structural sense."[9]

Not only is Brooks convinced that the exclusion of intellect and wit limits the potentialities of poetry, but he also argues that such a strategy inevitably leads to sentimentality. "The sentimentalist," Brooks contends, "takes a short cut to intensity by removing all the elements of the experience which might conceivably militate against the intensity.... To put the matter in terms of the poet's accuracy and fidelity to experience, the sentimental poet makes us feel that he is sacrificing the totality of his vision in favour of a particular interpretation. Hence the feeling on reading a sentimental poem that the intensity is the result of a trick" (p. 46). Rather than writing poetry of high seriousness, the sentimentalist actually trivializes his experience by simplifying it beyond credibility. By contrast, the poet who makes use of wit and irony is fundamentally more serious than the sentimentalist: the former *earns* his vision by testing it against the complexity of genuine experience; the latter merely *proclaims* deep sentiments with a pristine but uncompelling sincerity.

If *Modern Poetry and the Tradition* is divided about evenly between critical theory and textual analysis, *The Well Wrought Urn* (1947) is weighted more heavily toward the latter. In this his most famous work, Brooks does close textual readings of ten English poems, from Donne's "The Canonization" to Yeats's "Among School Children." Throughout, his critical notions and values are essentially the same as in *Modern Poetry and the Tradition*.

As the title of his first chapter suggests, Brooks sees the language of poetry as being fundamentally "the language of paradox." Whereas it is the duty of the scientist to purge contradictions from his statements about reality, the poet must embrace contradictions and make them part of a larger imaginative synthesis. Accordingly, Brooks shows how good poets of various ages—not just the metaphysicals and the moderns—have used paradox and irony in rendering their vision of the world. Indeed, if the outlook of *The Well Wrought Urn* differs in any significant respect from that of Brooks's earlier work, it is in the author's greater appreciation of the extent to which the basic structures

---

[9]Cleanth Books, *Modern Poetry and the Tradition* (Chapel Hill: University of North Carolina Press, 1967) 26.

of eighteenth- and nineteenth-century English poetry reflects—however obliquely—the same qualities he admires in the verse of the seventeenth and twentieth centuries.

In the appended chapters of *The Well Wrought Urn* Brooks demonstrates a willingness to distinguish his positions from those of other critics and to defend his views from various attacks. (Indeed, much of Brooks's critical writing involves just such an ongoing dialectic.) In Appendix I—"Criticism, History, and Critical Relativism"—for example, Brooks establishes some distance between himself and several other scholars. Although the specific arguments involved are too detailed to be summarized here, we can note some of Brooks's basic convictions. To begin with, he is intent on evaluating poetry in wholly aesthetic terms. While it may be necessary to go outside the poem to acquaint oneself with the language in which the poet is writing, whether it be Old Icelandic or Elizabethan English, that poet's use of his language can be judged by objective, universally applicable criteria.

Furthermore, a poem as a dramatically unfolding organism is always different from the sum of its parts. Thus, any attempt to understand these parts except in relation to the whole is wrongheaded. Here, Brooks faults even such New Criticism allies as Yvor Winters and John Crowe Ransom. While not minimizing the evident differences between them, Brooks contends that *both* Winters and Ransom err in asserting the existence of a denotative, paraphrasable element in poetry. By isolating such an element—even in a provisional way—Winters and Ransom seem to infer a form-content dichotomy that falsifies the essential unity of a poem. In Brooks's view, a poem has no prose meaning separable from its poetic context. For him it is the context itself that determines what a poem means.

Over the years Brooks has been attacked from a number of camps. In recent times, for example, those who feel that scholarship—and, indeed, language itself—should be the handmaiden of ideology have depicted him as an aesthete and ivory-tower reactionary. (J. L. Dillard in his book *Black English* has criticized an early linguistic work by Brooks—*The Relation of the Alabama-Georgia Dialect to the Provincial Dialects of Great Britain* (1935)—for its failure to recognize the African influence on black and white speech in the American South. The invidious implication here is that Brooks is at least a closet racist.) Most frequently, however, Brooks's critical perspective has been slighted by more traditional scholars who distrust its alleged antihistorical bias. A case in point is the debate between Brooks and Douglas Bush concerning their respective interpretations of Marvell's "Horatian Ode."[10]

The poem in question was written by Marvell as a celebration of Oliver Cromwell's rise to power and his triumphal return from Ireland. In his essay Brooks attempts to determine what Marvell's poem actually says about Cromwell as opposed to what purely historical evidence might indicate the poet personally thought about the British Lord Protector. "For to ascertain what Marvell the man thought of Cromwell," Brooks writes, "and even to ascertain what Marvell as poet consciously intended to say in his poem, will not prove that the poem actually says this, or all this, or merely this. . . . There is surely a sense in which any one must agree that a poem has a life of its own, and a sense in which it provides in itself the only criterion by which what it says can be judged" (p. 322).

Brooks provides us with a close critical reading of Marvell's poem, one in which he tries to indicate the ambiguity and complexity of the poetic speaker's attitude toward Cromwell. In doing so Brooks emphasizes the dramatic character of the "Horatian Ode." "It is not a statement—an essay on 'Why I cannot support Cromwell' or on 'Why I am now ready to support Cromwell.' It is a poem essentially dramatic in its presentation, which means that it is diagnostic rather than remedial, and eventuates, not in a course of action, but in contemplation" (p. 336).

For purposes of illustration the critic cites Shakespeare's *Macbeth* as an example of a similarly complex contemplation of an ambiguous personality. "What, for example, is our attitude toward Macbeth?" he writes. "We assume his guilt, but there are qualities which emerge from his guilt which properly excite admiration. I do not mean that the qualities palliate his guilt or that they compensate for his guilt. They actually come into being through his guilt, but they force us to exalt him even as we condemn him. . . . [Indeed,] the kind of honesty and insight and whole-mindedness which we associate with tragedy is to

---

[10]See *Seventeenth-Century English Poetry: Modern Essays in Criticism*, ed. William R. Keast (New York: Oxford University Press, 1962) 321-58.

be found to some degree in all great poetry and is to be found in this poem" (p. 336).

Unconvinced by Brooks's analysis, Douglas Bush questions him on the reading of a number of specific lines. For Bush, Marvell's opinion of Cromwell was one of unambiguous admiration. The purpose of Brooks's elaborate discriminations, he argues, is simply to impose a needlessly complex interpretation onto a relatively straightforward poetic statement, in effect "to turn a seventeenth-century liberal into a modern one." "This is one reason," Bush concludes, "why historical conditioning has a corrective as well as a positive value" (p. 351).

In reply to Bush's critique, Brooks attempts to respond to many of the specific arguments raised against his analysis of Marvell's poem. However, he also contends that "Mr. Bush is stalking bigger game" (p. 353). Essentially, Brooks sees the bias against his critical approach shared by such disparate figures as the historical critic Bush and the archetypal critic Leslie Fiedler as being different sides of the same coin. "In their concern for the break-up of the modern world," he writes, "Mr. Bush, Mr. Fiedler and a host of other scholars and critics are anxious to see literature put to work to save the situation" (p. 357). For Cleanth Brooks, however, such a prescription mistakes poetry for religion, and in so doing, does a disservice to both: ". . . though poetry has a very important role in any culture, to ask that poetry save us is to impose a burden upon poetry that it cannot sustain. The danger is that we shall merely get an ersatz religion and an ersatz poetry" (p. 358).

Having established early in his career his belief in the distinctive nature of poetry and in the proper function and limits of criticism, Brooks has seemed intent in his most recent works on eradicating the image of the New Critic as one "trapped in a cell without windows or door, staring through a reading glass at his literary text, effectually cut off from all the activities of the world outside—from history and science, from the other arts, and from nature and humanity itself."[11] In any event, his last five books clearly invalidate such a view of Cleanth Brooks. *The Hidden God* (1963) is concerned with the religious dimen-

---

[11] See Cleanth Brooks, *A Shaping Joy* (New York: Harcourt, Brace, Jovanovich, 1971) xi. For a more recent statement of Brooks's views on the New Criticism, see "The State of Letters," *Sewanee Review* 87 (Fall 1979): 592-607.

sions of literature, while his studies of Faulkner (1963, 1978, and 1983) and *A Shaping Joy* (1971) "are, in their different ways, richly historical."[12]

It would be wrong, however, to assume that Brooks has repudiated the critical faith of his early career simply because his more recent works do not seem as revolutionary as *The Well Wrought Urn*. Rather, the New Criticism has been so successful that yesterday's insurgency has become today's orthodoxy. Consequently, Brooks—who has always been more judicious and more eclectic than his detractors were willing to admit—has been able of late to pursue his various critical interests free of the polemical responsibilities of one who speaks for a new and suspect point of view.

As practitioner and popularizer of the New Criticism, Brooks has achieved a secure reputation. (His very ability to evoke controversy is perhaps a measure of his professional stature.) Although not as systematic a theoretician as Richards or Ransom, he is not primarily a derivative thinker. If the generation that came before him produced the *kerygmatic* theologians of the New Criticism, Brooks is clearly cast in the role of apologist. Like all good apologists, he has reshaped his doctrine to fit the facts of experience. The criticism of Cleanth Brooks, like the poetry it most reveres, is a tightly argued synthesis of experience that—to echo the critic's own comment about Faulkner—is "eloquent of the possibilities of order."[13]

Robert Penn Warren:
Foul Rag and Bone Shop of the Heart

In *Babel to Byzantium* James Dickey writes, "Opening a book of poems by Robert Penn Warren is like putting out the light of the sun, or like plunging into the labyrinth and feeling the thread break after the first corner is passed. One will never come out in the same Self as that in which one entered. When he is good, and often even when he

---

[12]This observation comes from Monroe K. Spears's essay "Cleanth Brooks and the Responsibilities of Criticism," in Simpson, 231. Although this essay was published prior to Brooks's second and third volumes on Faulkner, that study also substantiates Spears's point.

[13]Cleanth Brooks, *William Faulkner: The Yoknapatawpha Country* (New Haven CT: Yale University Press, 1963) 368.

is bad, you had as soon read Warren as live. He gives you the sense of poetry as a thing of final importance to life."[14] Although others might not express themselves as enthusiastically as Dickey has, the reception of Warren's verse has been such that he is easily America's most honored living poet. He has won the Edna St. Vincent Millay Prize, the National Book Award, the Bollingen Prize, the National Medal for Literature, the Van Wyck Brooks Award, the Emerson-Thoreau Award, and the Pulitzer Prize, twice for poetry and once for fiction. No less an authority than Harold Bloom asserts that in Warren "our nation . . . once again has a living poet comparable in power to Stevens or Frost."[15]

In approaching Warren's poetry we might do well to begin with his criticism; for, in the words of Victor H. Strandberg, Warren's essays have "maintained a running gloss on his creative literature."[16] Of particular interest are "Pure and Impure Poetry" and "A Poem of Pure Imagination," the entries which respectively begin and end Warren's *Selected Essays* (1958). The first of these endorses—in slightly different vocabulary—the poetry of inclusion advocated by Richards and Brooks. "Poetry wants to be pure," Warren writes, "but poems do not. At least most of them do not want to be too pure. The poems want to give us poetry, which is pure, and the elements of a poem, in so far as it is a good poem, will work together toward that end, but many of the elements, taken in themselves, may actually seem to contradict that end, or be neutral toward the achieving of that end."[17]

These neutral and recalcitrant elements, however, are not to be regretted as mere indications of human frailty; nor are we to conclude that in a perfect world there would be no "dross" in poems. Indeed, "poems include, deliberately, more of the so-called dross than would appear necessary. They are not even as pure as they might be in this imperfect world. They mar themselves with cacophonies, jagged rhythms, ugly words and ugly thoughts, colloquialisms, clichés, sterile technical terms, headwork and argument, self-contradictions, clever-

---

[14]James Dickey, *Babel to Byzantium* (New York: Farrar, Straus and Giroux, 1968) 75.

[15]"The Year's Books," *The New Republic*, 20 November 1976, 20.

[16]Victor H. Strandberg, *The Poetic Vision of Robert Penn Warren* (Lexington: University Press of Kentucky, 1977) 34.

[17]Robert Penn Warren, *Selected Essays* (New York: Random House, 1958) 4.

nesses, irony, realism—all things which call us back to the world of prose and imperfection" (pp. 4-5). Like his colleague Brooks, Warren rejects the notion of an inherently poetic subject matter. For him, "poetry does not inhere in any particular element but depends upon the set of relationships, the structure, which we call the poem.... Nothing that is available in human experience is to be legislated out of poetry" (p. 26).

In "A Poem of Pure Imagination"—a long interpretative reading of Coleridge's *Rime of the Ancient Mariner*—we gain further insight into Warren's conception of poetry. Summarizing his subject's metaphysical position as it pertains to his artistic practice, Warren notes Coleridge's contention that "the creativity of the human mind, both in terms of the primary and in terms of the secondary imagination, is an analogue of Divine creation and a proof that man is created in God's image" (p. 210). Accordingly, "the world of Nature is to be read as a symbol of Divinity, a symbol characterized by the 'translucence of the eternal through and in the temporal,' which 'always partakes of the reality which it renders intelligible; and while it enunciates the whole, abides itself as a living part in that unity of which it is representative' " (p. 210).

Essentially, Warren sees Coleridge as possessing a "sacramental" vision of life and art. A sacrament, when viewed in terms of its specifically Christian connotation, is—of course—a *material* vehicle of Grace, an occasion for the "translucence of the eternal through and in the temporal." The "believer" who repudiates material reality—a Puritan or a Manichean, for example—thus abjures any possible mediation between our fallen world and the Kingdom of Heaven. He is like the "pure" poet who by removing himself from the vicissitudes of life, from what Yeats calls the "foul rag and bone shop of the heart," cuts himself off from the resources of the spirit rather than attaining to them.[18] In contrast, the orthodox believer—and, by implication, the

---

[18]Allen Tate sees Poe as such a figure. In commenting on him, Tate writes, "Since he refuses to see nature, he is doomed to see nothing. He has overleaped and cheated the condition of man. The reach of our imaginative enlargement is perhaps no longer than the ladder of analogy, at the top of which we may see all, if we still wish to *see* anything, that we have brought up with us from the bottom, where lies the sensible world. If we take nothing with us to the top but our emptied, angelic intellects, we shall see nothing when we get there." See *Essays of Four Decades* (Chicago: Swallow Press, 1968) 422.

truly imaginative poet—manages to forge a synthesis of the physical and the spiritual. Such a synthesis amounts to a sacramental understanding of life, an understanding that—purged of its specifically theological trappings—can stand as a metaphor for the human imagination.

True to his critical convictions, Warren has produced a body of poetry that contains elements of the physical and the spiritual joined in impure but sacramental synthesis. An early example of this synthesizing faculty can be found in "The Return: An Elegy," published in Warren's first collected volume, *Thirty-Six Poems* (1935). Here, the speaker is a young man traveling by train to his mother's funeral. Part of him tries to come to terms with his grief, while other parts seek to avoid doing so. The psychological drama of the conflict and its ultimate resolution constitutes the action of Warren's poem.

At one level of consciousness the speaker tries to focus only on immediate perceptions, ignoring entirely the larger reality of life and death. At a second level he acknowledges the fact of death, but tries to distance himself from it with a sort of blustery cynicism. He says, for example,

> give me the nickles off your eyes
> from your hands the violets
> let me bless your obsequies
> if you possessed conveniently enough three eyes
> then I could buy a pack of cigarettes.[19]

It is only at a third level of consciousness, rendered in italics, that the speaker is able tentatively to realize that his mother—as all of nature must—has succumbed to the laws of mortality. Halfway through the poem he is able to speak her name: "*does my mother wake*" (p. 317); but then he wrenches his attention back to the sights outside his Pullman car. He sees these sights with new eyes, however. He is able to feel compassion for the lost and hungry people who once lived along the road he is passing. He is also able to recall the child he once was and acknowledge the reality of his mission. By the end of the poem he has achieved a mature and complex appreciation of life and death.

---

[19] Robert Penn Warren, *Selected Poems 1923-1975* (New York: Random House, 1976) 316.

He tells us to "honor thy father and mother in the days of thy youth / for time uncoils like the cottonmouth" (p. 318). No doubt, the snake is intended here to remind us of the Fall and of death. The imminence of death challenges us to act responsibly in the present and to value life while we have it. Armed with his new realization, the speaker is able to declare his love for his mother; and yet, the limits reality places on the deeds of love force him to speak in subjunctive fragments.

> If I could pluck
> Against the dry essential of tomorrow
> To lay upon the breast that gave me suck
> Out of the dark the dark and swollen orchid of this sorrow.
> (p. 318)

An even more complex dialogue of consciousness is effected in one of Warren's most ambitious and controversial poems, "The Ballad of Billie Potts" (first published in *Selected Poems* 1923-1943). In "Billie Potts" there is an interplay between the old Kentucky folktale that constitutes the poem's action and a philosophical meditation on that tale. The two diverse strands of narration certainly introduce an element of impurity into the poem; however, there seems to be no consensus as to whether these impurities are effectively synthesized into a larger poetic conception. Strandberg, for example, argues that next to *Brother to Dragons*, "Billie Potts" "is probably Warren's best poem, and certainly his most important" (p. 163). Ransom contends, however, that the work is seriously marred in its philosophical stanzas by "a gloss far more implausible than that which Coleridge wrote upon his margins" in *The Ancient Mariner*.[20]

The story Warren tells is basically simple. Young Billie Potts is the impetuous son of a tavernkeeper-highwayman. Although the elder Billie routinely lures his unsuspecting lodgers into a trap in which they are robbed and killed, the younger lacks his father's expertise and is forced to flee when he botches his own maiden attempt at crime. A decade later young Billie returns, so changed in appearance that he is taken for a wealthy stranger from the West. Seeking some fun at his parents' expense, Billie withholds his true identity, only to be slain for

---

[20]Quoted by Strandberg, 3.

his money. Too late, his mother and father realize that they have murdered their only son.

Although restrictions of space preclude a detailed analysis of this extremely rich poem, we can at least identify its principal theme and narrative structure. Essentially, the poem presents a quest for identity which is worked out in terms of Billie's journey to the West and back. In this respect "The Ballad of Billie Potts" resembles several of Warren's other narratives, both in prose and in verse. As Joe Davis points out, the journey West serves a crucial thematic function in *Night Rider, All the King's Men, World Enough and Time, Band of Angels*, and *Brother to Dragons* as well as in "Billie Potts."[21]

Historically, the movement of civilization has always been westward. In addition to the economic and demographic factors involved, there is mythical significance in this migration. Since the exile of our first parents to the *East* of Eden, the journey West has been a movement toward the recovery of our lost innocence. Only within the last century—with the closing of the frontier and the settling of California—have we in America come to realize the illusory nature of this geographical eschatology. (The Old World—at least as it is depicted in the novels of Henry James—came to such a realization much earlier.) Thus, the myth of an American Adam and of a New World Eden remain vivid memories in our national psyche; Warren makes effective use of these memories.

Calling our attention to Billie's origins in "the land between the rivers," Strandberg writes, "Mesopotamia, which translated means 'the land between the rivers,' has long been regarded in Semitic myth, including the Garden of Eden story, as the birthplace of mankind. So Warren subtly implies as early as line 2 of this poem the origin and outcome of the myth he is recreating in the context of New World innocence and its Fall" (p. 150). In seeking the promise and anonymity of the West, young Billie is trying to escape the legacy of his father—the old, fallen Adam. However, in terms of Warren's "sacramental" vision, such an escape involves a movement away from life and toward a false purity. Postlapsarian man has no choice but to accept the reality of evil, to be reconciled with what Strandberg calls "the hidden self."

---

[21]See "Robert Penn Warren and the Journey to the West," *Modern Fiction Studies* 6 (Spring 1960): 73-82.

Literature of Tennessee 103

The quest for identity figures as a key theme not only in the folk ballad part of Warren's poem, but in the meditative stanzas as well. The principal figure in these stanzas is a reader created by Warren and addressed as "you." As the poem progresses, however, "you" gradually becomes merged with Billie Potts. At the end of his stay in the West this figure looks at his reflection in the river, only to realize that the river is always in a state of flux.[22] He then returns home to seek a more stable and permanent identity.

Upon returning home Billie becomes an ironic integration of personality as both son and victim. The latter role is immediately suggested because he is dressed in black. At the beginning of the poem, the elder Billie's generic victim was described as a "Man in black coat, riding bay mare with star" (p. 273). The full implications of this role are realized when young Billie—again leaning toward water—is felled by his father's hatchet. For him, the flux of identity finally has been resolved in the permanent stasis of death.

It is only then that "the stranger" is revealed to be the elder Billie's son. After encountering a family friend in whom young Billie had confided his hoax, the father digs up his victim's corpse and finds the identifying birthmark, a discoloration under the heart. (Ironically, had this mark been evident before, it might, like Cain's, have preserved its bearer from harm.) Young Billie Potts has returned from the illusion of the West "To kneel in the sacramental silence of evening / At the feet of the old man / Who is evil and ignorant and old" (p. 284), to assume the burden of a fallen humanity.

Warren's major work in the poetic genre—and, in the opinion of Randall Jarrell, his "best book"[23]—is his "tale in verse and voices," *Brother to Dragons* (1953).[24] This poetic dialogue tells the story of Thomas Jefferson's nephew, a settler in western Kentucky named Lil-

---

[22]In "Ode to the Confederate Dead" Tate uses the Narcissus image as a metaphor for the condition of modern man.

[23]See "On the Underside of the Stone," *New York Times Book Review*, 23 August 1953, 6.

[24]In 1979 Warren published a substantially revised version of *Brother to Dragons*. Although the considerable development in his poetic technique that had occurred in the twenty-six years between the two versions of his *magnum opus* is evident in the revised *Brother to Dragons*, Warren's thematic concerns have remained essentially the same.

burn Lewis. "On the night of December 15, 1811," Warren writes in his Foreword, "—the night when the New Madrid earthquake first struck the Mississippi Valley—Lilburn, with the assistance of [his brother] Isham and in the presence of his Negroes, butchered a slave named George, whose offense had been to break a pitcher" prized by Lilburn's dead mother, Lucy Jefferson Lewis.[25] Although the brothers agreed to kill each other to avoid being hanged, only Lilburn died. Isham survived, spent some time in jail, escaped, and eventually was killed in the Battle of New Orleans. Because there is no historical record of Jefferson's reaction to his nephews' brutality, Warren has created an imaginative one in *Brother to Dragons*.

If we are to understand this poem and Warren's other writings, it might be useful to define the author's attitude toward the grand myth of American innocence. We know from reading R. W. B. Lewis and others that in the nineteenth century many serious writers saw the New World as a second Garden of Eden and viewed the American as a new Adam, "a figure of heroic innocence and vast potentialities poised at the start of a new history."[26] Such writers (Emerson, Thoreau, Whitman, et al.) constituted what Emerson called a "party of hope." Diametrically opposed to this group and its historical and moral optimism was a "party of memory," preoccupied with human depravity and Original Sin. However, mediating between the simplistic extremes of both these "parties" was an infinitely more complex vision, one which affirmed both the reality of a fall from innocence and the possibility of redemption. This third position, which Lewis attributes to a "party of irony," seems to be the one with which Warren is most closely aligned.

At the outset of his spiritual odyssey—prior to the "Any Time" of Warren's poem—Thomas Jefferson was clearly in the party of hope: he had believed in the goodness of man and in the possibilities of democracy. Upon discovering Lilburn's crime, however, he renounces these hopeful attitudes in favor of misanthropy toward his fellow man and profound pessimism about social institutions. In the course of *Brother to Dragons* Jefferson is forced to move one step further and

---

[25]Robert Penn Warren, *Brother to Dragons* (New York: Random House, 1953) ix.

[26]R. W. B. Lewis, *The American Adam* (Chicago: University of Chicago Press, 1955) 1.

abandon his *jejune* stance of despair and alienation which he has adopted. He moves beyond hope and memory to a position which is, in Lewis's sense, ultimately ironic: he acknowledges his own complicity in the world's evil and comes to see himself—in the words of the Book of Job—as "a brother to dragons and a companion to owls" (Job 30:29, King James Version).

The catalyst for Jefferson's conversion to the party of irony is his encounter with another family member, his philosophical heir Meriwether Lewis. Enthralled by Jefferson's idealistic view of human nature, Meriwether went West unprepared for the brutal reality of life in the wilderness or the news of corruption from back East. His vulnerability and disillusionment led ultimately to despair and suicide. When confronted with the destructive consequences of his previous philosophy of innocence, Jefferson comes to see that he shares in the burden of human guilt; he can no longer condemn Lilburn from a position of moral aloofness. Indeed, as Dennis M. Dooley points out, "Jefferson comes to realize that his repudiation of Lilburn is analogous to his nephew's butchering of the slave; both are attempts to deny the complex imperfection that is man."[27]

Like Jefferson, the narrator of Warren's poem—a choric figure named R. P. W.—also undergoes conversion from an attitude of pessimism to one of affirmation. This conversion is worked out in three digressions from the main action of the poem; each serves as a counterpoint to the depiction of Jefferson's transformation and earns R. P. W. the right to comment on that transformation. In his detailed and perceptive discussion of the narrator's role in *Brother to Dragons*, Dooley notes that "by having Jefferson's spiritual progress also acted out by R. P. W., the issue of the poem ceases to be simply an issue of the Nineteenth Century." "By enclosing the past within the frame of the present," Dooley concludes, "Warren is able to transcend mere past and present and to create his poetic 'Any Time' " (p. 163).

Although Warren published no verse between his *Selected Poems, 1923-1943*, which included "Billie Potts," and *Brother to Dragons*, he has more than made up for that hiatus in the past quarter century. During that time he has published *Promises: Poems 1954-1956; You, Emperors,*

---

[27]Dennis M. Dooley, "This Collocation of Memories: The Poetic Strategy of Robert Penn Warren" (Ph.D. dissertation, Vanderbilt University, 1970) 147.

and Others: Poems 1957-1960; Selected Poems: New and Old 1923-1966; Incarnations: Poems 1966-1968; Audubon: A Vision (1969); *Or Else— Poem/Poems 1968-1974; Selected Poems 1923-1975; Now and Then: Poems 1976-1978, Being Here: Poetry 1977-1980; Rumor Verified: Poems 1979-1980;* and *Chief Joseph of the Nez Percé* (1983). In each of his volumes of "selected poems" Warren has emphasized his later work by arranging the poems in reverse chronological order. And, as Monroe Spears points out, more than five-sixths of the most recent of these selected poems—"268 of its 325 pages—dates from 1954 or later." Moreover, since 1954, "Warren's poems have grown steadily more open, more unabashedly personal, more overtly psychological and religious, and more interdependent."[28]

There is probably no single reason for Warren's shift from the highly structured verse forms of his Fugitive years to the more flexible poetics of his middle and later years. Spears correctly observes that even in his early poetry, "Warren was more open in texture and more personal in tone" than Ransom and Tate and that when Warren returned to poetry in 1954 these qualities were simply accentuated. In part, no doubt, this transformation was due to some of "the same pressures that produced the 'confessional' movement at about the same time," as well as to "private and internal developments" (Spears, 38).

One might argue that, having assimilated the teaching of Ransom, Warren moved on—over the years—to find a poetic style more distinctively his own.[29] Indeed, such a movement away from early models is neither a surprising phenomenon nor one unique to Warren's career. A number of poets—including Ransom's other gifted student, Robert Lowell—have experienced a similar pattern of development. Whether or not Warren's particular evolution is an instance of what Harold Bloom calls "the anxiety of influence" is an intriguing question that deserves critical pursuit, although it is beyond the scope of the present study.

---

[28]Monroe K. Spears, "Immersed in America," *New York Review of Books*, 20 April 1978, 38.

[29]As we can see from his comments on "Billie Potts," Ransom was not always pleased with Warren's later poetry. Nor, for that matter, was he an unqualified admirer of his student's fiction. For a sampling of Ransom's comments on Warren's early novels, see Thomas Daniel Young, *Gentleman in a Dustcoat* (Baton Rouge: Louisiana State University Press, 1976) 413.

If Warren's poetry has become more original, more stylistically accomplished, more vividly realized in recent years, the same cannot be said of his fiction. Here his earlier work remains by far his best. Louis D. Rubin, Jr., maintains that Warren's "one persistent problem with his fiction . . . has been that of discovering the proper form for getting his fascination with ideas and values into an integral relationship with his interest in tale-telling—plot, characterization, motives, and action."[30] Increasingly, Warren's fiction has come to rely less on image and action than on abstract and sententious pronouncement.[31] The path from *Night Rider* (1939) to *A Place to Come To* (1977) is one of cumulative— though not steady—decline.

In *Night Rider* Warren remains close to the "dark and bloody ground" of his childhood. The enveloping action of his story deals with the efforts of Kentucky tobacco farmers to maintain an adequate price for their crop by organizing a growers' cartel. Eventually resorting to violence, this cartel forms bands of marauding night riders to destroy the crops of independent growers. Ultimately, though, Warren's novel is less about the public controversies in which the farmers are involved than it is about the deep spiritual alienation of one man—Percy Munn.

Munn, who is referred to impersonally throughout the novel as *Mr.* Munn, finds himself gradually becoming involved with the cartel— first as its attorney, then as one of the night riders. Unable to find satisfaction in his profession or in his marriage, Munn devotes himself increasingly to the abstract ideal of justice. In the course of the novel he becomes an adulterer, a murderer, and finally a fugitive from the law. The end of Munn's story comes when he leaves his hideout—the farm of a backwoodsman named Willie Proudfit—and sets out to murder Senator Tolliver, a politician who has betrayed the growers' association. Munn, however, cannot bring himself to kill Tolliver; instead, Munn is killed by a posse while fleeing Tolliver's house.

---

[30]Louis D. Rubin, Jr., *The Wary Fugitives* (Baton Rouge: Louisiana State University Press, 1978) 357.

[31]A similar progression from the concrete to the abstract, from the objective to the discursive, can be found in the careers of a number of modern writers. In *The Flesh and the Word* (Nashville: Vanderbilt University Press, 1971), Floyd C. Watkins discusses this phenomenon in reference to Eliot, Hemingway, and Faulkner.

The action of *Night Rider* is well-paced and credible; the characterizations are strong and the dialogue authentic. Of equal importance to the success of Warren's novel, however, is the effectiveness of his third-person limited narration. Although Percy Munn is the principal center of consciousness in the novel, Warren's narrator is able to maintain sufficient ironic distance that we are never tempted to regard Munn as a moral norm. Indeed, to the extent that the novel can be said to have a moral norm, that function is served not by Munn but by Willie Proudfit—the backwoods farmer who hides Munn when the latter seeks to avoid capture.

In an interpolated story which lasts for an entire chapter, Proudfit tells of a trip he made to the West and back. Like Meriwether Lewis in *Brother to Dragons*, Willie encounters brutality and hardship in the wilderness; but, unlike Meriwether, he is able to learn from his experience. Willie Proudfit returns to the land of his fathers a wiser and more tolerant person than when he left. His fully integrated personality is vastly different from that of Percy Munn or, indeed, of any of the other characters in *Night Rider*.

In Warren's most recent novel, *A Place to Come To*, however, there are *no* characters with fully integrated personalities, nor even any who are consistently believable in their various neuroses. Although this novel is not without merit, it suffers greatly from comparison with its author's earlier work. Whereas the prose style of *Night Rider* is relatively laconic and precise, that of *A Place to Come To* is inflated and murky. Whereas Warren's earlier novel possessed a reasonably tight structure and a plausible narrative line, his later one is a sprawling mass of gratuitous improbabilities. In attempting to depict the confusion and irresolution of his protagonist, Jed Tewksbury, the author falls prey to what Robert Penn Warren the critic might call the fallacy of imitative form.

Actually, the first third, even the first half, of this novel is quite promising. The death of Jed's first wife and the suicide of his German professor are compelling incidents movingly depicted, but they seem to have disproportionately little impact on Tewksbury's later life. When Jed moves to Nashville and begins his affair with a childhood flame named Rozelle Hardcastle, however, *A Place to Come To* goes downhill fast. No doubt, much of the problem has to do with the character of Rozelle herself. A Southern belle who is half again as tiresome as Scarlett O'Hara at her worst, Rozelle is accurately described by Anatole Broyard when he says of her, " ... she is equipped with that peculiar inscrutability that girls in some Southern novels seem to possess, as though she has sprung up out of a nameless crack in our culture.... Filled with dark presentiments, Rozelle is capable only of the 'Gothic' satisfactions of star-crossed love.... She is less like a love affair than a bad debt."[32]

After Jed leaves Rozelle and Nashville, his descriptions of his experiences become sketchy and episodic. Finally, late in life, he is able to return to his hometown and make an uneasy truce with his past. Although the book's epigraph is from Hopkins's "Carrion Comfort," Warren might just as easily have chosen those famous lines from Eliot's "Little Gidding": "We shall not cease from exploration / And the end of all our exploring / Will be to arrive where we started / And know the place for the first time."

The message of this novel seems to be that you not only *can* but *must* go home again. It is an interesting proposition and one which Warren, who has been part of the dispersion of Southern intellectuals to the North, is uniquely equipped to write about. Unfortunately, his thematic interests are too frequently reduced to bald statement or lost entirely in the midst of a story line whose movement is often tortuous and whose content is largely beside the point.

If *A Place to Come To* is a less than successful work of fiction, it and others like it could not fatally damage Warren's reputation as a novelist. For more than three decades that reputation has remained secure on the basis of what most observers think is his finest literary achievement—one of the great novels of American literature, *All the King's Men*.

This novel tells the story of a young newspaper reporter, Jack Burden, who undergoes a profound spiritual transformation while witnessing the rise and fall of a complex, demagogic politician named Willie Stark. What Jack finally learns from his experience with Willie and others is quite similar to what Jefferson learns in *Brother to Dragons*. In *All the King's Men*, as in his narrative poem, Warren is a spokesman for the party of irony. The full structure of Jack Burden's

---

[32]Review of *A Place to Come To, Cincinnati Enquirer*, 13 March 1977, F8. This review was distributed by the *New York Times* News Service.

experience amounts to a secular version of the paradox of the Fortunate Fall.

Among the lessons Jack learns in the course of the novel are the dangers of excessive innocence and of excessive cynicism. The first of these he learns from his lifelong friend Adam Stanton. As Warren's name-typing would suggest, Stanton exists in a sort of psychic Eden. Although he may realize intellectually that evil exists in the world, he feels that world must be different from the one he inhabits. He is an aristocrat and a Southern gentleman, unable to comprehend the corruption and vulgarity of a Willie Stark. Cut off from the creative ambiguity of human experience, Adam sees everything in scientific abstraction. He is philosophically akin to the "pure poet," spiritual heir to Hawthorne's Aylmer and to Hardy's Angel Clare.

When Adam finally discovers that his sister has been Willie Stark's mistress, he goes berserk and murders Stark in the capitol rotunda. In the process, Stanton is gunned down by Stark's body guard, Sugar-Boy. Adam thus destroys himself through an unwillingness to recognize the taint of imperfection in his sister. (If unfallen innocence involves an ignorance of good and evil, then it is a particularly willful form of such innocence that incapacitates Adam Stanton.) When confronted with the existential knowledge of good and evil, he falls and dies unredeemed.

Willie Stark's problem would seem to be just the opposite of Adam's. If Stanton is too innocent to deal effectively with the evil of a fallen world, one suspects that Stark is so flawed with cynicism that he is incapable of seeing anything but evil. When the Boss tells Jack to dig up some dirt on Judge Irwin and Jack suggests that this might not be possible, Stark replies, "Man is conceived in sin and born in corruption and he passeth from the stink of the didie to the stench of the shroud. There is always something."[33] Of course, Stark has not always been of this opinion. At the outset of his political career, Stark is the naive and idealistic "Cousin Willie," a public servant who wants to enlighten the populace and govern honestly. Only after such an approach fails does he decide to operate as a ruthless pragmatist.

Willie does not realize the error of his moral vision, however, until his son Tom is injured in a football game and becomes permanently

---

[33]Robert Penn Warren, *All the King's Men* (New York: Random House, 1946) 12.

paralyzed. At this point Willie tries to reform. He attempts to extricate himself from political corruption, and he leaves his mistresses, Anne Stanton and Sadie Burke, to return to his wife. Unfortunately, Willie's final enlightenment comes too late to save him from physical destruction. On his deathbed he forgives Adam Stanton and tells Jack, "It might have been all different. . . . And it might even been different yet. . . . If it hadn't happened, it might—have been different—even yet" (p. 425).

For Jack Burden it *is* in fact very different from the way it has been with his friends Adam Stanton and Willie Stark. Like Adam and Willie, Jack begins his spiritual development from a position of innocence and, like his two friends, he is forced by circumstances to abandon that innocence. Unlike Adam and Willie, however, Jack is eventually able to achieve a degree of wisdom and maturity by confronting the actual complexity of experience, which Warren calls "the awful responsibility of time."

Although Jack's attitude toward life evolves from a broad range of experience, three crucial events seem to mark distinct stages in that evolution. Jack's refusal to consummate his seduction of Anne Stanton and the subsequent breakup of their relationship leads to a period of lassitude and withdrawal, which he calls the "Great Sleep." By refusing to violate a fixed ideal of innocence, Jack retreats from the realm of adult responsibility. The "Great Sleep" is like a return to the womb, and Jack's philosophy of Berkleyan Idealism is simply a glib rationalization of his desire to remain as innocent as a "clammy, sad little foetus which . . . wants to lie in the dark and not know, and be warm in its not knowing" (pp. 11-12).

Jack is able to maintain this sort of detachment only until he learns of Anne Stanton's affair with Willie Stark. Fearing that he may somehow have driven Anne into Willie's arms and disabused of his belief in her purity, Jack then finds the actuality of evil impinging on his previously closed little universe. In reaction to this discovery he flees to the West, to Long Beach, California. There he gets drunk in a hotel room and goes into an abbreviated "Great Sleep." A few days later he returns from the West and, like so many of Warren's other characters who make a similar journey, he is a changed man. No longer able to believe in Anne's unqualified innocence, he denies that guilt and innocence have any objective meaning. For him all of reality has become a great mechanistic twitch.

Had Jack remained a believer in the "Great Twitch," his spiritual development would have been no more complete than that of Adam or Willie. He is brought one step closer to maturity, however, by an event roughly equivalent to the moment of recognition and reversal in a Greek tragedy. On orders from Willie, Jack blackmails Judge Irwin, thus precipitating the latter's suicide. When Jack's mother learns of the judge's death, she reveals to her son that Irwin was his real father. Just as Meriwether Lewis's suicide causes Jefferson to reevaluate his philosophy of life in *Brother to Dragons*, the judge's death has a similar effect on Jack Burden.

After the suicide of Judge Irwin, the novel moves through several smaller crises to its climax, the assassination of Willie Stark. In the final chapter Jack reflects on what he has learned and on the sort of person he has become. He is no longer a wet, clammy little fetus, warm in his not knowing. No longer is he an idealist, interpreting things solely in reference to his own perceptions; nor is he even part of a great cosmic twitch. Jack Burden's suffering has changed his picture of the world into one in which men are free moral agents. "History is blind," Jack's friend Hugh Miller tells him, "but man is not" (p. 462).

When asked to rank his contemporaries, William Faulkner frankly admitted that all, himself included, had been failures. But, he added, Thomas Wolfe "had made the best failure because he had tried hardest to say the most."[34] If all artists can be considered failures in the sense that all have fallen short of the ideal, then Robert Penn Warren is the most magnificent failure of the entire Fugitive group. Like only a handful of American writers (one thinks of Melville and Dreiser as well as of Wolfe and Faulkner), Warren is among those who tried hardest to say the most.

As Louis D. Rubin, Jr., points out, Warren "is not a fastidious writer" like Tate and Ransom:

> . . . his willingness to plunge ahead and not worry about getting everything in order ahead of time has made it possible for him to enjoy one of the longest, most varied, and most productive careers in Amer-

---

[34]See Richard Walser, "On Faulkner's Putting Wolfe First," *South Atlantic Quarterly* 78 (Spring 1979): 176.

ican literary history, but it has also meant that he has published work that is not always formally successful.... Warren is simply not the kind of writer who produces perfect work; his imagination is too bold, his mind too restless to allow him the kind of lapidary technique that would avoid all flaws and imperfections. (pp. 357-58)

Looking at the twentieth-century writers Brooks extols in *Modern Poetry and the Tradition*, one sees a revival of seventeenth-century techniques. In Warren's work, however, one sees the influence of the intervening centuries as well. In his poetry are the didactic and prosaic qualities of eighteenth-century verse, and in his fiction is a kind of Victorian earnestness. Moreover, the hard, gemlike flame of Romanticism burns throughout his writing. Although his light is one we generally associate with youth, Robert Penn Warren, youngest of the Fugitives and now the last, has entered an extraordinarily productive old age.

Selected Bibliography

Baumbach, Jonathan. *The Landscape of Nightmare: Studies in the Contemporary American Novel.* New York: New York University Press, 1965, pages 16-34.

Bohner, Charles H. *Robert Penn Warren.* New York: Twayne, 1964.

Bradbury, John M. *The Fugitives: A Critical Account.* Chapel Hill: University of North Carolina Press, 1958.

Casper, Leonard. *Robert Penn Warren: The Dark and Bloody Ground.* Seattle: University of Washington Press, 1960.

Crane, R. S., ed. *Critics and Criticism: Ancient and Modern.* Chicago: University of Chicago Press, 1952, pages 83-107, 138-44.

Davis, Joe. "Robert Penn Warren and the Journey to the West." *Modern Fiction Studies* 6 (Spring 1960): 73-82.

Dooley, Dennis M. "This Collocation of Memories: The Poetic Strategy of Robert Penn Warren." Ph.D. dissertation, Vanderbilt University, 1970.

Rubin, Louis D., Jr. *The Wary Fugitives.* Baton Rouge: Louisiana State University Press, 1978.

_____. *Writers of the Modern South: The Faraway Country.* Seattle: University of Washington Press, 1963, pages 105-30.

Simpson, Lewis P., ed. *The Possibilities of Order: Cleanth Brooks and His Work.* Baton Rouge: Louisiana State University Press, 1978.

Spears, Monroe K. "Immersed in America." *New York Review of Books,* 20 April 1978, 38-41.

Strandberg, Victor. *The Poetic Vision of Robert Penn Warren.* Lexington: The University Press of Kentucky, 1977.

Andrew Lytle

Charles C. Clark

Place, particularly the Cumberland Plateau of Tennessee and North Alabama, family, religion, history, and tradition have been controlling influences in the life and literary achievements of Andrew Lytle, novelist, critic, editor, and teacher. Man, according to Lytle, is "both good and evil, and . . . has a soul to win or lose. The defense against the evil within and without begins in a structure of a stable society. He must have location, which means property, which means the family and the communion of families which is the state."[1]

Born on 26 December 1902, in Murfreesboro, Tennessee, the town founded by his Revolutionary War ancestor, Captain William Lytle, Andrew Nelson Lytle was educated at the Sewanee Military Academy and Vanderbilt University. After a year of postgraduate study in France and two years at the Yale School of Drama under George Pierce Baker, he worked for a while as an actor in New York City.

At Vanderbilt, where he received his bachelor's degree in 1925, Lytle took part in the Fugitive-Agrarian Movement. Although not a poet, he was closely associated with some of the Fugitives, especially Donald Davidson, Allen Tate, and Robert Penn Warren. Later he was to receive the donnée for his first novel from his fellow Agrarian and close friend, the historian Frank Lawrence Owsley.

---

[1]Andrew Nelson Lytle, "How Many Miles to Babylon?," *Hopkins Review* 6 (Spring-Summer 1953): 103.

Through his association with the Fugitives and Agrarians, Lytle realized that writing was his proper work. In 1930 he contributed an essay entitled "The Hind Tit" to the Southern Agrarian manifesto *I'll Take My Stand*.[2] This essay, which depicts the debilitating effect industrialization has had on modern man and extols the simple rural life needed to counteract it, has been praised for its literary quality and characterized as a rhetorical overstatement. Unfaltering in his adherence to the Southern Agrarian tradition, Lytle comments in an essay published in 1971, "Almost absolutely I would say that the great, at least lasting, literatures and representative arts are found in either a pastoral or agrarian society. The images and references which the arts find to hand are to things natural and supernatural: to men, animals, plants, winds, water, and fire, not indiscriminately used but always through their proper functions and necessities."[3]

In 1931 Lytle published his first book, *Bedford Forrest and His Critter Company*. The biography, which shows the agrarian influences in the life of the great Tennessee cavalry leader, advances a main thesis of the historian Lytle: "The fall of the Confederacy was due chiefly to Davis's military policy in the West, and particularly to his support of Bragg."[4] The book's structure is determined by history, of course, but Lytle so develops Forrest with an intermingling of narrative and sharply rendered scene that the reader often has the impression he is reading a novel. Lytle's dramatic experience, put to good use in this first book, was to prove invaluable to him in writing his novels and short stories, all of which exhibit a skillful balancing of panoramic summary and scene.

Lytle published his first work of fiction, a short story entitled "Old Scratch in the Valley," in 1932. The protagonist, a matriarch named Ju-

---

[2]In "They Took Their Stand: The Agrarian View After Fifty Years" [*Modern Age* 24 (Spring 1980): 114-20], Lytle says, " . . . we should have found a larger word than agrarian, for it was this country's Christian inheritance that was threatened, and still is." After observing that Christendom has reached its Satanic phase, as shown by the materialism of present-day society, he adds, "There is only one comfort, and it is the only thing that has been promised: the gates of Hell will not finally prevail."

[3]"The State of Letters in a Time of Disorder," *Sewanee Review* 79 (Autumn 1971): 489-90.

[4]*Bedford Forrest and His Critter Company* (New York: Minton Balch, 1931) 393.

dith Mebane, rules Long Gourd Valley, a Cumberland cove, until her death in 1908. She is "the last matriarch to sit on the richest acres in the Dipper and govern the opinion of her dependents and neighbors." Her antagonist is none other than Satan himself, who contests mightily with her for "the soul and body of her cousin Micajah Searcy." The story is told by an inhabitant of Long Gourd, who recounts and comments on the *Antigone*-like events of Micajah's blasphemy, death, and burial, which he witnessed as a child or heard about.

While a professor of history at Southwestern College at Memphis,[5] Lytle contributed an essay entitled "The Small Farm Secures the State" to the second Southern Agrarian symposium, *Who Owns America?* (1936). In his argument for the preservation of the family farm, Lytle points out that man must not try to conquer nature but must live and work in consonance with it. Lytle, a farmer's son, who for a while tried to combine farming and writing, ends the essay with a dictum on family and place: " . . . only when families are fixed in their habits, sure of their property, hopeful for the security of their children, jealous of liberties which they cherish, can the State keep the middle course between impotence and tyranny."[6]

The theme of family informs Lytle's first novel, *The Long Night* (1936). This often lyrical tale recreates the milieu of the Middle South of the last century, particularly the everyday lives of yeoman farmers and their families during times of peace and war. As Robert Penn Warren observes, "It says something about the world of the South not said elsewhere. . . . it offers its own special fascination and its own special pleasure."[7] Lytle renders this "world of the South" in an action reminiscent of Elizabethan tragedy, set in Georgia, Alabama, Mississippi, and Tennessee during the 1850s, 1860-1862, and—by means of the frame into which the narrative is placed—during a brief period in the 1880s or early 1890s.

---

[5]In 1938 Andrew Lytle married Edna Langdon Barker of Memphis, Tennessee; he has been a widower since 1963. His daughters are Pamela, Katherine Anne, and Lillie Langdon.

[6]*Who Owns America?*, ed. Herbert Agar and Allen Tate (Boston: Houghton Mifflin, 1936) 250.

[7]"Andrew Lytle's *The Long Night*: A Rediscovery," *Southern Review* 7 (January 1971): 139.

In Lytle's recasting of the tale Frank Lawrence Owsley once told him,[8] there is an early shift in point of view, with Pleasant McIvor, the protagonist, changing from first-person narrator to third-person central intelligence or—to use Lytle's term—"roving narrator." The story the elderly Pleasant tells his nephew Lawrence, a young man on his way to south Alabama to become a teacher, is a bizarre one. The McIvor patriarch, Cameron, is forced by legal difficulties to sell his Georgia farm and move. Intending to take his family to Texas, he stops near Wetumpka, Alabama, where a landowner named Lovell (patterned on the infamous John Murrell) persuades him to interrupt the journey to make a crop on shares.

Because he has discovered that Lovell and his forty or more followers, some of whom are respected citizens, are speculators (men who steal and sell slaves and livestock), the upright Cameron is harassed and murdered by the gang. Young Pleasant learns the identities of the killers from his mother (an eyewitness), from his observations of spectators at his father's funeral, and from his father's ghost, whose voice he hears at the gathering of the clan and afterwards. Methodically the youth begins tracking down and killing the murderers.

The influence of Shakespearean tragedy on *The Long Night* is evident not only in the inclusion of the murdered father's ghost but also in the use of tall tales, anecdotes, and lyrical descriptions of country life to relieve tension. For example, the story the sheriff's wife tells a friend at the wake about her bibulous husband's bringing a horse into the bedroom one night and hitching it to a bedpost has an effect on the reader similar to that which the "knocking at the gate" scene in *Macbeth* has on the playgoer.

When the Civil War breaks out, Pleasant continues his quest within the ranks of the Confederate army, attempting to reconcile private and public commitments. However, the Battle of Shiloh has such a trau-

---

[8]Although the frame of *The Long Night* has been considered an invention of Lytle's, the introductory letter from Lytle to F. L. Owsley is not a product of Lytle's imagination; Pleasant McIvor is a fictionalized "Uncle Dink" McGregor, F. L. Owsley's great-uncle. "Uncle Dink," having killed many of the members of the gang that had killed his father in Georgia in the 1850s, told the story of his quest to F. L. Owsley's father (not F. L. Owsley, as some critics have it). According to Owsley family history, "Uncle Dink" told the story in his old age not to achieve catharsis, as the novel suggests, but to persuade his young auditor to kill the few remaining gang members.

matic effect on him that some time later, near Murfreesboro, he cannot squeeze the trigger when he has in his sights a Confederate picket who had been a member of Lovell's gang. This abortive effort causes him to delay making his scouting report on a concentration of Federal troops, and the delay results in the death of his comrade and friend, Roswell Ellis. He tortures himself with the thought that he has failed both his father's ghost, whose voice he no longer hears, and his friend Roswell: "Twice he had loved—once the dead, once the living, and each by each was consumed and he was doomed." He looks southward:

> Far to the south the hills of Winston rose close and stubborn out of the lowlands ... There he would go. There in the secret coves, far away from the world and vengeance, a deserter might hide forever. ...

Lytle's novella *Alchemy* (1942) involves a different kind of quest, one based on avarice and pride. Telling the story many years after the conquest of Peru, the first-person narrator, who had been one of Pizarro's soldiers, ironically fails to understand the meaning of what he relates, although as M. E. Bradford points out, he seems to realize that the devil's will, not God's, prevailed.[9] In this novella, in which the structure is largely determined by Prescott's *The Conquest of Peru*, Lytle portrays Hernando de Soto as the epitome of the man of will.

Lytle continues to fictionalize the career of de Soto in *At the Moon's Inn* (1941), rendering the Adelantado's abortive conquest of Florida through the viewpoint of a "roving narrator," Tovar, a young officer blooded by an arrow at Cuzco. The story of de Soto, the man of will, as it affects Tovar, the man of sensibility, can be read as an allegory that admonishes modern man to remember the medieval concept *de contemptu mundi*.

At a banquet in San Lúcar, an embittered Cabeza de Vaca declares that he will not join the expedition, giving Providence as his reason. De Soto drives his dagger into the table, saying, "There is one fortune I trust, Señor . . . this!" At the same banquet, a young priest arises to

---

[9] "Toward a Dark Shape: Lytle's 'Alchemy' and the Conquest of the New World," *Mississippi Quarterly* 23 (Fall 1970): 407-14. Reprinted in *The Form Discovered: Essays on the Achievement of Andrew Lytle*, ed. M. E. Bradford (Jackson MS: University and College Press of Mississippi, 1973) 57-63.

warn de Soto against the sins of avarice and pride and to predict that de Soto will bring the people of Florida the sword instead of the Word.

In Havana, de Soto peremptorily reduces Tovar in rank for seducing the lady-in-waiting to de Soto's wife, Doña Isabel, who is to remain in Havana to govern in the Adelantado's place while he leads the expedition on the quest for another Peru. The trek, which begins on the beach in Florida, proceeds through much of the southeastern part of the North American continent, the narrative closely following the accounts of members of the expedition.[10] Unlike the Incas, the Indians through whose lands the Spaniards pass fight to the death rather than submit to the armor-clad invaders, mounted on strange beasts and equipped with crossbows, lances, and swords. With Juan Ortiz, a survivor of the ill-fated de Narvaez expedition who had lived with the Indians for twelve years as interpreter, de Soto, sometimes using force, sometimes guile, strives to gain wealth and power by subjugating a people whose main concern is to live in harmony with nature.

After reaching Cutifichiqui (a Cherokee town on the South Carolina side of the Savannah River) and finding a treasure house of pearls to which they plan to return, the Spaniards, still seeking gold, move westward across the Appalachians, then southward. At the fortified town of Mauvilla, they win a Pyrrhic victory over the giant Tascaluça and his warriors. Both officers and men wish to abandon what is obviously another ill-fated quest and return to Cuba, but their monomaniacal leader will not accept defeat.

The Mass of Thanksgiving that de Soto orders to be given for the Mauvilla wounded, now recovered, is the climactic scene of the novel. In the middle of the service, Father Francisco abruptly orders de Soto in the name of the Lord, "Go out of this land!" De Soto remains adamant: "Heed me, priest. . . . I believe it is God's will that this land be pacified. Pacified it shall be."

Considering the situation from an orthodox point of view, Tovar sums up his thoughts.

> He [de Soto] had set his private will outside the guidance and the discipline of the Church, the will which, unrestrained, serves only the

---

[10]The accounts are by Ranjel, de Biedma, and "The Gentleman of Elvas." See *Narratives of the Career of Hernando de Soto*, tr. Buckingham Smith, ed. Edward Gaylord Bourne, 2 vols. (New York: Allerton, 1922).

senses, as the senses only the flesh. He, a layman, had undertaken to interpret God's mind.... From here it is only one step further to supplant God's will by man's and call it divine—man made God, man with all his frailties and pride setting up the goods of the world over the goods of heavenly grace.

Tovar's assessment of the meaning of the scene represents a definition of the form of modern gnosticism that Voegelin and others have called "the puritan heresy," the equating of the private will with God's purposes.[11]

The north wind that chills Tovar after de Soto's heresy portends death and corruption. Returning to the east bank of the Mississippi, near present-day Natchez, to report to de Soto on a massacre of the Nilco Indians to the north, Tovar finds that the fever-stricken de Soto has died. He has a vision in which de Soto's ghost tells him, "There's only one time at the Moon's Inn." To this enigmatic statement he replies, "I did not fail you.... The will remains." And then he hears:

"The will is not enough. It is not enough for one bent on his own destruction. Did I lead the chivalry of Spain to the sacred groves, the blessed land of Jerusalem? No, I am the alchemical captain, the adventurer in gold.... Pursuing, I found the world's secret, the alkahest and the panacea. They are one and the same. The universal menstruum is this..." [i.e., this dust to which all men return]. Slowly from the ground the arm raised up, the bony hand reached forth, white and shining, and the voice, thin and distant, "Only the dead can prophesy."

Tovar, like the old-soldier narrator of *Alchemy* a limited central intelligence, never fully understands the meaning of his vision. His last words to de Soto's ghost are, "My lord, say you have forgiven me that one time in Cuba...." Had he understood what the ghost of "the alchemical captain" told him, his words might well have been, "My lord, say you have forgiven me for all that I did to help bring us to this predicament." Symbolically, in the last sentence of the novel, Tovar moves forward into the partially illuminating moonlight.

---

[11]See Eric Voegelin, *The New Science of Politics* (Chicago and London: University of Chicago Press, 1952) 133-61. Also see Lewis P. Simpson, *The Dispossessed Garden: Pastoral and History in Southern Literature* (Athens: University of Georgia Press, 1975) 76-78.

Using Henry James's *The Turn of the Screw* as a sort of frame, Lytle again renders the theme of modern gnosticism in his next novel, *A Name for Evil* (1947). Showing that he possesses what Allen Tate describes as "the peculiarly historical consciousness of the Southern writer,"[12] he renders the attempt of Henry Brent, his psychotic first-person narrator, to recreate history. Henry and his wife, Ellen, buy and move to The Grove, a run-down house and farm in a tobacco- and grain-growing area in the southeastern part of the United States, sometime during World War II, proposing to regenerate the place as soon as possible. A middle-aged, none-too-successful writer, Henry equates the regeneration of the house and land with the realization of order in his life.

Attempting to achieve catharsis by describing his search for order, Henry reveals the cause of his failure: his solipsism. By his presentation (appropriately discordant in style) he demonstrates that he is the creator of his world in the act of perceiving it,[13] and it is in this egocentric world that he is compelled to oppose his ancestor, the Satanic former owner of The Grove, Major Brent, dead seventy-five years.

From Johnny, the Negro hired hand, Henry learns that Major Brent disinherited his sons, deeded The Grove to his daughter, whom he kept a spinster, brought the grain fields to a state of perfection only to allow the grain to stand until it rotted, and committed "that last affront to tradition, the unmarked grave." Henry's hyperactive imagination feeds on information from the superstitious Johnny, who seems to confuse in his mind the stories his father told him about the major with present events.

On several occasions Henry sees Major Brent, who wears a wide-brimmed black hat (a mark of authority), and believes that the fierce-looking gentleman is a threat to his nephew Moss, his heir, and to Ellen. Moss has mysteriously come to The Grove, without Ellen's knowledge, from military service in the South Pacific. After Henry learns that the army has notified Moss's parents that Moss has been dead for three months, he becomes fearful that Major Brent is now concentrating on

---

[12]"A Southern Mode of the Imagination," in *Essays of Four Decades* (Chicago: Swallow, 1968) 583.

[13]See Tate, "Narcissus as Narcissus," *Essays of Four Decades*, 595-96.

possessing Ellen, who after years of marriage is now pregnant for the first time. Seeing the Satanic, tradition-despising major hovering over the coals in the tobacco-curing barn makes him certain that the major intends to harm Ellen and the unborn heir.

In January, after a snow and ice storm, Henry takes Ellen into the garden, which earlier she had been regenerating as a surprise for him, to show her its eerie beauty. They become lost in a fog; and in an attempt to find the gate, he leaves her near the springhouse, with its serpent fountain (an Ouroboros about which the six graves of Major Brent's wives and housekeepers are arranged like the spokes of a wheel). Unable to find the gate, he begins walking in circles to find her. When he sees her, head down, apparently listening to something, and screams her name in warning, she looks up and backs away, moaning "No." He sees Major Brent, dressed like a bridegroom, beckoning to her and rushes forward. Frantic, she leaps onto the rotten platform of the springhouse and falls through it to her death. After rendering (in a style similar to that of a Poe narrator) the emotions that seized him upon reaching the corpse and searching for signs of life, Henry concludes: "Already I knew what it was I held in my arms, and I knew that at last Major Brent had triumphed and I was alone."

The circling that Henry does to find his wife is symbolic of his solipsism, as is the mandala-shaped, Edenic-Jungian garden. Ellen, a frail woman, nervous because of her husband's mental condition, her pregnancy, and the eeriness of the garden, may think before she leaps that she is seeing Major Brent. This possibility is a part of the enriching ambiguity of the novel; but whatever she thinks, Henry Brent, in effect, has become Major Brent: he is the jaguar betrayed by his own image.[14] Henry Brent's distorted view of tradition, which impels him to attempt to recreate the past, can bring about only one result—catastrophe.

Lytle began his masterpiece, *The Velvet Horn*, in 1948 and, aided by a Kenyon Fellowship in 1956, completed it in 1957. The novel, dedicated to John Crowe Ransom, is divided not into chapters but into five parts that exhibit a high degree of concinnity. This representation of "the world's body," often expressed in lyrical flashbacks, is at once a *Bildungsroman* and a rendering of the archetypal Edenic theme in the

---

[14]See Tate, "Ode to the Confederate Dead," lines 82-83.

form of a theodicy reminiscent of *Paradise Lost*. In "The Working Novelist and the Mythmaking Process," Lytle explicates the controlling symbol of the novel.

> ... the action itself [of a novel] must be symbolic of the archetypal experience. This, I consider, was the most important thing *The Velvet Horn* taught me. The symbol must be more than an inert sign or emblem. [Symbols] represent the entire action by compressing into a sharp image or succession of images the essence of meaning. For example, in animal nature, the horn stands for both the masculine and feminine parts of being. ... Add velvet to this and you posit the state of innocence.

Continuing the explication of his Edenic-Jungian imagery, Lytle says,

> The velvet grows about the feminine end of the horn, and it bleeds as it is rubbed away. ... In human nature the horn would be the hermaphrodite, Hermes and Aphrodite contained within the one form. Their separation, Eve taken from Adam's side, at another level continues the cycle of creation.[15]

As Lytle points out in his essay, the novel has no beginning, middle, or end in the Aristotelian sense. Each of the five parts tells almost the entire story, with Sol Leatherbury, "the woods boss," saying the first and last words. In Cumberland vernacular Sol announces that a great white oak crushed Captain Joe Cree to death. As Thomas H. Landess observes, "The tree which falls on Joe Cree ... is of course the archetypal tree of knowledge: Cree has discovered that Lucius is not his son but the product of [his wife] Julia's illicit conduct prior to marriage. This discovery is too much for the proud man to bear; and so, in an act perfectly symbolic, he commits suicide, destroyed by his new understanding of an old sin."[16]

The point of view in the first part, "The Peaks of Laurel," is Lucius Cree's, and the reader assumes for a while that he is following a Cumberland *Bildungsroman* of the latter part of the nineteenth century. But the protagonist is not Lucius; rather it is Lucius's mentor, his maternal

---

[15] Lytle, *The Hero with the Private Parts: Essays of Andrew Lytle* (Baton Rouge: Louisiana State University Press, 1966) 185-86.

[16] "Unity of Action in *The Velvet Horn*," *Mississippi Quarterly* 22 (Fall 1970): 354. Or see *The Form Discovered*, 8.

uncle, Jack Cropleigh, a scholarly bachelor addicted to jesting, whose consciousness serves as a means of unifying the five parts. On a trip up the mountain with this uncle, who is going to "witch" a water well, Lucius loses his virginity in the arms of Ada Belle, daughter of a poor white family, the Rutters, who live in a dogtrot house on the property of a wealthy bachelor, Pete Legrand, an outsider and a modernist. The next morning, after Leatherbury has arrived and notified Jack that Captain Cree has been killed, Jack, before awakening Lucius, tells Ada Belle's mother, "Old Ada," what he has learned. She comments that Cree was no man to die because of carelessness. Jack shushes her, but she continues:

> "You Cropleigh brothers. Smarter than other folks. A-branging up a little sister in man's rough company. No woman to holp her. And her growing up thinking she was no different from a boy until she's lost in the woods with Pete Legrand. He learned her, and your brother Duncan cut his guts out. . . . And that doctor brother sewed them back in. I've heard he made as purty a stitch as aer woman."

When Jack whispers, "Nobody saw," Ada replies,

> "You think Doctor Cropleigh sewed Legrand's clothes on him, too? You think a body can wear a scar, and it looped on his belly keen as a new moon, and nobody know it?"

Ada Rutter's comments, including the reiteration of backwoods gossip, sum up a crucial part of the action. Jack, Beverly, Dickie, and Duncan Cropleigh, left to shift for themselves after the death of their parents in a steamboat explosion, while on a deer hunt discover their sister, Julia, sleeping in the arms of Legrand. After Duncan nearly kills Legrand in a knife fight, Dickie saves the seducer. Soon the brothers marry their sister off to their quiet, industrious cousin, Joe Cree.

Coming down the mountain, Lucius, brooding over Cree's death, says, "When I did it up there with that girl, I knew. I knew something would happen." Lucius has "reenacted the sin of his mother" and Jack Cropleigh "recognizes the intrinsic relationship of the two actions."[17] Later, in the penultimate part, "The Wake," Jack, half-drunk and taking a walk to get some air, falls into Joe's open grave during a thunder-

---

[17]Landess, 357.

storm and sees in a vision something that he has imagined but has not been willing to admit the possibility of—the act of incest between Duncan and Julia on the hunting trip, when Julia wore a tight-fitting doeskin garment that Duncan had made for her. Appropriately, "The Wake" ends with an ironic confrontation between Legrand and Lucius, with Legrand offering to back Lucius, whom he regards as his son, in business.

In the last part of the novel, which bears the Jungian title "The Night Sea Journey," Lytle renders the final testing of Lucius and Jack Cropleigh's self-sacrificial act, which gives Lucius, the sole heir of the Cropleighs, the opportunity to carry on the family line. To ask for time to fulfill his late father's timber contract, Lucius visits his Aunt Amelie, Duncan's widow, owner of the timberland, who surprises Lucius by telling him that she had not set a time limit for performance. Lucius now knows that Cree did not commit suicide because of financial difficulties.

When Legrand asks Julia to marry him and speaks of Lucius as his son, Julia asks, "How do you know he is your son?" And she confesses that on the night before Legrand received his knife wound she and Duncan committed incest. Legrand, incredulous, whispers, "What are you telling me?" She answers, "What I told my husband that day." She adds, "I never saw him alive again." At the end of the novel, Legrand feels that Lucius may be his son after all; but at this point, in a state of shock, he is almost certain that Lucius is an incestuous bastard. Lucius, having learned of the fight between Legrand and Duncan, considers himself Legrand's bastard; and when he learns that Ada Belle is pregnant, he elopes with her, for he is determined that *his* child shall have *his* name. In the family confrontation that results from the elopement, Jack, "the victim-redeemer," steps in front of the pistol of Ada Belle's demented brother, Othel, to protect Ada Belle, who has stepped in front of Lucius. Dying, Jack speaks free verse that echoes John 20:15, 19-20; the self-sacrificial act of this man of words, which preserves the family, presumably wins him union with the Word.[18]

---

[18]Family, place, initiation, Christianity, and the Edenic myth are also themes in Lytle's carefully crafted stories, four of which—"Jericho, Jericho, Jericho," "The Mahogany Frame," "Mr. MacGregor," and "Ortiz's Mass" (from *At the Moon's Inn*)—are collected, along with *Alchemy* and *A Name for Evil*, in *A Novel, a Novella and Four Stories* (New York: McDowell, Obolensky, 1958).

Much of Lytle's literary criticism written while he was professor of English at the University of the South and editor of the *Sewanee Review* appears in *The Hero with the Private Parts* (1966). Particularly helpful to students of Lytle's fiction are three of the essays in this collection: "The Image as Guide to Meaning in the Historical Novel"; "Caroline Gordon and the Historic Image"; and the essay that explicates *The Velvet Horn*, "The Working Novelist and the Mythmaking Process." Allen Tate describes "The Working Novelist" as the "most brilliant example of ... formalistic-historical criticism" that he knows; he adds that it is "an essay from which contemporary novelists may learn a good deal more than James offers them in the *Prefaces*."[19]

Although there is no "heresy of the didactic" in Lytle's fiction, the Tennessean's beliefs concerning man's proper attitudes toward nature, history, and religion are evident in his novels, created around controlling images of archetypal experiences: Pleasant McIvor's quest for vengeance in *The Long Night*, Hernando de Soto's strivings toward self-anointed godhead in *Alchemy* and *At the Moon's Inn*, Henry Brent's search for order through an attempt to recreate history in *A Name for Evil*, and Jack Cropleigh's Tiresias-like encompassing of all the aspects of his brothers' and sister's and nephew's searches for wholeness and identity in *The Velvet Horn*. Lytle represents all of these quests without preaching. As he observes, "It should be obvious that polemics is one discipline and fiction another ... if you want to bring about political reforms, run for office: social reforms, behave yourself and mind your manners."[20]

Lytle renders these archetypal experiences, which define the human predicament, by means of fiction that is regional. Even *Alchemy*, though it takes place in Peru, is related to the other works in that it was written as the prologue to *At the Moon's Inn*. Flannery O'Connor, who studied fiction under Lytle at the University of Iowa,[21] observes that the best American fiction has a regional quality. She reports that

---

[19]Foreword to *The Hero with the Private Parts*, xvi.

[20]*A Novel, a Novella and Four Stories*, x.

[21]Another Southern writer, Madison Jones, studied fiction under Lytle at the University of Florida while completing work on his M.A. degree. Lytle taught at Iowa from 1946 to 1948 and at Florida from 1948 to 1961; he was editor of the *Sewanee Review* from 1961 to 1973 while teaching at the University of the South.

Walker Percy, on receiving the National Book Award, answered a question about why there were so many good Southern writers by saying, "Because we lost the War." She adds,

> He didn't mean by that simply that a lost war makes good subject matter. What he was saying was that we [the writers of the South] have had our Fall. We have gone into the modern world with an inburnt knowledge of human limitations and with a sense of mystery which could not have sufficiently developed in the rest of the country.[22]

This "inburnt knowledge of human limitations" is evident in Lytle's fiction and in his criticism, along with what O'Connor calls "anagogical vision," which she describes as an "enlarged view of the human scene," concerned "with the Divine life and [human] participation in it."[23] Lytle's recognition of human limitations and his "anagogical vision" are among the factors that set his novels and stories apart from those of writers whose ideas and techniques have influenced him—Henry James, Joseph Conrad, Ford Madox Ford, and James Joyce—not one of whom can be termed a religious writer. Lytle's fiction, from "Old Scratch in the Valley" through *The Velvet Horn*, is concerned in one way or another with the idea of God and with a sacramental sense of the world as God's gift.

Allen Tate, in his poem "The Oath," has his old friend Lytle ask, "Who are the dead? / Who are the living and the dead?" In *A Wake for the Living: A Family Chronicle* (1975), Lytle elaborates the answer suggested in the poem. This book, of course, is much more than a conventional family record. Containing a wealth of history (familial, local, and national) and folklore, it is written in a style that interweaves the erudite diction of a distinguished man of letters and the vernacular of a Middle Tennessee-North Alabama countryman, who, like Pleasant McIvor of *The Long Night*, has sat before the fire and spellbound his audience with the power of his narrative. At the beginning of *A Wake*, Lytle the traditionalist, after referring to his daughters, makes the Burkean statement "If you don't know who you are or where you come from, you will find yourself at a disadvantage." And fittingly, Lytle the

---

[22]Flannery O'Connor, *Mystery and Manners*, ed. Sally and Robert Fitzgerald (New York: Farrar, Straus and Giroux, 1969) 58-59.

[23]O'Connor, 72-73.

Christian artist concludes with a prayer his drama of characters in time and place and eternity.

Selected Bibliography

Lytle, Andrew. *Alchemy*. Winston-Salem NC: Palaemon Press, 1979.

———. *At the Moon's Inn*. Indianapolis and New York: Bobbs-Merrill, 1941.

———. *Bedford Forrest and His Critter Company*. New York: Minton Balch, 1931.

———. *The Hero with the Private Parts: Essays of Andrew Lytle*. Baton Rouge: Louisiana State University Press, 1966.

———. "The Hind Tit." In *I'll Take My Stand: The South and the Agrarian Tradition* by Twelve Southerners. New York & London: Harper, 1930.

———. *The Long Night*. Indianapolis and New York: Bobbs-Merrill, 1936.

———. *A Name for Evil*. Indianapolis and New York: Bobbs-Merrill, 1947.

———. *A Novel, a Novella and Four Stories*. New York: McDowell, Obolensky, 1958.

———. "The Small Farm Secures the State." In *Who Owns America?*, edited by Herbert Agar and Allen Tate. Boston: Houghton Mifflin, 1936.

———. "The State of Letters in a Time of Disorder." *Sewanee Review* 79 (Autumn 1971): 477-97.

———. "They Took Their Stand: The Agrarian View After Fifty Years." *Modern Age* 24 (Spring 1980): 114-20. Reprinted as *Reflections of a Ghost: An Agrarian View After Fifty Years*. Dallas: New London Press, 1980.

———. *The Velvet Horn*. New York: McDowell, Obolensky, 1957. Reprint. Sewanee TN: University of the South, 1983.

──────────. *A Wake for the Living: A Family Chronicle*. New York: Crown, 1975.

Polk, Noel. "Andrew Nelson Lytle: A Bibliography of His Writings." *Mississippi Quarterly* 23 (Fall 1970): 435-91.

──────────. "An Andrew Lytle Checklist." In *The Form Discovered: Essays on the Achievement of Andrew Lytle*, edited by M. E. Bradford. Jackson MS: University and College Press of Mississippi, 1973.

Wright, Stuart. *Andrew Nelson Lytle: A Bibliography 1920-1982*. Sewanee TN: University of the South, 1982.

James Agee

Victor A. Kramer

In a manuscript written in conjunction with *A Death in the Family*, James Agee (1909-1955) emphasized his realization that he had been formed in the absence of his father. Although this phrasing is ironic, there is an important truth in his insight because so many circumstances of his life did develop as a result of his father's early death. Agee's earliest years were a combination of experiences which he drew from two families: his mother's, associated with a relatively comfortable Knoxville urban setting, and his father's, in the rural community of La Follete, Tennessee. After his father's death, when Agee was six years old, he was inevitably drawn more into the circle of his mother's family and into the values associated with her, including firm Christian belief. As he matured he came to realize that had his father lived, he would surely have been different because of the productive tension provided by both parents. Agee's best-known work, the posthumously published *A Death in the Family*, grew out of this realization. Compensations, however, flowed from changes in his life brought about by his father's abrupt death. Brought closer to members of his mother's family who valued religion, education, and art (Mrs. Agee's brother, Hugh Tyler, was an artist), the child developed a strong spiritual and aesthetic sense. Agee became increasingly aware of the importance of such facts in later years.

Agee's first eight years were spent in Knoxville; however, in 1918, just two years after his father's death in an automobile accident, his mother decided to enroll him in St. Andrew's School near Sewanee, Tennessee. He remained there through 1924, and those years proved valuable. During this period the child developed a strong appreciation of the Anglo-Catholic Church and came to know Father James Harold Flye, a history teacher at the school and a man who became his lifelong friend. After Agee died, Father Flye gathered letters, written to him over a thirty-year period, and published them under the title *Letters of James Agee to Father Flye* (1962).[1] This collection is useful as an overview of Agee's life and as a testament of his affection for Father Flye. These letters provide a succinct introduction to Agee and his writing because they manifest the tension that was always present in his life, tension caused by a desire to live to the fullest and an equally compelling desire to be a great artist. Some critics have argued that Agee never resolved that tension. If this is true the tension was a positive force, for he was able to produce a large amount of work within many categories—poetry, autobiography, criticism, screenplays, and articles.

In the earliest letters to Father Flye, Agee's hope to be a writer is evident, and during that period, when he was only sixteen or seventeen years old, he demonstrated his wide range of interests—books, music, visual art, movies, language, education, religion, popular culture, psychology. Clearly, Agee sensed early that he would probably not be content to pursue a single set of interests. This fact is indicative of some of the difficulties he would later face as a writer who could always imagine an enormous variety of worthwhile projects. From his earliest years when he was ambitious and wrote prolifically, until the very end of his life, he found it difficult to decide which project to choose. Agee constantly sought ways to reconcile forces within himself that almost seemed to promise too much.

It is only speculation, but not without a basis in fact, that Agee's mother might have chosen St. Andrew's, a boarding school run by the monastic order of the Holy Cross of the Episcopal Church, to curb his

---

[1] *Letters of James Agee to Father Flye*, ed. James Harold Flye (New York: George Braziller, 1962). The second edition of this book contains a new preface and additional letters of Father Flye to Agee (Boston: Houghton Mifflin Co., 1971).

impulsiveness and enthusiasm. She must have sensed that the young boy would profit from the rigor of religious teachers who would provide guidance in the absence of a father, and according to Father Flye, one of the reasons Mrs. Agee chose St. Andrew's was the presence of male teachers on the faculty of that isolated mountain school.[2] It is significant that Agee's mother did not return to Knoxville, but instead took up residence adjacent to the school grounds. Passages Agee wrote for *The Morning Watch* approximately a quarter century later make clear that the atmosphere of the school was important for young Agee, yet it was an atmosphere qualified by his mother's proximity. She too had found a place which was satisfying aesthetically and religiously. Such associations remained important for both mother and son throughout their lives. Although Agee drifted away from formal connections with the Church in his adult life, his Christian belief always remained important. This influence can be seen in all his major writings, as well as in his contribution to the *Partisan Review* symposium "Religion and the Intellectuals" (1950) which emphasizes a continuing attempt to accommodate natural and supernatural impulses.[3]

By the time Agee was ready to leave St. Andrew's in 1924, much of his attachment to belief and ritual in the Anglo-Catholic Church had been formed. At that time, when he was about fourteen years old, he had not yet decided to be a writer. The following year, he returned to Knoxville for a year of high school before enrolling at the Phillips Exeter Academy. During the summer of 1925 he and Father Flye traveled in Europe, and during that trip Agee first expressed an interest in writing. In the three years that followed, the incipient literary career began to unfold. Agee wrote in large quantity and a considerable amount was published in *The Phillips Exeter Monthly*. In his earliest sketches, some of which are based on what he had seen in France, Agee already sought to go beyond fiction and document a world observed.[4] A careful reading of his Exeter writings reveals an eye for detail that also characterizes much subsequent writing—articles, poetry, and autobiography.

---

[2]Interview with Father James Harold Flye, New York City, 29 December 1968.

[3]"Religion and the Intellectuals," *Partisan Review* 17 (February 1950): 106-13.

[4]Various stories and sketches published in *The Phillips Exeter Monthly* are based on the trip to Europe. See, for example, "The Scar," 30 (January 1926).

Just as early, his primary interest was to focus upon the immediacy of the particular; fundamentally, Agee's entire career can be described as a continuing attempt to reconcile his intense appreciation of life with a desire to express a vision of life in language (or film). Finally, Agee would acknowledge the inability of words to express fully the dignity of life, but he also knew that attempts to reconcile such forces were at the heart of what he always did best as a writer.

The early literary productions published in the *Exeter Monthly* include fiction, poetry, drama, and reviews. That material, never edited for republication, sets a tone and pace for the varied career which followed. Agee was never content to work quietly in one safe haven of a writer's calling. This earliest literary work is often derivative, yet the variety of the fiction, satire, drama, and poetry published at Exeter from November 1925 to June 1928 clearly demonstrates success with what later became both help and hindrance—a stubborn insistence on nonspecialization. Within this earliest work is exhibited his penchant for careful observation, wit, and irony. For example, his story "Knoxton High" seems to be based on memories of the year he spent in Knoxville in 1924-1925 and satirizes small-town provincialism. This humorous story is an experiment with stream-of-consciousness. Other stories with Tennessee settings are sometimes somber, but are quite tightly executed. "The Circle," which seems to have been influenced by Sherwood Anderson, is about a young man trapped by his father's death. Still others of these earliest stories reflect wide reading and a thorough knowledge of classical literature.

Another important work is the manuscript poem "Pygmalion," probably the same piece Agee mentions in a letter to Father Flye in 1928. "Pygmalion" is a sustained example of early abilities and an objectification of doubts about what artists accomplish. While this early work cannot be dated exactly, it is significant because much of his later literary career involved devising methods that would reflect a personal vision of actuality. Many of his best works are attempts to catch the texture of ordinary life, and his classic documentary *Let Us Now Praise Famous Men* is largely about the impossibility of communicating what has been experienced. A similar problem is central to "Pygmalion," a soliloquy spoken by the Creator, who describes his inception, formation, and destruction of a world, his "glorious dream."[5] In the young artist's imagination the world seems so beautiful that the Creator must "strain" to alleviate His agony, yet such a magnificent caress results in a "bruised and broken" world. "Pygmalion" demonstrates that early in his career Agee was struggling with questions about appropriate artistic form; and just a few years later, during the 1930s, he was to find it increasingly difficult to rely upon a traditional framework, either of Christian thought or of a conventional poetic form. This is already evident in work he accomplished while a student at Harvard.

Agee's apprentice writing published in *The Harvard Advocate* included poetry, fiction, and reviews written over a four-year period, 1928-1932; during his senior year he was editor of the *Advocate*. The twenty-six poems written for *The Harvard Advocate* illustrate the manner in which Agee assimilated traditional writers. Almost all of these poems appear in *The Collected Poems* but only eight of the Harvard poems were included in Agee's first book, *Permit Me Voyage*, seven as revisions for a sonnet sequence. Much more important for illustrating Agee's development is the undergraduate prose. Fitzgerald states that the Harvard poetry never seemed to possess the rhythm and power of the fiction.[6] The prose is powerful because it reflects Agee's convictions about the difficulty of good writing. One can separate the undergraduate prose into two groups: stories that rely heavily on imagination and others that grow out of personal experience, or at least are limited to experiences someone as young as Agee could adequately present. "Boys Will Be Brutes," about the slaughter of tiny birds taken from their nest, is successful because its apparent basis is clearly an actual, or a believably portrayed, experience.

The writing completed at Harvard indicates that Agee early mastered conventional modes of writing. Two things about his undergraduate writing are especially significant: he was at ease with standard forms while he was continually seeking to develop new ways of writing.

---

[5]The complete text of "Pygmalion" has been edited. See my "Agee's Early Poem 'Pygmalion' and His Aesthetic," *Mississippi Quarterly* 29 (Spring 1976): 191-96.

[6]Two of Agee's best Harvard stories are in *The Collected Short Prose of James Agee* (Boston: Houghton Mifflin, 1968). See "Death in the Desert" and "They That Sow in Sorrow Shall Reap," 61-75 and 75-98.

The story "They That Sow in Sorrow Shall Reap" is therefore an example of a story that suggests states of consciousness as ideas flow from one person to another. Throughout the story Agee is able to suggest consciousness by focusing upon things observed. A completely different example is Agee's skillful engineering of a parody of an issue of *Time* magazine, an exercise that helped him secure a job as a writer for *Fortune* after he left Harvard. These two types of writing, an experimental attempt to suggest the complexity of individual consciousness and a humorous parody of a news magazine, suggest the range of Agee's ability.

It is clear that throughout his Harvard years and into the 1930s Agee sought to develop new ways of writing. These attempts account for his interest in a Byronic experiment, "John Carter," which he began at Harvard, as well as for the accomplishment and frustration of much of his writing for *Fortune*. Both the long poem and the unsigned articles reflect a fundamental division that remained within him as a writer. When he graduated from Harvard and began writing for *Fortune* in 1932, he was surely happy to have a job. But he had taken the position at *Fortune* with no intention of staying; during his first year there he applied for a Guggenheim Fellowship. One of the projects he hoped to finish was the long poem, "John Carter," a work which was, in his words, to be "a complete appraisal of contemporary civilization, and a study of the Problem of Evil." This poem is as ambitious as *Famous Men*. Agee's satire attacks a society that has lost reverence for tradition; "John Carter" emphasizes the hypocrisy that informs what passes for religion and art.

During these early years, while he was supporting himself as a journalist, Agee was also distancing himself from much of what was held to be of value in conventional journalism and poetry; an unpublished essay about his first published book emphasizes this separation. Agee's book of poetry had appeared in the Yale Series of Younger Poets, and a more conventional "young poet" might have been content to express gratitude that his poetry had been chosen for such a prestigious series. The unpublished essay is significant because it clearly demonstrates his ambivalent attitude toward *Permit Me Voyage* (1934). Agee wrote the essay as if he were reviewing the volume; essentially he suggested that *Permit Me Voyage* stands as a record of things accomplished, but also as a record of ventures that he did not want to

Literature of Tennessee 139

repeat. His dissatisfaction also clarifies how and why he chose to write as he did in the decades which followed. Two of his comments are of special value because they demonstrate what he had accomplished and show how he was ready to go one step further.

> Putting the ms. together in the first place was a good deal of trouble. I had done poems and verses in many lengths and tones: all put together they would not only burst the requisite limit of the volume; they would jangle more than even I could care for. I had for instance the first chunks of a long, loose, obscene, satirical, moral, dramatic-narrative, metaphysical, lyrical poem ["John Carter"] which, were I to let it loose at this time, would knock your eye out....
>
> One of the heaviest problems and contradictions within me is that of the human being vs the artist. Which resolves itself, ultimately, into the Battle of the Centuries: God vs Art. Granted that they can be neck and neck, and granted that they breed as well as murder one another, I am finally in favour of art, and I believe that in ways, and for reasons, which I shall not enter upon here, they are the same. Yet their struggle is violent enough to blow the brain where it goes on. In the interests of such truths as I was able to apprehend, it was therefore inevitable that both kinds of poetry should go into this volume.[7]

Other parts of his "reflections" provide additional comments about specific parts of the book, its "derivative" faults, and its ambitious innovations. In some ways Agee's attitude about this first book seems to be similar to his attitude as a journalist. Both conventional poetry and formal journalism could be accomplished, but they seemed "crystallized," and while he could produce such facile work, he really wanted to concentrate on "his own writing."

Dwight MacDonald recalls that Agee was regarded as *Fortune*'s specialist in "rich, beautiful prose," yet that prose usually revealed his personality.[8] Articles such as "The American Roadside" reveal Agee's consciousness of possibilities everywhere available for analysis. His

---

[7]"Reflections on *Permit Me Voyage*." Typescript, Humanities Research Center, The University of Texas at Austin Library. The kind permission of the James Agee Trust has been granted for use of selected quotations from this and other manuscripts used throughout this article.

[8]Dwight MacDonald, "James Agee," *Against the American Grain* (New York: Random House, 1962) 165.

article about the Tennessee Valley Authority takes the reader back to the hills of Tennessee and the small city of Knoxville, which he remembered from childhood, and describes how the surrounding area was changing with the arrival of the Tennessee Valley Authority. Agee wrote twenty-five articles for *Fortune*, usually not on subjects he would have chosen; it was only with the assignment in 1936 to go to Alabama to do a survey of cotton tenantry that he received a chance to do the type of writing that he felt was really pioneering. It was not that he did not write well as a journalist or that he did not value his accomplishments within such conventional modes of writing, but rather that he saw so much else that could be done. A remark made by his first wife, Olivia Saunders, makes his ambition clear. She recalled that during the time they were married, she realized that writing was the most important thing for him, and perhaps, she implied, that was why the marriage did not last.[9]

Agee's "Plans for Work," which accompanied a second application for a Guggenheim in October 1937, indicates how passionately he was interested in writing. The application must have seemed quite odd to the selection committee. Included was an elaborate outline for forty-seven proposed projects, and predictably, no fellowship was forthcoming. Agee explained how he planned to do various pieces of fiction, in addition to notes on photography, music, theater, and revues. Five of his proposals were suggestions for fiction, but he also wished to write serious stories "whose whole intention is the direct communication of the intensity of common experience." Other proposals contained outlines for various analyses, poems, and collections of data. Agee was clearly fascinated with the possibilities the ordinary world offered for analysis and as a challenge to communication.[10]

Much of what he actually accomplished in the 1930s and later is an extension of his fascination with the complexity of ordinary emotion and consciousness. An unpublished story, "Before God and This Company" (1939), a draft for a piece never finished, stands as a further example of how he sought to use an analytical journalistic method to

---

[9]Indirect quotation of a remark made by Olivia Wood in the film *Agee* by Ross Spears (1978).

[10]See *The Collected Short Prose of James Agee* (Boston: Houghton Mifflin, 1968) 131-48.

record the "commonplace" events that surrounded him.[11] Agee's subject is marital love, and interestingly these were years when his marriage to Via Saunders ended in divorce, and only a few years later a second marriage to Alma Mailman also disintegrated. In method, the sketch foreshadows the concentration of detail basic to *Let Us Now Praise Famous Men*, a manuscript probably in process when the sketch was written. Agee's draft matter-of-factly records specific events during a Saturday night party. Couples fight and talk, and people go about their business barely aware that their actions affect others.

Let Us Now Praise Famous Men (1941) has been described in innumerable ways—and it is finally *the* documentary that surpasses others of that genre. Agee knew it was impossible to catch the "*un*imagined," but he knew this was a chance to document what he had lived. Critics sometimes assert that the presence of Agee's tortured consciousness makes his text too personal. However, he knew that there was no way for him to be both honest and "objective," and such a realization accounts for the success of this unusual text. In large part Agee's text is a parody of the very type of journalism that had probably frustrated him from 1933 through 1939. In *Famous Men*, we see his awareness of the journalistic constrictions that had sent him South to observe a "typical" farm family. He had been told to get facts, but in realization of that impossibility, he sought to inundate editors and readers with facts. Through this technique, he reveals his doubts about stock assumptions, and the text becomes, among other things, a condemnation of those who confidently think they might get at the essence of reality through language.

Almost predictably, when *Famous Men* was published in 1941, no one seemed particularly interested in Agee's experiment in communication. His method of reporting, in gestation for years, finally included the total experience. The writer's confrontation with myriad distortions is at the heart of the book. A fundamental assumption undergirding the text—ironically a work of "Art," despite Agee's insistence that it is not—is that any attempt to provide an accurate record of what is observed is doomed. The basic notion to be communicated was that while distinct persons and events were apprehended, Agee

---

[11]"Before God and This Company, or Bigger than We Are." Pencil Manuscript. Humanities Research Center.

knew that he too had been definitely affected by what was experienced, and *his* reactions were equally important. *Famous Men's* aesthetic, therefore, focuses attention on details as remembered, but modified by the writer's reflection. Agee knew that what he experienced could never be fully communicated; he even says that, if it were possible, there would be "no writing at all."[12] His insistence on being present throughout *Famous Men* violates accepted criteria for journalism and documentaries, as well as for Art. A section-by-section analysis of his text reveals how he voices questions about what he is doing.

In part two of his text, which provides "Findings and Comments," Agee writes about money, shelter, clothing, education, and work. His method emphasizes divisions within his mind. He clearly respects language and uses it carefully, but simultaneously he doubts the success of ever communicating the essence of what he has experienced. Agee realized that much could be implied about his Alabama experience. He also hoped that *Famous Men* was only a beginning, perhaps the first of several volumes. His "Work" chapter demonstrates his success with expansion of this material. Unpublished notebook material also indicates that he seriously thought about using the techniques he had developed for *Famous Men* in analogous projects.[13] In a sense his film criticism became that analysis.

Throughout the 1940s Agee's writing was often about, or for, the movies. His film criticism might well be thought of as an extension of methods developed for *Famous Men*—most importantly a procedure for examining the culture as observed through one particular medium such as film. Agee thought of his writing about movies as the work of an "amateur" in the best sense of that word—one who cultivates a particular pursuit. His work as a movie critic and journalist at *Time* in the 1940s helped him become more aware of the complexity of both his culture and his own life as he moved toward more autobiographical writing and toward storytelling for the movies. A specific example is the essay printed under the title "James Agee By Himself," written in 1942, but published after his death. Assertive and caustic, it speaks

---

[12]*Let Us Now Praise Famous Men* (Boston: Houghton Mifflin, 1941) 13. All subsequent quotations for *Famous Men* are noted parenthetically.

[13]The complete "Work" chapter has been edited. See my article and text in *The Texas Quarterly* 15 (Summer 1972): 27-48.

Literature of Tennessee   143

for itself, simultaneously providing a record of an ambitious writer's frustrations and skill. While this portrait reveals Agee's anger with his apparent failure to write as much or as well as he wished, it also shows how he was slowly coming to realize that his best subject was analysis of culture and analysis of self.[14] Examination of the numerous book reviews he wrote between 1939 and 1942 reveals how his career developed as his skills as an observer developed. Through the experience of writing *Famous Men*, reviewing books and movies, and becoming increasingly analytical about the culture as a whole, Agee was gradually perfecting skills that allowed him to reconcile at least some of his great affection for the world with analysis and evocation of that world. He wrote one hundred reviews for *Time*, covering a wide range of books. Each reviewer could choose what he would review, and Agee's method was akin to that he later refined for the movie criticism—always seeking ways to relate the work to wider movements within the culture.

An examination of the many stories Agee wrote for *Time*, both published and unpublished, also reveals how he systematically sought to provide analysis of a culture which, he feared, had in some fundamental ways become lost. Two rejected pieces about popular culture, medicine deemed too strong for publication in the mass-circulation magazine, reflect Agee's increasing concern that "the world's history, and the daily and future destiny of every individual, are given shape, by the thousands of great and trivial assumptions, taboos, fears, prejudices, which men in effective numbers believe so fully that they act accordingly."[15] The malformed opinions Agee listed ranged from views about the "nobleness" of war and "democracy" to the conviction that groups and races can be guilty as groups or races or that it is possible "to enjoy the benefits of materialism without being liable to its hazards." Such "beliefs" were, he feared, what really caused people to act. Seldom did they act out of personal conviction or religious belief. More often than not, they simply adopted the thoughts of others and other groups. Other manuscript materials outline projects Agee hoped to accomplish by standing back from the culture as a whole. One is a long

---

[14] "James Agee By Himself," *Esquire* 60 (1963): 149, 289-90.

[15] "Consider the lilies . . . " Typescript. Humanities Research Center.

outline of a proposed evaluation of culture; those ideas could even today become a model for intelligent criticism of a nonreflective society.[16] Another manuscript, a letter written as a preface to a statement of eighteen pages to Archibald MacLeish, then Librarian of Congress, is about a project to preserve films as examples of the best (and worst) the culture had generated. Insights from these manuscripts help us to understand Agee's critical procedure and his mature creative works.

As has been established, Agee's career was always a combination of impulses that reflected a wish to live well and to be a successful writer. Yet as he lived through World War II and its aftermath, he came to feel that it was getting harder and harder for individuals to act responsibly. Such a realization increasingly influenced much of his mature writing. His personal convictions about the difficulty of acting as an individual were intensified by the horrors of the atomic bomb; in his opinion the war, and the cynicism connected with it, had been too easily accepted. His most succinct literary treatment of the demise of individualism is the satire "Dedication Day, a Rough Sketch for a Motion Picture," which satirizes an imagined dedication of a monument to the discovery of the atom's destructive power. The partly autobiographical "1928 Story" also grows out of related thinking and foreshadows later autobiographical fiction.[17] "1928 Story" catches the spontaneity and enthusiasm of an earlier time in Agee's life and corroborates significant facts about him as a mature writer. It is the first sustained attempt after *Famous Men* to recreate a time from his own life. As this story opens, Irvine, a writer, listens to old records that remind him of happier years when the same music was heard in an altogether more hopeful atmosphere. The story, like *The Morning Watch*, is a step toward *A Death in the Family* and shows how Agee learned to focus on the particularities of his own life. Thus, while the story begins with a mood of frustration and disappointment, Agee refines those emotions into the art of remembrance. An interesting point, therefore,

---

[16]"Notes and Suggestions on the magazine under discussion." Humanities Research Center.

[17]"1928 Story" has been edited. It is part of a special section of *The Texas Quarterly* 11 (1968). See my "Agee's Struggle To Be a Writer" within the section entitled "Agee in the Forties," 9-55.

is that just as *Famous Men* grew out of a journalism assignment for *Fortune*, the final fiction was, to some degree, the result of frustrations experienced during years as a journalist and writer in New York City ten years later. "1928 Story" might therefore be thought of as a preliminary exercise for *The Morning Watch* (1950) and *A Death in the Family*.

In *The Morning Watch* Agee returns to memories of St. Andrew's two decades earlier to evoke a high point of religious experience for a twelve-year-old boy. The novella takes place during the early hours of Maundy Thursday and celebrates his experiences. Fictionalized and heightened, Agee's account becomes far more than a record of a few hours on a religious day. It is a celebration of the mystery of living developed through the awareness of the main character, Richard, of developing strengths, biological and aesthetic, that impinge upon a religious sensibility.

Agee's most famous autobiographical work is *A Death in the Family*, a novel which was incomplete at his death. He probably began work on this book late in the 1940s (at approximately the same time as he wrote "1928 Story"). His marriage to Mia Fritsch and the promise of a family of his own may have triggered his desire to fictionalize his own childhood. Possibly the writing of a successful Omnibus television series about the life of Abraham Lincoln reminded him of his father. The fictional Jay is compared to Lincoln in the novel. More than likely Agee's sense of his own impending death as he approached age forty and felt he had not accomplished as much as he had wished sent his imagination back to these earlier years.

A Death in the Family should be thought of as a continuation of this writer's double awareness: a desire to write, but a doubt about how this might be accomplished. In this final book, Agee's emphasis is upon remembrance, and fittingly the word "poetic" occurs in critics' descriptions. It is poetic because its construction is unlike that of most novels; its primary concern is with evoking earlier moments. Agee had written about his father's death as early as age sixteen, and some of his best writing of the 1930s relies on remembrance of family. Thus, the 1935 sketch "Knoxville: Summer of 1915" was chosen by Agee's editor, David McDowell, as a prelude for *A Death in the Family*. This sketch evokes the peaceful atmosphere Rufus and his family enjoyed; however, recollection of such peacefulness is not the only fact that generated Agee's fictional remembrance. Another mood that contributed to the novel is evident in the excluded fragment called "Dream Sequence." This story suggests that through a work of art some harmony with life is achieved, but the artist must first exorcise the nightmare of contemporary life before a peacefulness like that of the summer of 1915 can come. The dream of Agee's narrator is a frightening piece of writing reminiscent of Celiné, yet it is also fiction ending with the evocation of a peacefulness that leads the son-narrator to resolve to write well of all he can remember about childhood and his father. Agee's decision to honor the memory of his father became the autobiographical project *A Death in the Family*.

A Death in the Family is an unusual novel because it is both a detailed remembrance of specifics and an archetypal depiction of events within any family. It is a book about marital love and loss, about initiation of children into life, and about maturation and loss for adults. It is a book about religious faith and the need for religion. It is a book about the urban and rural conflict so many Americans have experienced in this century. Yet, while it is all of these things, it is Agee's specific documentation of his life when he was four, five, and six years old. The book is a demonstration of how art can be produced from the tension of a changing world.

Still another example of Agee's creative response to problems observed in his contemporary world is a screenplay he hoped to do for Charlie Chaplin. This working draft, "Scientists and Tramps," included sketches for many scenes.[18] Some dialogue was projected; several scenes were outlined; the prologue was worked out in detail. The prologue was to be composed of newsreel clips and accompanied by a satirical speech. Its opening harangue of democracy, given by a "Grand Old Man," is a beautiful example of parody, which Agee relished. The speech illustrates what occurs if people pretend they are individuals when they are only members of an unthinking herd. This screenplay was only sketched, yet the extant notes provide insight into many aspects of Agee's final years as a scenario writer. His recognition as a screenwriter began in the late 1940s with *The Quiet One*, a documentary about a boy from Harlem who is sent to a correctional institution.

---

[18]"Scientists and Tramps" is catalogued "Unidentified television or screenplay." Autograph manuscript working draft with autograph revisions (62 pp.). Humanities Research Center.

Agee suggested that city streets be used in this film and that nonactors be employed to catch the reality of that city. Also, he foresaw that continuous dialogue would not be necessary.[19] All of these elements have combined to make this film a classic. Much additional successful screen work followed, including the adaptation of works by various fiction writers. Five of Agee's screenplays are included in *Agee on Film*, volume two.

Agee's career produced a varied corpus, but the nine books he left are of value because in all his projects he sought and found ways to honor the life he loved. Whether in poetry or for the screen, whether in journalism or in fiction, he found ways to evoke actuality. Through art, which creates new moments, he gives us glimpses of a constantly changing world.

---

[19]Details of Agee's writing for *The Quiet One* can be observed in the manuscript materials available for this scenario catalogued as "Wiltwyck Movie." Humanities Research Center.

Selected Bibliography

Barson, Alfred. *A Way of Seeing, A Critical Study*. Amherst: University of Massachusetts Press, 1972.

Kramer, Victor A. *James Agee*. Boston: Twayne, 1975.

Larsen, Erling. *James Agee*. Minneapolis: University of Minnesota Press, 1971.

Madden, David, ed. *Remembering James Agee*. Baton Rouge: Louisiana State University Press, 1974.

Moreau, Genevieve. *The Restless Journey of James Agee*. New York: Morrow, 1977.

Ohlin, Peter H. *Agee*. New York: Obolensky, 1966.

Seib, Kenneth. *James Agee: Promise and Fulfillment*. Pittsburgh: University of Pittsburgh Press, 1968.

ated to the same office, after Robert Love Taylor moved on to the United
Peter Taylor

Clayton Robinson

Peter Hillsman Taylor is a member of a distinguished Tennessee family. His grandfather, Robert Love Taylor, defeated his own brother, Alfred, in a celebrated gubernatorial campaign in 1886 and served three terms as governor; and later, in 1921, Alfred himself was elected to the same office, after Robert Love Taylor moved on to the United States Senate. Peter's father, Hillsman Taylor, was speaker of the Tennessee House of Representatives in 1909, and at the time of the author's birth in Trenton in 1917, he was attorney general for the Thirteenth Judicial Court.

When Peter was six, his parents moved from Trenton to Nashville and three years later to St. Louis, where his father was an insurance executive. Then came a move back to Tennessee in 1932 and Peter's graduation from Memphis's Central High School in 1935. The various places of boyhood residence all appear in his fiction, and the interval in St. Louis seems particularly important. His birthplace, Trenton, becomes the Thornton of his fiction, a rural village closely tied to the past, while the fictional Chatham seems to be a composite of the cities he has known. St. Louis was special in that it provided him with a non-Southern perspective. In effect, it intensified his vision. In his only novel, *A Woman of Means*, set in St. Louis in the early part of the century, the rural Tennessee background of the principal characters is a determining factor in the meaning of the work.

Peter Taylor began his college career in the spring of 1936 under the direction of Allen Tate at Southwestern at Memphis. That fall he left for Vanderbilt to study under John Crowe Ransom. A year later, after persuading his father to allow him to attend a Northern school, he followed Ransom to Kenyon College and, like Tate, Ransom, and others of the Vanderbilt School, went on to combine writing with college teaching. In 1940 Robert Penn Warren accepted one of his stories for *Southern Review*, and in 1948 Warren wrote an introduction to Taylor's first book, *A Long Fourth*. Since then, while establishing himself as a regular contributor to *The New Yorker* and other journals, he has maintained an academic career—at the University of Chicago, Kenyon College, the University of North Carolina at Greensboro, and Harvard. From 1967 until 1983 he was Commonwealth Professor of English at the University of Virginia, and in the fall of 1983 he was writer in residence at Memphis State University.

Although he was published as early as 1937 in a little magazine at the University of Mississippi, *The River*, it was not until 1948 that his book *A Long Fourth* established his reputation. Since 1948 he has published five more collections of short stories: *The Widows of Thornton* (1954), *Happy Families Are All Alike* (1959), *Miss Leonora When Last Seen* (1963), *The Collected Stories* (1969), and *In the Miro District* (1977). In addition, there have been a novel, *A Woman of Means* (1950), and two volumes of plays, *Tennessee Day in St. Louis* (1957) and *Presences: Seven Dramatic Pieces* (1973).

Most of his fiction is set in Tennessee, not, as he explains, in the "hard-bitten, monkey-trial world of East Tennessee," where some of his ancestors came from, but in the "gentler world" of the Cumberland Great Basin.[1] In this country of Middle Tennessee with a reaching westward toward the Mississippi Valley, Taylor makes his fictional home. He has been charged with lack of incident—nothing much seems to happen in some of his stories—and with paucity of characterization. To a large extent his characters act the way they do because of where they live. This quiet interplay of character and place in the Middle South in the first half of the twentieth century is the most distinctive quality of his fiction.

---

[1] Peter Taylor, "In the Miro District," *In the Miro District and Other Stories* (New York: Knopf, 1977) 161.

Rebelling against the romanticized view of the past that had marked the earlier literature of the region, William Faulkner and his contemporaries turned to a kind of realism that in its own way was as extreme as the myth they tried to replace. They presented a South defeated by history, unable to cope with an urban, industrialized world. To many Southerners all this seemed false to the life they knew. Why, they asked, don't Southern authors write about average people like ourselves and our friends?

To such readers, the appearance of Peter Taylor in the 1940s was a pleasant surprise. *A Long Fourth*, wrote Hubert Creekmore in the *New York Times Book Review*, was "a cheering and welcome confirmation" of the existence of the average twentieth-century Southerner.[2] Taylor, said Robert Penn Warren, writes about "the contemporary, urban, middle class world of the upper South, and he is the only writer who has taken this as his province."[3] Despite the urban setting, there is "the hint of rural life not far away."[4]

While ignoring the extremes of class or caste, Taylor, like his contemporaries, *is* concerned with the clash of values embodied in the myth of the region's cultural decline. His first book gives us, according to Warren, "a world vastly uncertain of itself and the ground of its values, caught in a tangle of modern commercialism and conventions gone to seed."[5] Thus his writing is not so different after all, in that while he avoids the sensational and writes about average people, often in a city setting, he is concerned with the issues and moral values that engage most Southern writers.

Despite the political importance of his own ancestry, Taylor rarely writes about politics—nor about the equally important institution of religion. It is the family, says Ashley Brown, "its slow decline and its occasional survival," that most engages Taylor.[6] The interaction of gen-

---

[2] *New York Times Book Review*, 21 March 1948, 6.

[3] Robert Penn Warren, "Introduction," Peter Taylor, *A Long Fourth and Other Stories* (New York: Harcourt, Brace, 1948) vii.

[4] Ibid.

[5] Ibid.

[6] Ashley Brown, "The Early Fiction of Peter Taylor," *Sewanee Review* 70 (Autumn 1962): 589.

erations—grandparents, parents, children—provides the dramatic confrontation in some of his best and most characteristic stories. He grants the older characters what Hubert Creekmore calls "a rueful, personal triumph of character" because they most often represent the old values and rural heritage.[7]

For the title story of his first collection, he chose a 1946 publication from *Sewanee Review*, "A Long Fourth," about an ordinary family living on semirural acreage near Nashville during World War II. A doctor's wife, Harriet Wilson, endures the long holiday weekend of the Fourth of July when her son, a New York publisher, brings home a woman editor of a birth-control magazine with whom he is having some sort of affair. Harriet is worried about his impending entrance into the army. When Harriet's maid Mattie suggests that her own BT's going away to work in a war factory is "like you losin' Mr. Son," Harriet flares up in anger at the comparison of her son with the maid's irresponsible nephew. The middle-class matron is an eccentric person, in some ways comic, but Taylor takes us beneath the surface as she comes to an awareness that she and her maid have more in common in their ties to traditional values than she and her own children, including her daughters who condescend to her.

Thus the most effective scenes involve the destroyed hopes of both mistress and maid. When Son comes to see his mother, she hopes it is "to tell me what it is in his heart," but he turns away in embarrassment. Mattie, waiting up for BT, turns out a Nashville prostitute he brings with him. Reciting the Lord's Prayer over and over, she goes to her mistress with grief in her eyes, "and something beyond grief ... an unspeakable loneliness for which she could offer no consolation." Harriet comforts Mattie, but is herself left in despair, shut off in isolation from her children.

Taylor had already taken up the clash of values between the generations in a short story published in *Southern Review* in 1941. In "The Fancy Woman," a Memphis floozie hopes to join the rich and respectable world of her middle-class lover and is foiled by his son, an aspiring artist who retains some sense of the old values. When he asks her to pose for him, she assumes it is to be in the nude as a prelude to intimacy; however, the boy is appalled. Her old past revealed, she

---

[7]*New York Times Book Review*, 21 March 1948, 6.

winds up like the women in "A Long Fourth," a lonely victim. Similarly, in "The Scoutmaster," published in 1945, Taylor focuses on the boy initiate, in this case the unwilling witness to his sister's indiscretion. His uncle the scoutmaster explains the changing values of a generation that no longer respects "the teachings and ways of our forefathers." To him the Scouts represent a holdover from "the golden days" when a different breed of men lived in the country. The boy's father, on the other hand, an advocate of the new times, scoffs at the scoutmaster as being out of touch with reality, "unable to deal realistically with people."

This is a theme Taylor worked with again and again and which in his early fiction seemed fresh and original because of the urban setting and his quiet approach to the material. He deals with this theme at length in his only novel, *A Woman of Means*, in which the values of city and country are brought into direct confrontation. The story is told from the point of view of a boy from rural Tennessee, taken by his father to St. Louis, where the father makes a lucky marriage to a St. Louis divorcée who is heir to a brewery fortune. At first all goes well, but when the marriage begins to break up and the city loses its appeal, the boy remembers the Tennessee farm of his grandmother, who wants to keep the boy on the farm because country life is what he needs and "what people need." The father disagrees. He has married Mrs. Lauterbach to give his son the supposed advantages of a mother "who has never seen a farm" and a city school "where they teach you something." He recalls his own upbringing on a "poor ridge farm" in Tennessee and how little that he learned there has been of use to him. He is a complete convert to the city life his new wife represents. The boy remains loyal to his father but is haunted by the affectionate memory of life in the country with his grandmother and his Negro playfellows.

Ironically, the boy's attractiveness for the stepmother rests largely on associations with this rural world of the past. She senses something lacking in her own life and hopes that he can fill the void. When her daughters patronize him as an "adorable little Rebel," she reminds them of his old family name and its respectability, whereas Lauterbach, however well known in the world of finance, will always be linked with the brewery business. For his twelfth birthday, his grandmother sends him his grandfather's watch, which leads his father to reflect on the long, honorable history of his family. But the watch and his long

Southern name prove embarrassments at school, where he becomes known for his "reeyul Southern accent" and where at Chapel every face turns toward his when a Negro spiritual or a Southern folk tune is sung. He then begins to strike a pose of Southerness, which in his better moments he scorns as affected. In the struggle to fix his identity in an alien world, he expresses doubt as to whether the South and the order of life dimly recalled from his early years "really did exist." At length he shuts off his mind to the subject and drops the "Southern business," refusing to talk about it. In the end, however, with his life in the city breaking up, he entertains the "fantastic" notion of returning to the farm. His father and stepmother no longer seem the towers of strength he once thought them—in fact, he has nothing left but memories of a vanished past that from the point of view of the city seems more and more unreal. The novel ends with the boy's future in doubt, but Taylor has made his point: whether or not it is possible to make one's way back to the values of the past, the modern world fails to satisfy a deep longing, apparently perennial, to know who one is, where one is going, and what one stands for.

Taylor's third book is another collection of short stories, *The Widows of Thornton*, which continues and makes more explicit the concerns he had voiced in his first two volumes. His intention, he said, was

> to write a group of stories dealing with the histories of four or five families from a country town who had migrated, during a period of twenty-five years, to various cities of the South and the Midwest.... I wanted to present these families—both Negro and white—living a modern life while continuing to be aware of the old identities and relationships. I wanted to give the reader the impression that every character carried in his head a map of that simple country town while going about his life in the complex city . . . to show, in fact, how old patterns, for good or bad, continued to dominate many aspects of the people's lives.[8]

Of the eight stories and one short play, only two are set in the small Tennessee town of Taylor's fiction; the others are set in cities—St. Louis, Chicago, Detroit, Nashville, Memphis. However, all involve characters with small-town backgrounds. Thornton, or at least the rural or

---

[8] Quoted in Alfred J. Griffith, *Peter Taylor* (New York: Twayne, 1970) 73.

Literature of Tennessee 155

small-town past it symbolizes, is the spiritual center, and the focus is on family life. The title of the book is metaphorical, as Albert J. Griffith has pointed out. The whole village of Thornton—and by extension the modern South—has been widowed, remaining stubbornly tied to what the rest of the world has long since given up.[9]

In "Their Losses," three old women friends, reunited by chance on a train to Memphis, reminisce about their girlhood days and the changes that have taken place during their lifetime. One is taking her dead mother to Brownsville for burial; another is taking an invalid aunt to Thornton where she can spend her last days in familiar scenes; the third, Mrs. Werner, is returning from her own mother's funeral. They differ in their attitudes toward what has been lost. The two maiden ladies mourn, not only the passing of their families, but the world they have seen disappear, with "good towns, fine towns" like Grand Junction, Moscow, and La Grange now reduced, as Mrs. Werner reminds them, to dismal outposts of Memphis. Mrs. Werner, married to a successful Jewish banker in Memphis, is cynical about her loss, recalling that her mother was "tied to things that were over and done with before she was born." She herself is committed to the new and seems unaware of what the others are talking about and what she herself has given up. The title of course is metaphorical. The ladies' loss is really that of a whole generation as the civility of the past gives way to the anonymity of the city and a different set of values.

In one of Taylor's most powerful stories, "What You Hear from 'Em?," the aged Negro servant of a distinguished Thornton family, the Tollivers, has seen her favorite charges, "Mr. Thad and Mr. Will," move on to prosperity in Memphis and Nashville, while successful "strangers from up North" manage the Piggly Wiggly, the five-and-ten, and the roller-skating rink. Aunt Munsie, pulling her wagon through the streets to collect garbage for her pigs, asks her white neighbors: "What you hear from 'em? When are they coming home to live in Thornton?" She refuses to be placated by their short visits, the cards and gifts she never opens, and the argument that they are doing well in the city. "If they were going to be rich, they ought to come home where their granddaddy owned land and where their money counted for something. How could they be rich anywhere else?" The Tolliver

---

[9]Ibid., 83.

brothers conspire to get a law passed banning the keeping of hogs in the city—for the old woman's safety, but she is not fooled. "I tell you what the commotion's about. They *ain't* coming back. They ain't never coming back. They ain't never had no notion of coming back." And she will not follow them to the city, because "I ain't nothin' to 'em in Memphis, and they ain't nothing to me in Nashville." Another metaphorical widow of Thornton, Aunt Munsie gives them up like William Faulkner's Dilsey, the black matriarch who tries to hold her family together and fails. This theme of social disintegration runs throughout Taylor's early fiction.

Although his stories had been appearing in literary reviews for several years, his first in 1937, Peter Taylor's writing career began in earnest only after his return from the war. In 1948 he published his first story in *The New Yorker*, where he became a regular contributor and where most of the stories in his second collection originally appeared. This period in which he published two collections of short fiction and a novel—from the end of the war until 1954—is not only his most productive in output but his most original in achievement.

Taylor is not a prolific author. In the quarter of a century since *The Widows of Thornton* he has published only four books of fiction, and two of these are mainly composed of work that had already appeared in earlier volumes. In the meantime, he has tried his hand at drama. In 1957 his first full-length play was produced at Kenyon College, and in 1961 he accepted a fellowship for a year's study at the Royal Court Repertory Theatre in London. The result was a small volume of short plays, published in 1973, which, in the eyes of the critics, has not enhanced his literary reputation.[10] "Most of the situations are clichés," says Richard D. Olson, neither dramatic nor actable, since Taylor's plays are only fiction in a different guise.[11] In his last book, he tries still another form, blank-verse poetry, for four of his eight stories. These diversions are interesting as experiments but mark nothing original and, in fact, raise a question about the direction of his literary career.

His reduced production and turning to other genres suggest a wavering of impulse and perhaps of inspiration. His undramatic, matter-

---

[10]*New York Times Book Review*, 2 May 1954, 5.

[11]*Library Journal*, 1 January 1973, 83.

of-fact style, which in the beginning set him apart from the Gothic school, often appears in his later work drawn out, prosy, sometimes contrived, instead of developing organically from setting. The half-hearted attempt at new forms does not indicate inner development or growth; with only slight variation he still deals with the same theme, the effect of change on Southern life. In a 1958 story, "Je Suis Perdu," he writes about a professor, like himself, who at the age of thirty-eight has said all he has to say. Although Mr. Taylor is still writing, his best work seems to be that small body of fiction he produced in his early thirties.

In this work he established himself as the chronicler of the urban Southern middle class, creating his own fictional world by keeping within self-imposed limitations. But now, perhaps to avoid repeating himself, he broke out, not just into new forms but with new matter—uncomfortable and uncertain—as in the O. Henry First Prize story, "Venus, Cupid, Folly, and Time" (1959). He worked on this story, he says, for months,[12] and it shows the signs of struggle—unlike the earlier work which has the quality of being remembered, where art conceals art in the naturalness of expression.

It is the story of an eccentric old couple, brother and sister, who attempt to relive their youth by inviting newly pubescent children of their well-to-do neighbors to an annual party. But there is something odd about them. Both they and their great Gothic house recall too easily Miss Emily of Jefferson, Mississippi, in the same unpleasant manner, for brother and sister are too close, at least in the minds of the townspeople and of the young people who attend their parties. The open declaration that they are lovers by a couple of bold youngsters is the main incident in the story—but not the most important thing Mr. Taylor is trying to say, if indeed he knew quite what he wanted to say.

Toward the end he leaves the pathetic old couple for a look at the city at large. They are failures; other members of the family have left Chatham and done well for themselves in other cities. They and others like them, who had "to stay on here and pretend that our life had meaning which it did not," represent the very essence of Chatham, a middle-sized city, part Southern but more generally American. There

---

[12]Stephen Goodwin, "An Interview with Peter Taylor," *Shenandoah* 24 (Winter 1973): 9.

is confusion as to whether the state seceded from the Union—nobody seems to remember. So Taylor closes with an afterthought on the emptiness of modern industrial civilization, not out of keeping with the theme of earlier stories but here muddled with alien and embarrassing details. What is the reader to think about the two old people reduced to the grotesque at home when the rest of the family did better outside, or at least became rich and rootless in the modern American pattern? And what purpose does incest serve except to shock the sensibility?

The Gothic note was to appear frequently thereafter. Old Miss Dorset is not only her brother's mistress; she has been seen by the paperboy pushing the vacuum cleaner across the living-room floor stark naked. Taylor strains for effect with the Gothic and outré, homosexuality, masturbation, and various kinds of violence—even black humor, which does not come easily to him. "An Overwhelming Question" (1962) begins with a comic situation—the determination of a young woman to seduce her lover in the few days remaining before their wedding—and ends as a tragedy that borders on the absurd, the death of the young man in a freak accident. Here at least "he was safe from Isabel at last, poor fellow."

One of the more bizarre of Taylor's tales appears as a blank verse story poem in his most recent book. "The Hand of Emmagene" (1975) is startling not only for indelicacy of subject but for its violent conclusion. Emmagene is brought up in the hill country outside Nashville according to strict puritan principles. While visiting her cousins in the city, she becomes involved in a petting love affair with a boy. Innocent enough by most modern standards, the "affair" in Emmagene's mind has brought a corruption into her life. It must be purged, violently—the hand that fondled must be cut off. And so it is. Taylor is obviously on his old theme, the waning sense of moral values in the modern city as opposed to the country with its roots in the past; but for all that, the story is unconvincing.

Aside from innovation, however, Mr. Taylor persists in his concern with moral values, which finds a more subtle statement in "In the Miro District," the title story of his 1977 collection, than in earlier work. The story is about an old man and his grandson, the past and the present. The old man, who fought with Forrest in the Civil War, lives in a "drafty, unheated farmhouse, where he and his father before him had been born." He comes into Nashville occasionally to visit his daughter and family, who are modern and urbane, but they cannot comprehend why he prefers the primitive life in the country. The difference is brought sharply into focus in the relationship between the old gentleman and his grandson, a free-wheeling young man whose easy morals are calculated to offend the grandfather. But the old man is no narrow puritan. He looks with a tolerant eye on drink and women and, after surprising the boy at a wild party in the house when the rest of the family are away, ignores the matter after ordering the boy to clean up and dismiss the drab he has brought in off the streets. On another occasion, however, the grandfather's reaction is different. He discovers the boy in a casual affair with a young lady of his own class, which to the grandfather is a very different matter.

Taylor handles the predicament with great care, the sort of situation—psychological nuance with a firm moral underpinning—that he likes best. This experience is a revelation to the old man, who understands well enough women of a certain stamp. What he has not understood is that their morals now pervade a whole society, from top to bottom. When he finds the youth in an affair with a young lady of the country club set, he leaves the house without a word. Later he announces that he is moving from the country to live "like all the other grandfathers" with his family in the city. The grandfather's capitulation results from his awareness, as James Barnes Casey notes, "that traditional moral authority built on the Southern woman's code of honor is dead in the grandson's generation."[13] Mr. Taylor is not concerned with the effect on the youth. With great reticence, of which he is master in his best moments, he suggests that the grandfather has at least given up the fight and reconciled himself to things as they are.

This story is the most important in his most recent volume. It marks a return to the mode of his early fiction, but with a difference. It is a quiet story; nothing much seems to happen, but in reality everything has happened, and not for a happy ending. But there is no lament, no nostalgia, and on the surface no regret. If the grandfather is more acquiescent than Mr. Taylor's characters in earlier stories, it is because he recognizes and accepts the fact that moral relativism is at last pervasive. His gentle compliance and seeming acceptance of a

---

[13]John Barnes Casey, "A View of Peter Taylor's Stories," *Virginia Quarterly Review* 54 (Spring 1978): 225.

condition which in fact he can never accept is perhaps Mr. Taylor's most eloquent statement of the dilemma that underlies all his fiction. In the old man, one is reminded of Aunt Munsie worrying about when her "white children" will return from the city and make the old home place live again. In the earlier story, Taylor makes dramatic use of the traditional Southern locale; in "In the Miro District" he cuts clean. There are no effects, only the stark truth. Change involves suffering and loss, without promise of recompense.

In a 1970 interview, Taylor recalled the advice of Randall Jarrell, fellow student at Kenyon, "to write about the South, to record it" because in a few years it would all be gone.[14] He thought of himself as a sort of historian, not as a critic of an old order or a harbinger of a new one. He was not trying to change the world. "It may be," he said, "that a writer's most important possession, after his talent, is his sense of belonging to a time and place, whatever the disadvantages or injustices or cruelties of the time might be."[15] In offering us glimpses of a modern world torn between change and the moral assurance of the past, Taylor has, in Jarrell's words, written "not just for literature but for posterity."[16]

---

[14]Goodwin, 11.

[15]Ibid.

[16]Ibid.

Selected Bibliography

Works by Peter Taylor

A Long Fourth and Other Stories. New York: Harcourt Brace and Co., 1948.

A Woman of Means. New York: Harcourt Brace and Co., 1950.

The Widows of Thornton. New York: Harcourt Brace and Co., 1954.

Tennessee Day in St. Louis: A Comedy. New York: Random House, 1957.

Happy Families Are All Alike: A Collection of Short Stories. New York: McDowell, Obolensky, 1959.

Miss Leonora When Last Seen and Fifteen Other Stories. New York: Ivan Obolensky, Inc., 1963.

The Collected Stories of Peter Taylor. New York: Farrar, Straus and Giroux, 1969.

Presences: Seven Dramatic Pieces. New York: Houghton Mifflin, 1973.

In the Miro District and Other Stories. New York: Knopf, 1977.

Secondary Sources

Brown, Ashley. "The Early Fiction of Peter Taylor." *Sewanee Review* 70 (Autumn 1962): 589.

Casey, John Barnes. "A View of Peter Taylor's Stories." *Virginia Quarterly Review* 54 (Spring 1978): 225.

Griffith, Albert J. *Peter Taylor.* New York: Twayne Publishers, 1970.

Smith, James Penny. "A Peter Taylor Checklist." *Critique*, vol. 9, no. 3 (1967): 31-36.

Shelby Foote

Helen White

Although his abiding interest as a writer is in his native Washington County and Greenville, Mississippi, Shelby Foote has a prominent place in the literature of Tennessee by virtue of his long residence in Memphis and his use of Tennessee locales in several works. As a product of that stretch of territory and shaper of human character, the Yazoo-Mississippi Delta, he has the Deltan's sense of Memphis as his own metropolis. For his Tennessee readers, this circumstance will revive the ancient recognition of a tripartite division of their state and remind them that in its southern exposure their most populous city looks to a fourth dimension.

Foote has been steadfast in his commitment to the creation of his fictional Jordan County and its seat at Bristol, modeled on the actual Washington County and Greenville, despite devoting more than half his life as an author to the production of a magnificent work of history, *The Civil War*, published in three volumes between 1958 and 1974. He signaled his faithfulness to the vocation of fiction by subtitling his imposing digression into the historical "A Narrative." The subject of his fiction has been historical, and the technique of his historiography derives from his fiction. Furthermore, the subject of the history he chose to write is the grand external event he sees as influencing the culture and personalities of the Delta.

After the publication of the third volume of *The Civil War*, Foote returned to fiction on Jordan County themes. He has yet to bring to full artistic realization his idea of Jordan County, which he has treated in novels, novellas, and short stories set at various dates. He gives promise of continuing development, unusual in a writer past sixty, and his readers nurse a pleasurable suspense with respect to his work in progress. This work, insofar as may be inferred from his few remarks about it, appears to be a major novel bearing the title *Two Gates to the City*, which deals with Jordan County in the late 1940s.

In his first novel, *Tournament* (1949), Foote consciously imitated William Faulkner, whom he came to know and who is on record as an admirer of Foote's work, in laying proprietary claim to Jordan County as Faulkner had to Yoknapatawpha County. *Tournament* is a young man's book, full of echoes of writers he admired, including not only Faulkner but Joyce, Wolfe, and others. He laughs about its exuberant vocabulary, which he says sent him and whoever read it to the dictionary numerous times.

But it was a considered invitation to comparisons, especially with Faulkner, rash perhaps but fundamentally serious, as Foote's career has proved. The differences of culture and character between Deltan and hillman, reflecting the differences between the cash-cropping, alluvial Delta land and the more straitened, subsistence-farming hills, gave the younger novelist room. Foote, born to the Delta as Faulkner was to the hills, distinguished his fictional property not only by cultivating his Delta garden but by deploying an autonomous style. In *Tournament*, occasional Faulknerian words or sentences emphasize his independence by their rarity. More fundamentally, Foote took a distinctive approach in narrative construction.

In the second volume of *The Civil War*, Foote memorably rendered the physical aspects of the Yazoo-Mississippi Delta in his narration of the campaigns of 1862-1863 from Shiloh to Vicksburg. He begins:

> This incredibly fertile, magnolia-leaf-shaped region, 200 miles in length and 50 miles in average width, bounded east and west by the two rivers that gave it its compound name, and north and south by the hills that rose below and above Memphis and Vicksburg, was nearly roadless throughout its flat and swampy expanse, was subject to floods in all but the driest seasons, and—except for the presence of a scattering of pioneers who risked its malarial and intestinal disorders

for the sake of the richness of its forty-foot topsoil, which in time, after the felling of its big trees and the draining of its bayous, would make it the best cotton farmland in the world—was the exclusive domain of moccasins, bears, alligators, and panthers.

Here he is concerned with Delta geography as a factor in military operations, but in his fiction he is concerned with it as an influence upon the scattering of pioneers and their descendants. Having obliterated the claims of the Indians, the people of his books contested and destroyed the dominion of moccasin, bear, alligator, and panther while substituting for malarial and intestinal disorders others of a psychological and spiritual description.

Himself an ironic and disabused descendant of antebellum exploiters of Delta topsoil, Foote also has roots in the literary Delta. By the 1930s, when he was in high school, Greenville possessed a literary culture owed in large part to the poet and memoirist William Alexander Percy. In Percy rather than William Faulkner the young Foote had an immediate model of the literary man, although he was already reading Faulkner enthusiastically. Percy was more or less responsible for the presence in Greenville of two other writers of note, Hodding Carter and David Cohn. As a neighbor of William Alexander Percy and friend of his adoptive sons, especially Walker Percy, Foote was at the center of the literary life of the town. The high school was of respectable academic quality, and Foote, as contributor to and editor of the school paper, *The Pica*, had an outlet for his talent. The paper was judged best in the United States while he was associated with it. During his two years at the University of North Carolina, 1935-1937, he published stories and reviews in *The Carolina Magazine*.

When he returned after service in World War II, Greenville continued to provide an environment favorable to developing literary talent. Foote had begun *Tournament* before the war and on returning revised and finished it. The town could even publish his first book, a story entitled *The Merchant of Bristol* (1947)—the material is used in *Tournament*—because Hodding Carter and the other literati had started the short-lived Levee Press. The local department store contained a good book shop, in which Ben Wasson, a writer and literary agent, was employed: he was a help in guiding Foote to a New York publisher. The Levee Press and the book shop implied a local reading public. When

Tournament was published by the Dial Press, the author had the satisfaction of seeing 750 copies sold in his hometown.

Between 1949 and 1954, Shelby Foote published three novels and a book of related shorter fiction which still comprise, pending publication of *Two Gates to the City*, the Jordan County fiction. These may be described as "takes" of Jordan County at different points in history from the first encounters between whites and Indians at the end of the eighteenth century to about 1950. All except *Tournament* have been reprinted. Foote does not intend to give this canonical status by reprinting it, for he sees it, affectionately, as juvenilia but also as a "quarry" from which to draw and develop material for other fiction and expects eventually to use it up in this way. Yet *Tournament* will remain a key, both technically and substantively, to Foote's work. Lacking familiarity with it, readers cannot fully appreciate the interrelationships of the Jordan County fiction.

Tournament is the story of the rise and fall of a postbellum planter, Hugh Bart, as told by his grandson, Asa, who seeks to understand how and why the grandfather was able to restore Solitaire, a baronial plantation sacked during the war, only to fail as husband and father, sell the land when his sons proved incompetent to farm it, and finally lose his fortune through imprudent investment and gambling. An arriviste in Jordan County, Bart marries the daughter of General Jameson, "the Delta's beau sabreur" of Civil War renown who had inherited Solitaire from his father Isaac, a pioneer settler. Bart acquires the plantation after the impoverished Jamesons have lost it and seeks to redeem the old order by marrying the Jameson daughter. Isaac, the general, and Bart loom heroically by comparison with Asa's feckless father and Asa himself.

As Asa grows up, he is discomfited and puzzled by the paltriness of the family's circumstances in Bristol and the sharp contrast they make with a past recent yet mythic at Solitaire. He suspects the explanation lies in the character of Hugh Bart, which he investigates. Asa's point of view, although not specifically invoked in the other Jordan County works, may be said to condition all of them. It is the point of view of the author's generation—Foote was born in 1916, and Asa is given a birth date of 1911—and autobiographical to a degree that has evidently influenced the decision to keep *Tournament* out of print.

The pattern of family history represented by the Bart-Jameson clan is a background theme developed in various ways in all of the Jordan County group. In subsequent works, as in *Tournament*, Foote explores the related theme of the thinness and inauthenticity of Delta culture, interwoven with another preoccupation, the relationships of fathers, father substitutes, and children—the children always suffering from deprivation stemming from male and paternal inadequacy. The testing of men, the attainment of male *virtú*, often through violence and especially war, and its dissipation are of central importance. Also recurrent, although only suggested by the figure of Asa Bart in *Tournament*, is the "portrait of the artist," often the potential artist who is balked or fails. Subsuming all of these is the grand theme that Asa announces and that recurs throughout Foote's work: the loneliness of the human condition and the inherent difficulty of building any kind of satisfactory life at all.

In manner as well as in matter, *Tournament* forecasts the later works of the Jordan County group, and indeed *The Civil War*. It is very consciously structured, with a carefully varied interplay of points of view and a design analogous to music in some respects. The narrative begins with an "overture" in Asa Bart's first person, shades into omniscience for the body of the novel, and moves back to Asa for the concluding commentary or "coda." The novel proper, dealing with Hugh Bart's career, comprises eight sections, meticulously deployed and balanced. The first two are devoted to Bart's rise and his acquisition of Solitaire, the middle four to his increasingly effective management as this is undercut by his incapacity for sustained commitment leading to ennui and the sale of Solitaire, and the last two to life in Bristol under the sign of the dollar and ultimate ruin. This complex pattern is enhanced by descriptions, flashbacks, and uses of symbols, all quite remarkable in a first novel.

Foote has worked from strong undergirding patterns in all of his fiction and history as well. In recent years, he has acquired French commentators who, sharing enthusiasm for arcane theories of structuralism, have ingeniously analyzed what one of them terms "*le jeu des structures*" in his novels and stories. Foote is not especially theoretical about his art, but the almost architectural development of material is a constant feature of his writing.

Follow Me Down (1950) is full of cross-references to *Tournament*, although these are not stressed but matter-of-fact and incidental to a very different narrative. The novel concerns Luther Eustis, a severely repressed, fanatically fundamentalist farmer working land that was part of Solitaire. The name of the old plantation begins to resonate. It was named by Isaac Jameson as an allusion to his bachelorhood at the time he acquired it. Hugh Bart was also a bachelor when he bought it after the Civil War, and though he married Florence Jameson with the intention of continuing the landed dynasty, he failed in human relations. Now in *Follow Me Down* the poor white Eustises inherit the consequences of what is stated to be "the failure of Love."

On a summer day in 1949, Luther, seized by passion for the young country whore Beulah, abandons his family and takes the girl to an island in the Mississippi where, after an Edenic interlude, he kills her. This crime and its causes and effects—immediate and inherited, personal, social, and historical—are presented through Foote's characteristically well-engineered narration. The design allows multiple points of view on Luther's "truly complicated" crime and punishment.

Foote has commented in connection with this novel, "I like to get out the same way I got in." He gets in—that is, approaches the central situation of Luther and Beulah—through successively more personally involved characters. The novel is organized in threes: three parts, each comprised of three points of view, with a variation in the second part. In part 1, the opening voice is that of the circuit court clerk, the next that of a newspaper reporter, and the third that of an afflicted boy who was on the island with Eustis and Beulah and informs the sheriff that Eustis is the murderer. The progression is from impersonal functionary through professional observer to an emotionally implicated person. The second and longest part is presented through Luther, Beulah, and a reprise by Luther. Then, in part 3, Foote "gets out" via points of view reversing the emphasis in part 1: the progression is through a personally involved party (Luther's wife), a professional (his lawyer), and finally an impersonal functionary (the turnkey of the county jail). This effect intensifies our involvement in the passion of Luther Eustis, culminating in an identification with the two principals, followed by gradual withdrawal to the social perspective imbued with humane sympathy generated by the narrative.

Having dealt with the failure of love in modern Jordan County among the poor whites, Foote extended this theme to "the quality" in a comic novel with cutting edges, *Love in a Dry Season* (1951). The time is 1929-1941. The degeneration of the upper class has rendered it vulnerable to the opportunism of an outsider, a Yankee of immigrant stock with an Anglicized name, Harley Drew. He sets out to marry the pathetic but wealthy spinster Amanda Barcroft, daughter of Major Barcroft, one of Jordan County's inadequate males, gone sour and snobbish. However, Drew sees a better opportunity in the flapper Amy Carruthers, wife of the impotent Jeff Carruthers and heiress of Briartree, a plantation near Solitaire, and abandons Amanda.

Treating this double triangle with Harley Drew as the common element, Foote again develops a complex, strongly articulated narrative meant to adumbrate a truth more "complicated" than those of the earlier novels. This ingenious construction has received the pleased attention of Simone Vauthier, one of Foote's French critics, who dwells upon the "superimposition" of "ternary and binary patterns." These involve an interplay of voyeurs and their objects, inversions and reversals of roles, so that seeing and being seen become "one of the metaphorical centers" of the novel. These people are speculators without heart, and if there is blood in their veins, it is cold. Harley Drew weaves deviously in and out of the Barcroft plot and the Carruthers plot, which cross only once, when Amanda sees Harley and Amy at a traffic light; but all the characters are held in the great "Eye of Bristol" symbolized by that same traffic light.

The representation of modern Bristol as a scene of anomie is repeated but without brittleness or any comic intention in "Rain Down Home," the first of the collection of stories entitled *Jordan County* (1954). Foote describes this as "a landscape in narrative" with "place for its hero and time for its plot." The stores are printed in reverse chronological order, and the reader is expected to infer explanations of the modern situations with which he starts as he finds himself in those that preceded. The alienated central character of "Rain Down Home" is a returning veteran of World War II who encounters one of those upper-class gentlemen of Bristol that we know from as far back as *Follow Me Down* "has ice water in his veins." The veteran makes a statement and asks a question that remain in the reader's mind as he reads the tales that follow and thinks about Foote's work as a whole: "I want to live in the world but I dont understand, and until I understand I cant live. Why wont people be happy? Not cant: *wont*." This is a variation on the question Asa Bart had asked about his family in *Tournament*.

There is little happiness, and that only momentary or precarious, to be found in the component stories of *Jordan County*. The longest is "Child by Fever," a novella filled with horrors, violence, cannibalistic women, madness, and death, which Foote describes as "my Gothic novel." The main character, Hector Wingate Sturgis, who is born in 1878 and hangs himself in 1911, is the impotent scion of a once-proud plantation family and an example of the failed artist. Ironically, his domineering, ruthless mother gives the city land for Wingate Park and is known as "the mother of Bristol." Another story in the *Jordan County* sequence, "Ride Out," is one of Foote's finest. It is about a real artist, a Negro jazz musician who briefly succeeds. This novella, set in the 1920s and 1930s, gains impact from the author's love of the jazz of his native region. The darkness of the tale, which ends in the protagonist's electrocution in the same jail where Luther Eustis was held, is somewhat mitigated by the proposition, emergent in the narrative, that the incomparable music he makes with his cornet is a function of the man's fate and fulfillment for him.

Whatever is wrong in the Yazoo-Mississippi region—Yazoo means "River of Death"—was wrong from the start, as the reader learns from "Pillar of Fire," the Civil War tale in the *Jordan County* sequence. Yankee troops raid Solitaire twice, and Isaac Jameson, now an old man, suffers a stroke between the attacks. His speech is affected. Since he does not understand the medical situation, he wonders whether he may be speaking in tongues as people did at religious revivals—"maybe God had touched him." However, he has no comfort in the idea, for "if it was God it was punishment, since it had not come through faith. He must be under judgment, just as maybe the whole nation was, having to suffer for the double sin of slavery and mistreatment of the land." But Isaac finally reverts to an explanation that had already occurred to him: "The earth, he thought, the earth endures. He groped for an answer.... The earth, he thought, and the earth goes back to the sun; that was where it began. There is no law, no reason except the sun, and the sun doesnt care. Its only concern is its brightness; we feed that brightness like straws dropped into its flame. Fire! he thought suddenly. It all goes back to fire!"

Whatever Isaac may have concluded as he dies with the flames of Solitaire reflected in his eyes, Shelby Foote implies that there was iniquity of the fathers specific to the Delta (but no doubt only a particular variant of a universal human quality), the effects of which are being visited upon the latest generations. The clearest suggestion of this theme comes in "The Sacred Mound," the story set first in time but last in *Jordan County*. Parallels to Isaac Jameson's ruminations about the sun are developed in the Indians whom Isaac and his kind displace. Furthermore, the Indians say of the French and Spanish that they "began to ask a strange thing of us, seeking to buy the land. Sell us the land, they said: Sell us the land. And we told them, disguising our horror: No man owns the land; take and live on it; it is lent to you for your lifetime; are we not brothers?"

At the end of *Jordan County* the reader registers a deeper and darker meaning in the poetic name Isaac Jameson gave his plantation: Solitaire. His punishment was not only the result of mistreating the land but of enslaving the Negro in the process. Not content with expelling the Indians, the white man mounted the ultimate assault on human brotherhood. The "failure of Love" ambient in the novels and stories of modern times is traced radically to the strongest white male personage of the early times. From him, apparently, his women, his sons and daughters, and all their progeny contract and inherit alienation.

During the period when Foote was producing the Jordan County series, he also wrote an elegant little historical novel, in the strict sense of documentable fiction, about a battle of the Civil War, that larger denial of brotherhood which so heightened the predicament of Jordan County. *Shiloh*, published in 1952 but written before *Follow Me Down*, is tied to the Jordan County fiction by the character Luther Dade, son of a farmer on Solitaire, grandfather of Luther Eustis. It provides an instructive transition to *The Civil War: A Narrative*. In a bibliographical note to the first volume of this work, Foote stated that he had combined the "separate methods" of the novelist and the historian, whom he saw as pursuing the same goal: truth. "Accepting the historian's standards without his paraphernalia," he said, "I have employed the novelist's method without his license."

In *Shiloh* the novelist's license permitted him to impose a theme on historical material—his subject is the testing of men in "the first great modern battle"—and develop it through the points of view of fictional characters. His account of the battle is meticulously researched. Foote has stated that the "historical characters . . . speak the words they spoke and do the things they did," that many minor incidents and phrases given to the fictional characters are also authentic, and that he hoped that even "the weather is accurate too." The novel is presented in strictly limited first person monologues by a variety of participants, Northern and Southern. The narratives are rounded, individualized stories of men tested to the utmost. The author's voice, which can be heard in ways that enrich his other fiction and the history as well, has no place here. Foote is all of the voices in *Shiloh* and at the same time no particular one, without bias or judgmental comment.

There are six main characters, one of whom is a composite of the twelve men of Company G in an Indiana regiment, part of a division commanded by Lew Wallace. The most important character, to whom Foote assigned opening and concluding sections that frame the others, is Lieutenant Metcalfe, an aide-de-camp on Albert Sidney Johnston's staff, whose position gives him a perspective more nearly inclusive than that of the other characters. Having participated in the production of the Confederates' romantic Napoleonic battle plan, he is especially qualified to indulge in poignant "spilt-milk thinking" when the battle disintegrates into bloody chaos. But he could still find comfort in the performance of Nathan Bedford Forrest, exemplifying "men who did not fight as if odds made the winner, who did not necessarily believe that God was on the side of the big battalions."

The fascination with individual experience, particularly with that of men under stress, is common to the Jordan County fiction, *Shiloh*, and *The Civil War*. Of the last, Foote has said he considers it a particular type of military history.

> [I]t is a military history in the same sense that the "Iliad" is a military history. I am more interested in the people than in the evolutions of the line, and I am intensely interested in what caused a battle to be fought and what its results were. Not so much in the military sense, but what was the effect on Lincoln? And what was the effect on Davis? And I like

very much to include the planning of a battle, so that when the two sides come together, you understand what's swinging in the balance.

The *Iliad* is a formal influence as well since it supplies the design. A book may not be a battle, but Foote plans his with great care, and the reader must analyze the planning to appreciate fully "what's swinging in the balance." *The Civil War* is organized like an epic in twenty-four books framed by a prologue and an epilogue, and the accounts of the campaigns in the east and west are interwoven in a narrative dialectic resulting in a vivid, suspenseful development of events now more than a century old.

Foote has observed that most academic historians never become serious about writing but skip "the sweatshop apprenticeship" through which alone they might obtain "command of language" and "a way of looking at the world: Proust called it 'a quality of vision.'" The quality of vision that shapes *The Civil War* can be described by a term usually employed in literary criticism rather than in judgments of history—"modern." It is the vision of a writer who approaches his work as a craft, to which, far from pretending impossible detachment, he brings the accidents of his own breeding as part of his materials. Foote's history, like his fiction, exemplifies the formalism—attention to structure and design, balance, symmetry, proportion—that distinguishes the great moderns and is a first tenet of modern criticism. The narrator is a distinct presence—balanced, generous—seeing many sides from many angles, and from a late position in a long tradition. The tone holds piety and ruefulness in a tension that issues in pervasive irony.

This is no doubt a particularly Southern quality in the book, disarmingly expressing the attitude of this historian of the war who happens to be an heir of the losers. The distinguishably Southern marks, which certainly do not include chauvinism, include abundant proofs of "the sense of place" which has been so much discussed in the work of Southern novelists. Through its economical, functional use of concrete details, the narrative, the human story, is anchored to "the world's body." A Southern relish for the humorous or absurd aspects of the narrated situations has dictated the choice of much of the matter and colored much more.

Imbued with a sense of place, a sense of history, a sense of literary tradition, *The Civil War* is most profoundly Southern in projecting the sense of tragedy. C. Vann Woodward has declared, "The experience of evil and the experience of tragedy are parts of the Southern heritage that are as difficult to reconcile with the American legend of innocence and social felicity as the experience of poverty and defeat is to reconcile with legends of abundance and success." Insofar as Foote's vision of the Civil War is Southern by virtue of the humorous, the ironic, and the tragic, it transcends the parochial and may prove to be the version of all Americans.

For all his amplitude—the work contains about 1,600,000 words—the book is compulsively readable as a result of firm organization and stylistic grace. Foote has erected the figures of Jefferson Davis and Abraham Lincoln in symbolic proportions, stationing them at the beginning and end and reverting to them frequently throughout. Beginning with Davis's farewell speech to the U.S. Senate on 21 January 1861, the prologue moves to Lincoln's furtive entrance into Washington after his election to the presidency. Volume 1 closes with the preparations of Davis, now president of the Confederate states, for his trip to "the troubled western theater" to rally his people as they began to apprehend the seriousness of the war. Foote follows this with an evocation of "the Lincoln music" in an account of his message to Congress in December 1862, in which the Union heard itself eulogized as "the last best hope of earth."

Volume 2 opens with Davis's trip west, which gives Foote an occasion to develop his Western-mindedness, not as a contribution to the sometimes biased debate as to the relative importance of Virginia and the rest of the South, but as a presentation of the whole Confederacy and its wishful assertion of a manifest destiny in the Southwest and Latin America. The immense work is brought to a climax in the Cincinnati conference between Sherman and Grant, the latter finally recognized by Lincoln after the fall of Vicksburg as the general who could "face the arithmetic" of modern war. Foote shows us the two Union generals as they concert the western and eastern strategies to bring the conflict to an end by waging it totally. Sherman and Grant are presented earnestly talking in a hotel room against the chiaroscuro of the Confederates' grieved liquidation of their pretensions to mount a second American Revolution. They had had to enact conscription some time back, feeling that in doing so they sacrificed classic rights to the necessities of "the Thing"—war monstrously grown beyond all romantic preconceptions. Now they had to extend conscription to all white males from seventeen to fifty, and Jefferson Davis mourned the necessity "to grind the seed corn of the nation."

The final volume, after moving inexorably with sustained narrative art to the laying down of arms on all fronts, comes to a quiet and thoughtful epilogue, a look into the future. The ghost of the murdered Lincoln is summoned, and Foote employs Lincoln's words to suggest his own motivation in writing a Civil War history: "What has occurred in this case must never recur in similar cases. Human nature will not change. In any future great national trial, compared with the men of this, we shall have as weak and as strong, as silly and as wise, as bad and as good. Let us therefore study the incidents of this, as philosophy to learn wisdom from, and none of them as wrongs to be revenged." Foote, I suspect, would approve the amendment of this by the addition of a phrase—" . . . or as complacencies to be defended." He goes on to quote Davis, the worn and hounded survivor, though acknowledging that he "could never match that [Lincoln] music, or perhaps even catch its tone," as he asserts at the end his love for America. The reader supplies, "All passion spent."

Foote has woven, stitched, and bound the parts of this vast work by using recurrent themes and personages, meant to function, he has said, like the armature within a sculpture. They do function in this manner; only through analysis can the reader become aware of the trusses beneath the surface of the finished work of literary art. The most pervasive theme, already mentioned, is the one Foote has said comes as near as he can to a thesis about the war, the redressing of the balance between the east and west theaters. A corollary theme is the changing character of the war, begun, especially by the Confederates, with illusions of individual honor only to develop into the prototype of mass technological warfare.

Foote makes themes cross-light one another, often with ironic effect. By narrating the changes in the character of the war he creates an occasion to illuminate another major theme, that of the searches by the two presidents for generals competent to understand modern war and execute it effectually. It is less obvious that, in giving thematic prominence to the contrast between Northern plenty and Southern poverty, he should have dramatized certain tactical issues faced by the presidents and their generals. There is powerful human interest in repeated senses of hungry, tattered Confederates falling ravenously upon abandoned Yankee supply dumps or stripping Yankee dead, not in Homeric lust for trophies but to obtain food to eat, shoes for bleeding feet, and guns to fire. Cumulatively, such scenes help the reader concretely understand that in certain circumstances what Foote terms their "philosophy of abundance" was a tactical drawback to the Union forces, who had to manage huge commissaries, while the Confederates, necessarily traveling light, could achieve stunning victories under officers such as Stonewall Jackson and Nathan Bedford Forrest.

Foote's human sympathies are so inclusive and his skill in recreating characters from the sources is so great that he brings historical personages hauntingly alive in a way that helps integrate the work. Their presence is felt even when offstage, with the result that they function as ligaments binding and articulating the narrative. As figures appear and reappear, Foote develops them in terms of their responses to successive crises and engagements. He never presumes to judge absolutely but is only fascinated to observe men of whom he declares, "It was their good fortune, or else their misery, to belong to a generation in which every individual would be given a chance to discover and expose his worth, down to the final ounce of strength and nerve."

In *The Civil War* Shelby Foote exhibits an undeviating interest in human character and enjoyment of human experience. He knows that there is always a mixture of qualities in men, that heroism is not exclusive. There *are* heroes in this narrative, however, North and South, no matter how ironic Foote's view may be and no matter how unfashionable the idea of the hero may be. There is magnanimity for the men who break or fail, such as the Wagnerian Texan, John Bell Hood, or the Union general William S. Rosecrans, who abandoned the field at Chickamauga. The tests they had to meet are rendered in all their formidableness. The reader is also prepared to credit the virtual apotheosis of Robert E. Lee when, after Chancellorsville, Foote presents "the jubilant Confederates, recognizing the gray-bearded author of their victory" and tendering him "the wildest demonstration of their lives." The reader is prepared to credit yet more when Foote, discreetly avoiding authorial assertion, quotes one of Lee's staff: "I thought that it must have been from such a scene that men in ancient times rose to the dignity of gods."

The Homeric quality of *The Civil War* causes one to look at the earlier Jordan County fiction in a new light and enhances expectations with regard to subsequent novels. Foote has revealed himself as an aficionado, not exclusively of war, but of the testing of men under extreme pressure of any description. Pressure may come from the weight of inherited error and have its cumulative effect in the day-to-day civilian life of Jordan County. The careful reader of Foote's work since the beginning may learn from *The Civil War* that his preoccupation with the testing of men derives from faith that some, at least, will rise to the occasion and set a standard, while others, if they fail, earn understanding and pity. This insight allows for some qualification of the pessimism and contempt implicit in, for example, *Love in a Dry Season*. Is it conceivable that Jordan County may yet produce its civilian Nathan Bedford Forrest and learn that it is possible to live in sustained happiness, as well as occasionally to fight, against the odds?

Such a possibility may be reasonably inferred by the development, under extreme testing, of the Kinships in *September September* (1978), the novel Foote wrote as "a conscious exercise" in order to "get his hand back in" after the long excursion into historiography. He wished to try his hand at treating "black bourgeois characters and the problem of their imitation of whites." In facing up to this problem, the Kinships prove their mettle.

Like all of Foote's fiction as well as history, *September September* incorporates a tremendous amount of information and, in particular, painstaking research into recent events. The setting is September 1957 in Memphis, accurately presented, sometimes street by street, although some of the scenes have already disappeared in urban renewal. The disastrous Edsel was introduced that month and appears briefly in the novel as a symbol of what might go amiss. It was the month when federal troops were sent to Little Rock, 135 miles to the west, to force the racial integration of Central High School. At about the same time, "the Russians put the sputnik up from Kazakhstan, a polished steel basketball with spike antennas, beeping in A-flat around and around a world that would never be the same."

The Memphis novel is linked to the matter of Jordan County, for the three main white characters are natives of it and join forces in Bristol to work out their scheme to kidnap a little black boy in Memphis, son of Eben Kinship but, more important, only grandson of wealthy and powerful Theo G. Wiggins. The conspirators think that the disturbance in Little Rock will so affect Memphis that they will be able to persuade a Negro family that it dare not seek the aid of the white police force. The Jordan County characters are Podjo, a gambler who has served time at Parchman; the woman Reeny; and Reeny's current attachment Rufus, an ex-convict and a drifter. The first two have a southern Jordan County background but have departed far from "the primary virtues" of the country; Rufus, a Bristol boy, has gone even further astray. The major black character, Eben Kinship, also has a Bristol background. His sexy sister precipitates a killing in "Ride Out."

The action moves quickly and steadily forward, and suspense is maintained through the last paragraph. With attention to both white and black characters, the author presents the backgrounds together with preparation for the crime; little Teddy Kinship is kidnapped and kept in the attic of a house on the bluff over the Mississippi River; he is eventually returned and a complex aftermath ensues. The destinies of all the characters take decisive turns. Rufus, the most alienated, meets the violent death he has long courted. Podjo and Reeny, who have some redeeming qualities, go off to further adventures. In the course of his ordeal, Eben Kinship defines his manhood in relation to his wife, Martha, who is really married to somewhat distorted and anachronistic white ideas of gentility, and against his domineering father-in-law. All of the characters are individualized, the most memorable being Theo G. Wiggins, who has learned how to live and prosper in a city dominated by the Crump machine, "using their own system to beat them with." He realizes that his way is "going fast," that his son-in-law will live his life in his own way, and that the world of his grandson will be different—perhaps even better.

September September is distinguished, like all of Foote's work, by skillful handling of narrative point of view. Four omniscient sections frame and alternate with three sections called "Voices": Podjo, Eben, Rufus; then Reeny, Martha, Reeny again; and finally Rufus, Eben, and Podjo. The women are framed by the men, the blacks by the whites. These first person parts provide intimate access to characters and motives, interesting variety of style and tone, and not a little of the humor and irony that pervade the novel. The crime has unexpected results, some of them beneficent. The cool, level tone of the omniscient narrator does not allow anything so rash as a happy-ever-after conclusion, but the Kinships are happier. There is no doubt that the two surviving villains will go on together; they, too, are "in orbit."

Foote's considerable following can look forward to *Two Gates to the City*. Beyond a few general statements, Foote does not discuss work in progress, and to speculate would be inappropriate. He has called it "a Mississippi Karamazov." Following the pattern of *The Brothers Karamazov*, one may suppose that it will be massive and comprehensive, on the great theme of fathers and sons. He has also said that it will be set in Bristol and treat "a struggle for values in the modern South"—again, Foote's grand theme. Those who are familiar with his work can be reasonably sure of certain qualities that they will find: a rich historical background against which the immediate story is enacted (Foote has said that the central characters will be Lundys, descendants of a Union soldier who took part in the burning of Solitaire in "Pillar of Fire"); a wide variety of intimately developed characters from "the melting pot" of the Delta, which contains a surprising number of different ethnic compounds; striking descriptions as functional parts of the story told; a wealth of allusion, especially to the Bible and liturgy; literary parallels and archetypes; and the use of music—all integrated in a novel that will attest to the author's love of language. Most impressive of all will be a complex, beautifully developed design. The novelist "has his hand in" again, and the Delta soil he works is rich and deep.

Selected Bibliography

Works by Shelby Foote

The Merchant of Bristol. Greenville MS: The Levee Press, 1947.

Tournament. New York: Dial Press, Inc., 1949.

Follow Me Down. New York: Dial Press, Inc., 1950.

Love in a Dry Season. New York: The Dial Press, 1951.

Shiloh. New York: The Dial Press, 1952.

Jordan County. New York: The Dial Press, 1954.

Three Novels by Shelby Foote. New York: The Dial Press, 1964. Includes *Follow Me Down, Jordan County,* and *Love in a Dry Season.*

The Civil War: A Narrative. Volume 1: *Fort Sumter to Perryville;* volume 2: *Fredericksburg to Meridian;* volume 3: *Red River to Appomattox.* New York: Random House, 1958, 1963, 1974.

September September. New York: Random House, 1978.

Criticism

Bradford, M. E. "Else We Should Love It Too Well." *The National Review,* 14 February 1975, 174-75.

Carr, John. "It's Worth a Grown Man's Time: Shelby Foote." In *Kite-Flying and Other Irrational Acts: Conversations with Twelve Southern Writers.* Baton Rouge: Louisiana State University Press, 1972.

Literature of Tennessee

Delta. No. 4 (April 1977). Review published by the Centre d'Etude et de Recherches sur les Ecrivains du Sud aux Etats-Unis, Paul Valéry University, Montpellier, France. This issue is devoted entirely to Shelby Foote.

Garrett, George. "Foote's *The Civil War*: The Version for Posterity?" *Mississippi Quarterly* 28 (Winter 1974-1975): 83-92.

Mississippi Quarterly: The Journal of Southern Culture. Special Issue on Shelby Foote: Essays, Interviews, and Bibliography. 24 (Fall 1971).

Rubin, Louis D., Jr. "Shelby Foote's Civil War." *Prospects: An Annual Journal of American Studies* 1 (1976): 313-33.

White, Helen, and Redding S. Sugg, Jr. "Shelby Foote's Iliad." *Virginia Quarterly Review* 55 (Spring 1979): 234-50.

White, Helen, and Redding S. Sugg, Jr. *Shelby Foote.* Boston: G. K. Hall & Company, 1982.

Woodward, C. Vann. "The Great American Butchery." *New York Review of Books*, 6 March 1975, 12.

10

Contemporary Writers

Dennis Loyd

Since 1950 Tennessee has produced several writers of considerable note. They have included Harry Harrison Kroll and Alfred Leland Crabb, whose prolific pens have created historical and regional novels almost by the score. There have been writers such as Wilma Dykeman and Harriette Arnow, whose visions of pioneer life have especially warranted critical attention. Dykeman's *The Tall Woman* and Arnow's *The Dollmaker* are impressive works. There are scholar-educator-writers such as Robert Drake, who has produced three fine collections of short stories while continuing his responsibilities as a professor of English at the University of Tennessee at Knoxville. At the same university, Richard Marius has completed two novels, *The Coming of Rain* and *Bound for the Promised Land*. Paul Ramsey, teacher and poet in residence at the University of Tennessee at Chattanooga for many years, has helped maintain a high standard for Tennessee poets with works such as his *In an Ordinary Place* (1965) and *The Doors: Poems of 1968* (1968).

At the western extreme of the state there are educator-writers, too. Two members of the faculty of Southwestern at Memphis who have published notable works of fiction are Jack D. Farris and John L. Farris. Although they share no blood relation, both men have found a kinship in their teaching and writing. Jack Farris is the author of *Ramey* (1953), a popular novel which was made into a television series a few years ago. John Farris has published at least eight novels. Shelby Foote, noted for his monumental history *The Civil War* as well as his fiction, has been treated in the essay preceding this one.

Other significant contemporary figures are Bette Greene, Joan Williams, David Madden, Cormac McCarthy, and Lisa Alther, whose single novel *Kinflicks* was a best seller in 1976. Finally, no one can overlook Alex Haley and his enormously successful *Roots*.

From the many, this chapter will concentrate on four writers whose reputations are well established—Jesse Hill Ford, Madison Jones, Ishmael Reed, and Nikki Giovanni.

Jesse Hill Ford

Ford was born in Troy, Alabama, in 1928 but soon moved to Nashville, where he was educated in private schools including Montgomery Bell Academy and Vanderbilt University. Tiring of public relations work, he began to write fiction. His first published work, *Mountains of Gilead* (1961), was set in a fictional locale that he was to use again and again. He called his county Sligo, with Somerton its seat. This setting was to serve him in *The Liberation of Lord Byron Jones*; parts of *Fishes, Birds and Sons of Men*; and *The Raider*.

The past and its effect on the present are felt in *Mountains of Gilead*, where the "mounds" of West Tennessee, presumably the work of Indians centuries before, inspired the title and much of the action. Grant Shafer, the novel's protagonist, is in Somerton because his anthropologist father had moved there to study the mounds. The story unfolds in June of 1950 at the wedding of Shafer and Eleanor Fite of Memphis. Shafer had dated Patsy Jo McCutcheon for fifteen years before deciding to marry Eleanor, and Tom McCutcheon, Patsy Jo's father, is determined that his daughter will not be spurned without some retaliation. He stops the wedding violently with the murder of the bride and his own suicide. Although he had originally planned to shoot Shafer, at the last moment his shot goes astray.

Ford's drama *The Conversion of Buster Drumwright* was produced by CBS in 1959. In continues the author's interest in rural people and their inner lives. Drumwright has been convicted of killing seventeen people, including Katherine Hedgepath and her infant son. He is waiting in the Trammel, Tennessee, county jail for his hanging three days away. Ocie Hedgepath comes home from Texas after a thirteen-year absence to avenge his sister's murder. Pretending to be a preacher intent on Drumwright's conversion, Hedgepath is committed to murdering the man. However, in his three visits, Hedgepath not only converts Drumwright, but also experiences a conversion of his own.

Somerton serves as the setting for *The Liberation of Lord Byron Jones* as it had for the earlier *Mountains of Gilead*. Published in 1965, *The Liberation of Lord Byron Jones* was Ford's first big financial success. It was chosen as a Book-of-the-Month selection in that year and was made into a movie in 1970. The novel presents the story of a serious racial conflict in the West Tennessee community. Amid the tension of the civil rights movement, Ford tells the story of a love affair between a black woman, the wife of Lord Byron Jones, Somerton's black undertaker, and Willie Joe Worth, a white lawman. Interwoven with this story is the search for revenge by Sonny Boy Mosby, who thirteen years before was beaten by Stanley Bumpas. The resolution of both elements of this novel occurs amid horror—Jones is the victim of a mutilation murder, and Bumpas dies after Mosby pushes him into a hay baler.

Fishes, Birds and Sons of Men, Ford's collection of short stories, appeared in 1967. Each story had been previously published in *The Atlantic Monthly*, beginning with "The Surest Thing in Show Business" (April 1959). Some of Ford's finest work is found in this volume in stories like "Bitter Bread," "How the Mountains Are," "The Highwaymen," "The Savage Sound," "To the Open Water," and the title story, "Fishes, Birds and Sons of Men."

"Bitter Bread" deals with the alienation brought about by racial discrimination and poverty. The story of Robert, a young black man, and his frantic effort to provide aid for his seventeen-year-old wife, Jeannie, who is pregnant, "Bitter Bread" delineates Robert's increasing desperation as he finds rejection at every turn. A midwife immediately recognizes her inadequacy and sends the couple to the hospital where Robert faces policy. Money opens hospital doors, but Robert has none. Frantically, he searches the black community for a loan so that Jeannie can be admitted. When he returns with the money, she is dead.

"The Savage Sound," the story of Bud Morgan's training his two whippets to hunt rabbits, emphasizes the underlying brutality in all of nature. The warm and loving animals are taken on their first hunt, and in their initial encounter with a rabbit they play with it until it runs away. Dismayed at his animals' apparent lack of hunting enthusiasm, Morgan tries them again. He is not prepared for the sudden reversal as they pounce on the rabbit and tear it limb from limb. When he tries to restrain them, one dog bites him. "The man was left with nothing but the awful blame, an uneasy feeling across the shoulders, like strange harness."[1] What began as an initiation experience for the whippets ends as a painful and poignant initiation for the man.

In *The Feast of Saint Barnabas* (1969) Ford changes his setting from Tennessee to Florida, but as in *The Liberation of Lord Byron Jones* he is again concerned with racial conflict. Although there is a varied cast of characters—blacks, Cubans, a Norse sailor of mythic suggestion—Ford never quite ties this book together. The action takes place in Woodyard, a black community in Ormund City, Florida, and the story is one of the influx of new people and new interests. The grocery store in Woodyard is the focus for much of the activity. Originally owned by Papa John, the store was next owned by Big Cuban. At Big Cuban's death, his son Purchase Walker takes over the store. These men provide part of the mythology of the community. Walker sells the store to Felton Watridge, a white man; in a fit of anger, Watridge kicks a black man into unconsciousness. Father Ned, a black preacher, in his St. Barnabas Day sermon tries to calm the tensions that are building to a race riot. Ford uses an actual riot that began in 1967 in Tampa, Florida, on the feast day of St. Barnabas, 11 June. As the fictional riot increases in fury, Ford reveals the personalities and the forces that have promoted this conflict, many of them for personal and financial gain. But there are also the real people, white and black, who suffer and agonize over the dissolution of a community.

Ford's most recent novel, *The Raider* (1975), is his most obviously historical work. Based on Nathan Bedford Forrest, the work is set in West Tennessee and describes the land as a kind of Eden, with Elias McCutcheon as its Adamic protagonist.

> Thus, the man, Elias, makes a tally. Of things that creep, of things that fly, and of growing things rooted in the wild earth. He walks swiftly on now, so swiftly that before dusk he has circled clean back to where he began, to the sycamore; and the tree has a different look. It has a tame look and a look of home upon it that was not there before.

---

[1] Jesse Hill Ford, *Fishes, Birds and Sons of Men* (Boston: Little, Brown, 1967) 192.

Literature of Tennessee

And he builds a fire. The first fire, and therefore not a fire like any other.[2]

The rigors of settling the land, the rise to prominence of McCutcheon and his family, and the defense of the land as the War Between the States encroaches become the focal points of this very readable book.

There are times when one thinks of a chronicler as one reads Ford, for characters are subtly introduced in one work only to be fully developed and analyzed in a later work. For instance, the black undertaker Lord Byron Jones appears in both *Mountains of Gilead* and "The Bitter Bread," one of the stories in the collection *Fishes, Birds and Sons of Men*, before Ford tells his complete story in the novel in which Jones is the title character. The incident developed in *The Conversion of Buster Drumwright* is only a possibility in *Mountains of Gilead*. And Tom McCutcheon, a significant character in *Mountains of Gilead*, is a descendant of Elias McCutcheon, a founder of West Tennessee in *The Raider*.

In all of his works, but especially in his West Tennessee works, Ford has dealt essentially with the same materials and concerns. He has seen family life and small-town life and noted their strengths and weaknesses. He has been concerned with a sense of the past and the responsibilities it always places on the present generation. He has been troubled by petty politics and the grip it has on a community. But overriding most of his work is his concern with racial problems.

In a 1969 interview, Ford commented on the varying personalities evident among Southerners. He noted, "Alabama people do not think like Tennesseans nor Mississippians or Georgians or Kentuckians." He went on to observe, "Tennesseans are like Swedes—they *like* to brood. They *hate* to *feel* well. They always like to be just a mite porely."[3]

This sense of brooding, of being "a mite porely," is frequently found in Ford's fiction. Characters are also likely to suffer some form of isolation: economic, social, racial, geographical, or political. Although there are quiet times in Ford's work when an individual pauses to reflect on the magnitude and majesty of the natural world, as in "How

---

[2] Jesse Hill Ford, *The Raider* (Boston: Atlantic-Little, Brown, 1975) 7.

[3] James Seay, "The Making of Fables: Jesse Hill Ford," in *Kite-Flying and Other Irrational Acts*, ed. John Carr (Baton Rouge: Louisiana State University Press, 1972) 201.

the Mountains Are" and *The Raider*, an encounter with violence is more likely. Murder and suicide run rampant through his work. A gloss for his treatment of this topic seems well verbalized in *Mountains of Gilead* when Patsy McCutcheon, thinking back over the horrors surrounding her own life, says, "I can wade up to my neck in blood."[4] Like her, Ford seems to wade up to his neck in blood.

Madison Jones

Madison Jones was born in the Nashville area on 21 March 1925. He was educated at Vanderbilt, with graduate training at the University of Florida, where he studied creative writing with Andrew Lytle. In more recent years Jones has served as writer in residence and faculty member in the department of English at Auburn University, Auburn, Alabama.

Jones has published six novels, all with Tennessee settings and all dealing with those themes most readily identified with contemporary Southern writing, such as family relationships, the power of the land, the fear of change, and violence. The Jones family lived for some time in Cheatham County, northwest of Nashville; his first novel, *The Innocent*, which is the most autobiographical of his novels, is set in a location drawn from that county. Described early in the novel as possessing only one eye, the protagonist, twenty-seven-year-old Duncan Welsh, obviously symbolizes the individual with limited vision. He has two goals: to own a great racehorse and to reestablish a respected family name.

Welsh finally achieves his dream of breeding a fine racehorse, only to see the horse killed. As one critic observed, there is some thought of Poe's "Metzengerstein"[5] when Welsh is revealed to be obsessed with the animal's birth and training. Later Welsh becomes involved with a woman, Nettie Roundtree, but Welsh's interests and ambitions do not include a romantic involvement. Instead, he comes under the influence of Aaron McCool, a moonshiner, who eventually prevails upon Welsh to make runs with him. In time, McCool seems to take over the personality of Welsh, controlling him in thought and action.

---

[4]Jesse Hill Ford, *Mountains of Gilead* (Boston: Little, Brown, 1961) 298.

[5]John Cook Wyllie, "Guilt-Ridden Dixie," *Saturday Review*, 23 February 1957, 18.

Literature of Tennessee

Forest of the Night (1962) understandably bears a dedication to Andrew Lytle, for it strongly reflects his influence. It incorporates Lytle's interest in the early history of the state, his fascination with evil and its impact on mankind, and his suggestion of the supernatural. *Forest of the Night* is set in 1802 and based loosely on the legendary historical characters the Harpe brothers, who robbed and murdered along the Natchez Trace.

The protagonist of the novel, Jonathan Cannon, comes into the wilderness near Nashville bringing with him books and the ambition to start a school to combat the ignorance of the region; however, his own first encounter is with violence, and he quickly learns that violence is a way of life on this frontier. He meets Judith Gray, a former mistress of one of the Harpes, and his fascination with her increases until she dominates his personality. She still functions under the spell of the evil Harpes and finally begins to believe that Cannon may be one of them returned from the dead. Soon some of the local citizenry also begin to believe that Cannon is one of the Harpe brothers returned in disguise. Although he starts his school, it soon collapses as Cannon's grasp on reality gradually gives way. Cannon's psychological descent takes on frightening proportions. Eli, a pioneer man of the wood, is the only character with real strength. Following the death of Judith, Eli insists that Cannon finally renew his educational pursuits. The novel ends on the hope that the night of ignorance (part of that forest suggested in the title) will slowly diminish for Cannon and the frontier.

In *A Buried Land* (1963) Jones looks from the past to problems in the modern South. Percy Youngblood returns home at the time the Tennessee Valley Authority, for which he works, is flooding the valley where he has lived most of his life. He sees the value of this kind of modernization, and he clashes with his father who does not want the change. As Louis Rubin observes, one of the best scenes in the book— one which Youngblood does not himself witness—is the moving of a family cemetery.[6]

Youngblood falls in love with Cora Kincaid, and her subsequent pregnancy sends him in search of an abortionist. When Cora dies fol-

---

[6]Louis D. Rubin, Jr., "The Difficulties of Being a Southern Writer Today: Or, Getting Out From Under William Faulkner," in *The Curious Death of the Novel* (Baton Rouge: Louisiana State University Press, 1967) 287.

lowing the abortion, Youngblood and his friend, Jesse Hood, bury her in one of those empty graves before the water floods that part of the land.

After an absence of a few years, Percy returns to the town to practice law. He learns that Fowler Kincaid is searching for his sister's murderer and believes that Jesse Hood was involved. Before long Youngblood is implicated. His guilt so consumes him that he finally returns with his mother to the edge of the lake where Cora is buried and confesses his crime.

This novel is concerned with progress, but progress at the expense of all forms of stability. People and the land are intricately interwoven. Youngblood sees progress as a way of totally destroying his past, but he never forgets. The land may be buried, but not his guilt.

In 1967 Jones wrote his short book *The Exile*. The story of Hank Tawes, sheriff of Rhine County, becomes another study in degradation and character deterioration as the sheriff falls under the spell of Ezra McCain, a local moonshiner. One recalls Aaron McCool in *The Innocent*. The events in this book, in addition to the similarity of titles, suggest Jones's continuing interest in the same topic. McCain uses his daughter, Alma, to lure Tawes and deceive him by her supposed affections. The depiction of "white trash" in the McCain family bears likeness to Jones's development of McCool and Hollis Handley in his next novel, *A Cry of Absence*. Like both of these characters, McCain has a hypnotic effect. Tawes seems helpless and does whatever McCain directs him to do.

The Exile is the only work by Jones to be made into a movie. Entitled *I Walk the Line,* the film version was shot in Tennessee and released nationwide in 1970. Later the novel appeared in paperback editions under the film title.

When *A Cry of Absence* appeared in 1971, it was immediately noted as Jones's civil rights novel. Taking his title from John Crowe Ransom's poem "Winter Remembered," Jones created the fictitious Cameron Springs, a small town resembling Franklin, Tennessee. A few months after publication of the book, there was talk of a movie version to be filmed in Franklin, but local opposition was too strong.

Hester Glenn, a divorcée with prominent Southern roots, has two fine-looking sons: Ames, a student at a nearby university, and Cam, a high school athlete, charming, handsome, and very strong. The resemblance of Cam and Ames to Cain and Abel is obvious. This family, excluding the father who has never fit in, sees itself as a preserver of Southern gentility. While the new South develops around them, Hester and Cam resent the new industry, civil rights leaders, and outspoken blacks in their town. They both look for a return to Fountain Inn, Hester's childhood home. In her dreams the place exists, still perfect in memory though nonexistent in reality.

At the novel's opening, a young black leader, Otis Stevens, has been chained to a tree and stoned to death. Gradually Ames suspects his own brother, a star pitcher on the high school baseball team. Hester refuses to believe such and denounces Ames for even thinking it. Finally Ames proves his contention implicating Cam and his low-life friend, Pike Handley.

When Hester realizes that Cam committed the act because it was what he thought she would want of him, she is horrified. Cam says to her, "You won't believe me, but I always did like I thought you wanted. As much as I could." Later he says, "Most boys don't respect their grandfathers, and all the old things, like I do. Like you taught me." And then he asks, "Why can't we go back being like we were?"[7] Hester leaves the motor running in her son's car, taking the life of the monster she feels she created, and then she commits suicide.

Madison Jones's most recently published fiction, *Passage Through Gehenna* (1978), is his weakest. A treatment of sex and sin, the novel is the story of Jud Rivers and his strong interests in women, beginning with the desirable but unavailable Lily Nunn, whose name belies her sinister nature. Jud turns to the local prostitute Goldie Poole as a substitute for Lily. Jud is arrested on drug charges and then released in custody of the local Baptist minister, who is the father of Hannah Rice. Rivers feels imprisoned by Hannah—he works in her garden and listens to her sermons. The expected happens as Jud seduces Hannah. When Hannah becomes pregnant and Jud insists on an abortion, Lily Nunn provides the doctor's name. After Hannah is struck by a truck and killed, Lily's role as the arch-villainess heightens as she dominates the mind and emotions of Jud. Finally, Jud's sense of guilt overcomes him, and he turns himself in to the judge and is jailed. After being re-

---

[7]Madison Jones, *A Cry of Absence* (New York: Crown, 1971) 190-91.

leased from prison, Jud goes to Hannah's grave penitent and thankful for her influence that has helped him find himself.

Jones, like Jesse Hill Ford, understands the power of Southern violence. At the same time, he is at his best in the creation of loners, isolates. Repeatedly his characters long for an involvement in a family unit but stand apart from it, never knowing how to be included.

In a review of *The Innocent*, Jones's first novel, Robert Penn Warren is complimentary with qualifications. Suggesting Jones's talent, he writes, "Just how considerable that talent is remains, of course, to be seen, but this exhibit is impressive, and it would be no surprise to find, in the fullness of time, this writer comfortably situated among the best of his generation."[8] Unfortunately, Jones has not yet reached such a plateau.

Ishmael Reed

Ishmael Reed has chosen satire as his means of expressing his feelings toward society. Using some of the basic materials found often in American fiction—college life, family life, the West, history—he has employed what one critic has called "the tension of dissonance."[9] Exaggeration in both language and character delineation and juxtaposition of disparate elements mark this writer's work.

Born in Chattanooga in 1938, the son of an auto worker, Ishmael Reed moved to Buffalo, New York, where he grew up. In recent years he has lived in New York, Berkeley, and Seattle. In his writings he has shown little attachment to his native state except in a single volume of poetry entitled *Chattanooga*, published in 1973.

His first novel, *The Free-Lance Pallbearers*, appeared in 1967. Using as his central character Bukka Doopeyduk, a college dropout who had hoped to be the first black expert in bacteriological warfare but who has now settled for the post of hospital orderly, Reed tells a disjointed and satirical tale of the overthrow of a corrupt and inept leader called Harry Sam, who has not been seen for thirty years. Bukka leads the crusade and is hanged. His body is cut down by the Free-Lance Pallbearers, the liberal whites and uncommitted blacks who never "get involved" in such social upheavals.

---

[8]Robert Penn Warren, "A First Novel," *Sewanee Review* 65 (1957): 347.

[9]Henry Louis Gates, Jr., "Parody of Forms," *Saturday Review*, 4 March 1978, 29.

Yellow Back Radio Broke-Down (1969) continues Reed's satirical attack on the establishment, but this time he introduces Loop Garou, a black cowboy, as his hero. The western town of Yellow Back Radio has been taken over by the children who have revolted against their parents. The parents, in turn, have allied with the corrupt Drag Gibson to help them regain their town. In a confrontation, Kid Garou (appropriately sided with the children) and Gibson meet almost as if it were the classic meeting of good and evil, with only a few of the children as survivors. While Reed employs as his vehicle the American western with its traditional emphasis upon hero and villain, he mixes too many myths in this work and somehow loses both his characters and his readers.

In 1972 Reed published another novel and his first volume of poetry. The novel, *Mumbo-Jumbo*, establishes in its title and subject matter Reed's determined interest in the supernatural and especially in folk mythology. In 1970 Reed published in the Los Angeles *Free Press* his "Neo-HooDoo Manifesto," in which he devised "a myth that divides history into a war between two churches, two communities of consciousness: the 'Cop Religion' of Christianity and the transformed Osirian rite, Voodoo."[10]

Mumbo-Jumbo is a composite narrative consisting of quotations from books, newspapers, and magazines. There are five pages of bibliography following the text of the novel. Central to the book's action is the recurrence of Jes Grew, the Osirian/Dionysian dance phenomenon, in New Orleans. Reed takes his term from James Weldon Johnson's comment in *The Book of American Negro Poetry* that "the earliest Ragtime songs like Topsy, 'jes grew.'"[11] A concerted effort is made by the Wallflower Order of the Knights Templar to destroy the effectiveness of Jes Grew, "to bleach its blackness and neutralize its force,"[12] as one critic says. The protagonist of this novel is Papa LaBas, an authority and devotee of Jes Grew.

---

[10] Neil Schmitz, "Neo-HooDoo: The Experimental Fiction of Ishmael Reed," *Twentieth-Century Literature* 20 (1974): 132.

[11] Schmitz, 135.

[12] Schmitz, 135.

The publication of Reed's first book of poetry, *Conjure: Selected Poems, 1963-1970*, gave him the opportunity to reveal in his poetry the same approach he had used in fiction. As the subtitle of the book indicates, some of his poems predate his first published novel by four years, suggesting that some of his fictional ideas were first expressed in his poetry. The title *Conjure* reveals Reed's continuing interest in African mythology. The foreword to the book is used by Reed as an opportunity to furnish the reader with the poet's personal reflections on the contents of the book, poem by poem. He explains how some were written, how some are to be interpreted, and how some are offensive to certain readers. Reed also includes in this collection his "Neo-HooDoo Manifesto" previously published in 1970. Among the tenets of this belief Reed cites:

> Neo-HooDoo is a "Lost American Church" updated.
> Neo-HooDoo is not a church for "ego-tripping"—it takes its "organization" from Haitian VooDoo.
> Neo-HooDoo believes that every man is an artist and every artist a priest.
> Neo-HooDoo is a litany seeking its text.
> Neo-HooDoo is a Dance and Music closing in on its words.
> Neo-HooDoo is a Church finding its lyrics.[13]

In another poem in this collection that explains, in part, the newly espoused philosophy of the Neo-HooDooism of Reed, "catechism of d neo-american hoodoo church," the poet speaks of himself:

> goodhomefolks gave me ishmael. how
> did they know he was d 'afflicted one'?
> carrying a gag in his breast pocket. giving
> d scene a scent of snowd under w/ bedevilment.[14]

In 1973 Reed published his second collection of poems, *Chattanooga*. The book is a loose compilation of occasional verse primarily covering Reed's experiences as a teacher and lecturer. Many of the individual poems reflect interests already developed in the novels. For example, there is a balladlike poem, "Railroad Bill, A Conjure Man,"

---

[13]Ishmael Reed, *Conjure: Selected Poems, 1963-1970* (Amherst: University of Massachusetts Press, 1972) 20-21, 25.

[14]Reed, *Conjure*, 40.

which presents Bill, who has the ability to conjure himself into many forms and does so in order to escape mistreatment. "Loop Garou Means Change Into" reminds the reader that he has already met Garou in the previously published novel *Yellow Back Radio Broke-Down*. Two poems deal with the author's birthdays and indicate his reflection on the coming of advanced age—"The Last Week in 30" and "The Author Reflects on His 35th Birthday."

In *The Last Days of Louisiana Red* (1974), Reed brings back Papa LaBas from *Mumbo-Jumbo* on his way from New York to Berkeley, the scene of this novel. Ed Yellings has moved to Berkeley to found the Solid Gumbo Works, a mysterious business whose produce is known only to the trusted employees. Yellings is killed and LaBas is sent to find the murderer. The Yellingses' four children—Wolf, Street, Sister, and Minnie—find their own places in the revolutionary world. Wolf replaces his father as the head of Solid Gumbo Works; Street is convicted of murder and flees America for Africa; Sister opens a boutique but soon gives way to the influence of Minnie who heads the Moochers. Louisiana Red is both a metaphor for inflicting psychological stress upon individuals and the name of a Southern mailorder house that undermines Yellings's business. Reed ties into this domestic-business novel the ancient story of Oedipus, aligning each member of the family with one of the Theban family.

Flight to Canada was published in 1976. Based upon the escape of three slaves from the Arthur Swille plantation in Virginia, the novel mixes and merges nineteenth- and twentieth-century elements. The literal-minded reader already expecting the unexpected in Reed's novels must come to grips with modern appliances in plantation homes. Neither should he be dismayed by slaves' fleeing in airplanes and automobiles. Canada offers the newly arrived immigrants "Ford, Sears, Holiday Inn, and all the rest." Time is meaningless, or at least it is relative. Abraham Lincoln, Jefferson Davis, and even Queen Victoria are subjects for satire. The hero of the novel, Robin Quickskill, whose very name suggests his youthfulness, just happens to be a poet, and his poem about the Swille plantation serves as the source for the title of the book.

In a volume of contemporary poets which he edited, *19 Necromancers from Now*, Reed explained his use of folk superstitions.

One has to return to what some writers would call "dark heathenism" to find original tall tales, and yarns with the kind of originality that some modern writers use as found poetry—the enigmatic street rhymes of some of Ellison's minor characters, or the dozens. I call this neohoodooism; a spur to originality, which prompted Julie Jackson, a New Orleans soothsayer, when asked the origin of the amulets, talismans, charms, and potions in her workshop, to say: "I make all my own stuff. It saves me money and it's as good. People who has to buy their stuff ain't using their heads."[15]

In an interview he explained his dissonant approach to his writings as being similar to an essay style the Sufistic Moslems call "scatter"—that is, moving from one subject to another. "That's the way my mind works. I'll go into one topic and then go into its ramifications. Sometimes I lose where I started from."[16] In that same interview Reed explained that his seemingly haphazard style, which permits him to move abruptly from one topic to another, is television influenced. "I've watched television all my life, and I think my way of editing, the speed I bring to my books, the way the plot moves, is based upon some of the television shows and cartoons I've seen, the way they edit."[17]

In *Yellow Back Radio Broke-Down*, Loop defines a novel, and that definition seems to describe the work and intention of Reed: "No one says a novel has to be one thing. It can be anything it wants to be, a vaudeville show, the six o-clock news, the mumbling of wise men saddled by demons. All art must be for the end of liberating the masses."[18] What Loop committed himself to do seems to be the aim of Ishmael Reed.

Nikki Giovanni

Nikki Giovanni, one of the most outspoken and popular of the Black Movement poets, was born in Knoxville, Tennessee, in 1943. The

---

[15] Ishmael Reed, Introduction, *19 Necromancers from Now* (Garden City NY: Doubleday, 1970) xvii-xviii.

[16] John O'Brien, "Ishmael Reed," in *The New Fiction: Interviews with Innovative American Writers*, ed. Joe David Bellamy (Urbana: University of Illinois Press, 1974) 140.

[17] O'Brien, 131.

[18] Ishmael Reed, *Yellow Back Radio Broke-Down* (Garden City NY: Doubleday, 1969) 36.

family later moved to Cincinnati, but Nikki graduated from Austin High School in Knoxville and enrolled in Fisk University in Nashville when she was sixteen. At Fisk she was soon placed on probation and then expelled at the end of her first semester. She later credited that experience with teaching her how to face reality and deal with it: "I went back to Fisk as a woman—not a little girl."[19]

When she returned to Fisk in 1964, she became actively involved in restoring Fisk's chapter of the Student Nonviolent Coordinating Committee (SNCC), which had been declared illegal on the campus. She received her B.A. in history in 1967 and then enrolled in graduate school at the University of Pennsylvania. After nine months, she quit that program.

Since the late 1960s she has been actively writing and publishing poetry primarily, but also some nonfiction and fiction. She has reestablished a wide acceptance for the oral presentation of poetry through her numerous stage appearances on college and university campuses and at public gatherings around the country for poetry readings and lectures. She has been seen frequently on national television and has produced an album of her readings accompanied by a choir singing hymns. In one of her later poems she accurately described herself as "a child of the sixties." The label is appropriate because of the forthrightness of her message concerning the rise of the black culture, her sense of public presentation, and her flexibility with language and subject matter.

Her best-known works are her books of poetry. Titles and publication dates for these include *Black Feeling Black Talk* (1968); *Black Judgement* (1968); *Re: Creation* (1970); *My House* (1972); *The Women and the Men* (1975); and *Cotton Candy on a Rainy Day* (1978). She has published two volumes of verse for children, *Spin a Soft Black Song* (1971) and *Ego Tripping and Other Poems for Young Readers* (1974), and one volume of autobiographical essays, *Gemini* (1971).

Upon reading Nikki Giovanni's early poetry, one immediately notes the ferocity of her verse. Its force, its passion, and its hatred startle, but the 1960s were startling years. Hers is a message of revolution, killing, changing. The cry is for a strong sense of individualism and for an individual who will stand up to effect the changes society demands.

---

[19]"Giovanni, Nikki," *Current Biography*, 1973, 149.

The combined volume containing the texts from her first two books, *Black Feeling Black Talk/Black Judgement*, illustrates this emphasis. A later volume, *My House*, is much more personal and concentrates on the influences at work on the poet.

The Women and the Men continues that sense of mellowing, of shifting focus and emphasis in the poetry, as the poet stresses personal contacts. It is interesting to note that many of her individual poems are dedicated to specific people, often identified by name or by initials. In the most recent volume, the mellowing is not only evident; it is the thrust of the book.

One critic of contemporary poetry praised Giovanni for her ability to use simple folk and blues rhythms and techniques.[20] That strength is evident in several of her verses about strong black women she has met. But perhaps none says it better than the opening verse in *My House*. The poem is called "Legacies."

> her grandmother called her from the playground
> "yes, ma'am"
> "i want chu to learn how to make rolls" said the old
> woman proudly
> but the little girl didn't want
> to learn how because she knew
> even if she couldn't say it that
> that would mean when the old one died she would be less
> dependent on her spirit so
> she said
> "i don't want to know how to make no rolls"
> with her lips poked out
> and the old woman wiped her hands on
> her apron saying "lord
> these children"
> and neither of them ever
> said what they meant
> and i guess nobody ever does[21]

There is a similarly impressive portrait in "Once a Lady Told Me" in

---

[20]Karl Malkoff, *Crowell's Handbook of Contemporary American Poetry* (New York: Crowell, 1973) 133.

[21]Nikki Giovanni, *My House* (New York: William Morrow, 1972) 5.

The Women and the Men. The speaker in the poem is old and weak but determined to remain in her own house even if the children do want her to move in with them. She reflects,

> but I shal pad around my house
> in my purple soft-soled shoes
> i'm very happy now
> it's not so very neat, you know, but it's my
> life[22]

Giovanni has even given the Tennessee reader something to reflect upon from her memories of home in Knoxville. In her first volume with all its furor and intensity, there is "Knoxville, Tennessee."

> I always like summer
> best
> you can eat fresh corn
> from daddy's garden
> and okra
> and greens
> and cabbage
> and lots of barbecue
> and buttermilk
> and homemade ice-cream
> at the church picnic
> and listen to
> gospel music
> outside
> at the church
> homecoming
> and go to the mountains with
> your grandmother
> and go barefooted
> and be warm
> all the time
> not only when you go to bed
> and sleep[23]

---

[22]Nikki Giovanni, *The Women and the Men* (New York: William Morrow, 1975) no page number.

[23]Nikki Giovanni, *Black Feeling Black Talk/Black Judgement* (New York: William Morrow, 1970) 65.

There is a pleasantness inherent in much of Giovanni's verse, a pleasantness increasingly evident in the later poems. In the early poem "Nikka-Rosa," she expresses the concern that memories of black childhood are supposed to be so dreary, but she confesses that she has no such reminiscences. And she concludes,

> and I really hope no white person ever has cause
> to write about me
> because they never understand
> Black love is Black wealth and they'll
> probably talk about my hard childhood
> and never understand that
> all the while I was quite happy.[24]

These four writers illustrate a considerable difference in interests, subject matter, and form. In their variety they are representative of the contemporary Tennessee writer—some with melancholic eyes to the past and tradition and some with a sharp probing of the future.

---

[24] Giovanni, *Black Feeling Black Talk/Black Judgement*, 58-59.

Bibliography

Jesse Hill Ford

Mountains of Gilead: A Novel. Boston: Little, Brown, 1961.

The Conversion of Buster Drumwright. Nashville: Vanderbilt University Press, 1964.

The Liberation of Lord Byron Jones. Boston: Little, Brown, 1965.

Fishes, Birds and Sons of Men. Boston: Little, Brown, 1967.

The Feast of Saint Barnabas. Boston: Little, Brown, 1967.

The Raider. Boston: Atlantic-Little, Brown, 1975.

Madison Jones

The Innocent. New York: Harcourt, Brace, 1957.

Forest of the Night. New York: Harcourt, Brace, 1960.

The Buried Land. New York: Viking, 1963.

The Exile. New York: Viking, 1967.

A Cry of Absence. New York: Crown, 1971.

Passage Through Gehenna. Baton Rouge: Louisiana State University Press, 1978.

Ishmael Reed

The Free-Lance Pallbearers. Garden City NY: Doubleday, 1967.

Yellow Back Radio Broke-Down. Garden City NY: Doubleday, 1969.

Conjure: Selected Poems, 1963-1970. Boston: University of Massachusetts Press, 1972.

Mumbo-Jumbo. Garden City NY: Doubleday, 1972.

Chattanooga. New York: Random House, 1973.

The Last Days of Louisiana Red. New York: Random House, 1974.

Flight to Canada. New York: Random House, 1976.

Shrovetide in Old New Orleans. Garden City NY: Doubleday, 1978.

Nikki Giovanni

Black Feeling Black Talk. Detroit: Broadside, 1968.

Black Judgement. Detroit: Broadside, 1968.

Black Feeling Black Talk/Black Judgement. New York: William Morrow, 1970.

Re: Creation. Detroit: Broadside Press, 1970.

Gemini: Extended Biographical Statement on My First Twenty-Five Years of Being a Black Poet. Indianapolis: Bobbs-Merrill, 1971.

Spin a Soft Black Song: Poems for Children. New York: Hill & Wang, 1971.

My House. New York: William Morrow, 1972.

Ego Tripping and Other Poems for Young Children. Westport CT: Lawrence Hill, 1974.

The Women and the Men. New York: William Morrow, 1975.

Cotton Candy on a Rainy Day. New York: William Morrow, 1978.

Selected Critical Bibliography

Jesse Hill Ford

Berryhill, Kenneth. "Jesse Hill Ford: His Motif of Death." *Tennessee Philological Bulletin* 10 (July 1973): 31.

Bradbury, John M. "Look Back to Dixie." *Saturday Review*, 30 December 1967, 26-27.

Clark, Anderson. "Violence in the Fiction of Jesse Hill Ford." *Tennessee Philological Bulletin* 10 (July 1973): 30-31.

Frady, Marshall. "The Continuing Trial of Jesse Hill Ford." *Life*, 29 October 1971, 56-68.

King, Larry. "No Jail Except the Prison of His Mind." *Today's Health* 49 (December 1971): 28-33, 69, 72.

Landress, Thomas H. "The Present Course of Southern Fiction: Part II." *The Arlington Quarterly* 1 (Winter 1967-1968): 62-70.

Matthews, Jack. "What Are You Doing There? What Are You Doing Here? A View of the Jesse Hill Ford Case." *Georgia Review* 26 (Summer 1972): 121-44.

Seay, James. "The Making of Fables: Jesse Hill Ford." In *Kite-Flying and Other Irrational Acts*, edited by John Carr. Baton Rouge: Louisiana State University Press, 1972.

Sugg, Redding S., Jr. "Tangled Irony: 'Now He Can Write About Hisself.'" *South Today* 2 (June 1971): 3.

Thomas, William. "The Liberation of Jesse Hill Ford." *Mid-South, The Commercial Appeal Magazine* 24 (April 1966): 4-7.

Weeks, Edward. *In Friendly Candor*. Boston: Little-Brown, 1959.

_____. "The Peripatetic Reviewer." *The Atlantic Monthly* (May 1959): 86-87.

White, Helen, ed. *Jesse Hill Ford: An Annotated Check List of His Papers*. Memphis: Memphis State University Press, 1975.

Madison Jones

Binding, Paul. *Separate Country: A Literary Journey through the American South*. New York: Paddington Press, 1979.

Meeker, Richard K. "The Youngest Generation of Southern Fiction Writers." In *Southern Writers: Appraisals in Our Time*, edited by R. C. Simonini, Jr. Charlottesville: University of Virginia Press, 1965.

Rubin, Louis D., Jr. "The Difficulties of Being a Southern Writer Today: Or, Getting Out From Under William Faulkner." *Journal of Southern History* 29 (1963): 486-94. Reprinted in *The Curious Death of the Novel*. Baton Rouge: Louisiana State University Press, 1967.

Sullivan, Walter. "The Continuing Renascence: Southern Fiction in the Fifties." In *South: Modern Southern Literature in Its Cultural Setting*, edited by Louis D. Rubin, Jr., and Robert D. Jacobs. Garden City NY: Doubleday, 1961.

Vauthier, Simone. "Gratuitous Hypothesis: A Reading of Madison Jones' *The Innocent*." *Recherches Anglaises et Americaines* 7 (1974): 191-219.

Warren, Robert Penn. "A First Novel." *Sewanee Review* 65 (1957): 347-52.

Wetzel, Donald. "Tale of a Dark Frontier." *New York Herald Tribune Book Review*, 13 March 1960, 10.

Wyllie, John Cook. "Guilt-Ridden Dixie." *Saturday Review*, 23 February 1957, 18.

Ishmael Reed

Abel, Robert H. "Reed's 'I'm a Cowboy in the Boat of Ra.' " *Explicator* 30 (1971): 81.

Ambler, Madge. "Ishmael Reed: Whose Radio Broke Down?" *Negro American Literature Forum* 6 (Winter 1972): 125-31.

Beauford, Fred. "Conversation with Ishmael Reed." *Black Creation* 4 (1973): 12-15.

Bush, Roland. "Werewolf of the Wild West." *Black World* 23 (January 1974): 51-52, 64-66.

Duff, Gerald. "Reed's 'The Free-Lance Pallbearers.' " *Explicator* 32 (1974): 69.

Emerson, O. B. "Cultural Nationalism in Afro-American Literature." In *The Cry of Home*, edited by H. Ernest Lewald. Knoxville: University of Tennessee Press, 1972.

Ford, Nick Aaron. "A Note on Ishmael Reed: Revolutionary Novelist." *Studies in the Novel* 3 (Summer 1971): 216-18.

Klinkowitz, Jerome. *The Life of Fiction*. Urbana: University of Illinois Press, 1977.

O'Brien, John. "Ishmael Reed." In *The New Fiction: Interviews with Innovative American Writers*, edited by Joe David Bellamy. Urbana: University of Illinois Press, 1974.

Reed, Ishmael. "The Writer as Seer: Ishmael Reed on Ishmael Reed." *Black World* 23 (1974): 20-34.

Schmitz, Neil. "Neo-HooDoo: The Experimental Fiction of Ishmael Reed." *Twentieth-Century Literature* 20 (1974): 126-40.

Whitlow, Roger. *Black American Literature: A Critical History*. Chicago: Nelson Hall, 1973.

Nikki Giovanni

Bailey, Peter. "Nikki Giovanni: 'I Am Black, Female, Polite.'" *Ebony* 27 (February 1972): 48-52, 53-54, 56.

Brooks, Russell. "The Motifs of Dynamic Change in Black Revolutionary Poetry." *CLA Journal* 15 (September 1971): 7-17.

Dusky, Lorraine. "Fascinating Woman." *Ingenue*, February 1973, no page number.

Lee, Don L. "The Poets and Their Poetry: There Is a Tradition." In *Dynamite Voices: Black Poets of the 1960s*. Detroit: Broadside Press, 1971.

Malkoff, Karl. *Crowell's Handbook of Contemporary American Poetry*. New York: Thomas Y. Crowell, 1973, 133-35.

Nazer, G. "Lifestyle." *Harper's Bazaar*, July 1972, 50-51.

Palmer, R. Roderk. "The Poetry of Three Revolutionaries: Don L. Lee, Sonia Sanchez, and Nikki Giovanni." *CLA Journal* 15 (September 1971): 25-36. Reprinted in *Modern Black Poets: A Collection of Critical Essays*, edited by Donald B. Gibson. Englewood Cliffs NJ: Prentice-Hall, 1973.

Whitlow, Roger. *Black American Literature: A Critical History*. Chicago: Nelson Hall, 1973.

BETHANY COLLEGE LIBRARY

MUP *Literature of Tennessee*

Designed by Alesa Jones
Composition by MUP Composition Department
Production specifications:
    text paper—60 pound Warren's Olde Style
    endpapers—Multicolor Adobe Dove Gray
    cover—(on .088 boards) Holliston Kingston Natural #35406
    dust jacket—Multicolor Adobe Dove Gray Text, Printed PMS 491U
Printing (offset lithography) by Omnipress of Macon, Inc., Macon, Georgia
Binding by John H. Dekker and Sons, Inc., Grand Rapids, Michigan